ATTIC ODYSSEY

Letters Tell A Tale or Two

By
Winifred Wardle Fiero

Kaaterskill Falls, Catskill Mountains. Copied from old plates of
James Harvey Van Gelder.

PHOTOGRAPHED BY

J. H. VAN GELDER, A. M.

ILLUSTRATED LECTURER,

CATSKILL, N. Y.

TERMS ON APPLICATION.

TABLE OF CONTENTS

PREFACE

I never would have tackled the hundreds of letters and family memorabilia if it had not been for my son's three children and my great grandchild.

I could never have picked my way through the jungle I called my attic with such determination if the "GDs," (Gradual Deteriorations), had not been working their gremlin tricks.

My only regret is that too many people and incidents have been left out because of limitations of space and time.

I never do any genealogical research. Fortunately, others have. But I do save all the little leads that come my way, and the Greene County Historical Society has saved many files of them for others to use in research.

Invaluable help has been generously accorded me by many dear friends. I wish especially to thank Dr. Dorothy Bruno, a good friend since we ran the Hot Line together, for her patience in typing my illegible copy, and in editing the final manuscript.

Richard Philp has shared his expertise with all the members of the Writers' Group, and I have especially welcomed it.

Vivian and Irving Rosenberg were friends indeed in the stress of the closing hours. Irving provided the artwork.

Winifred Clark photographed some of the illustrations with her skills that are truly professional.

The members of the Writers' Group have found each other most helpful with suggestions and encouragement. Their individual gifts and expertise have been a great help to me.

Winifred Wardle Fiero
Catskill, New York
July, 1985

PART I
INTRODUCTION

The lid on Grandpa's old pine chest creaked open after I took a chisel to the rusty lock. There lay hundreds of letters bedded down for many a year. A few light sleepers among them were already peeking out from their envelopes. I peeked too. Postmarks paced history from whale oil lamps to electric lights, from horseback and "shanks' ponies" to railroads, autos and airplanes, from sails to steamboats.

It boggled my imagination to see place names from far corners of the United States and much of the Far East. The only writer I had trouble linking closely to this grandfather I knew so well in his later years was a mystery Civil War soldier. But he was mentioned in a letter to Grandpa and had left a chest marked **Pelham** that sat in my cellar.

My attic had become a veritable ghetto of generations past and present. Ostracized from current living, chests and boxes had proliferated and vied with old furniture to make the path through the attic one vast obstacle course. My grandchildren are herewith warned. They are lineal descendants of packrats.

It was a day of autumn blue skies. One glance out the attic balcony door, and I escaped over the Rip Van Winkle Bridge to a quiet knoll beside Chancellor Robert Livingston's restored Manor House. He was the Patroon responsible in 1710 for feeding the Palatines, French Huguenots, and other refugees that Queen Anne had sponsored in a kindly but ill-advised venture to the New World.

Ten ships and 3,000 persons had embarked toward the end of January for the Hudson River. It was the largest exodus that ever embarked to a new land in colonial days. Their voyage was one of the most terrible in history. There were 470 who died at sea before they landed at both the East Camp and West Camp more than 100 miles north of New York City. But what was worse than all, according to Brink's **History of Saugerties,** a semi-serfdom awaited them. Their land had once been the garden spot of Europe. No one who has ever seen the documents signed by these refugees from the Palatine needs to be told they came from a land of schoolhouses. They were signatures of hands that were used to pens.

Bark and log huts were built for winter quarters. Here they shivered and suffered. But they built a church that very winter. And in January, three months after landing they had a school house . . . the relative needs of mind, body and soul were never more clearly seen, nor more quickly provided for than by these exiles — not even by the Pilgrims at Plymouth.

To the West I searched the long ridge that carried the Old King's Road on its back, hoping sharp eyes could pick out at least the slender spire of the lovely old Catsbaan Church, but the trees were too tall. A little north of it would be the land of the old Peter Van Gelder Farm. My grandfather, James Harvey, and his three older Van Gelder brothers were born there. His mother was the great granddaughter of Christian Myer, best known of all the early Palatines. He had had 25 sons and grandsons in the Revolution and signed the Articles of Association which were an attempt at reconciliation not a threat of separation from the King.

Like all good rivers this so-called Rhine of America, at my feet, reflected the bright blue skies above. The Catskills with their famous profile of the Old Man of the Mountains made a darker backdrop. That day I was not distracted by such awesome beauty. The letters still haunted me. I headed back to Catskill.

Looking west across the Hudson River at the Old Man of the Mountains. *Photograph by Winifred J. Clark.*

MYER HOMESTEAD
LAND DEEDED 1724 TO
CHRISTIAN MYER, PROMINENT
PALATINE SETTLER; EIGHTEEN
DESCENDANTS SERVED IN
REVOLUTIONARY WAR
STATE EDUCATION
DEPARTMENT 1938

Grandpa was sixteen when he left for the Seminary. Loaded down with his carpet bag, and once with a five-foot rosewood melodeon, he set out for the Seminary at Charlotteville way back of our mountains. It was a roundabout trip by way of Albany and probably by boat. From there he went by stagecoach. William Myer, his next older brother, was an artist when he was not a dirt farmer or a one-room school teacher. He was listed as Professor of Art in a brochure of the Ashland Seminary, thus earning some tuition. Two of his copies of Thomas Cole's famous Voyage of Life series now hang in the Bronck House Museum. The home of Cole, the founder of the Hudson River School of Art, is still preserved in Catskill and is now an historical landmark. Peter Van Gelder allotted these two youngest sons land and farm stock. They formed a "company" to raise money for their tuition. Sometimes they took turns at school and farm for a semester or two. Later William tried to make a living organizing art classes in other localities.

Homestead of Christian Myer, ancestor of Van Gelder family.

Peter's oldest son, David, became a master builder of covered bridges made completely of wood right down to the pegs that held them together. He also built an Octagon House of red brick, complete with a cupolo. This is the only one of these unique eight-sided houses in Greene County. It has been called the purest example of this type of architecture. The man who promoted them was not even an architect, but a phrenologist and author of many books, Orson Squires Fowler.

Jacob, next younger, made a name for himself as teacher, horticulturist, and as a specialist in commercial law and banking. His home was in Saugerties, from which town as well as from Catskill, the brothers often took a boat to New York City or to Albany.

William Myer was eleven years younger than his brother Jacob and wrote more letters to James Harvey than other relatives, friends, and fellow students. This favorite brother died when he was only 25 years

of age, the first year James was in Yale College. Peter had bought a farm in town and built a brick house. James Harvey graduated in the Class of 1864, cum laude, and with a prize for mathematics. One of the many friends who had enlisted in the Civil War, Bartholomew Mulligan, wrote a vivid description of the Battle of Chancellorsville in the Eastern theatre of the conflict. He wrote,

The moon shining with all its mild splendor, the constant blaze bursting forth from the mouths of numerous canon and the flash of thousands of muskets made a scene magnificently awful.

Meanwhile in the Western theater of war mystery surrounds the letters of Augustus Pelham, Jr. He is barely mentioned and only once in a letter from a student at Ashland Seminary. How did all his letters get bedded down with our family missives? There is no twig on the family tree where I can perch him.

According to Charles Dornbusch, an authority on Civil War records, Pelham's 110th regiment from Oswego, New York, is poorly documented. These letters are full of names and make the war come very much alive even today, both on the home front and on the battlefront.

The war and college over, James Harvey Van Gelder returned to Catskill and married his sweetheart of many years, Rebecca Pine. She had graduated from Charlotteville as valedictorian of her class in 1862. Together they established a private school in Catskill; but attendance was small; and the next year the family moved to a farm at Drummond Falls, Palenville. My mother, Carrie, was born there in 1865. They had planned to name her Abraham Lincoln.

The neighbors claimed Van Gelder was "too lazy to carry his own water," because he built a bucket line from the kitchen door to the falls. A reddish rock from the ruins of the old stone house is my "pet," sitting by the fireside. My favorite of all Grandma's paintings is of that stone house, and it hangs on my wall. The Van Gelder Genealogy says,

In 1872 they returned to Catskill and James Harvey took up the study of law, obtaining his LLB from Albany Law School in 1876 and an A.M. from Yale in 1886. At that time he built a large three story and basement residence on land bought from his mother and established a summer boarding house. This was quite a lucrative business in this area and many notables came from New York City and other places for the season. He increased his business along these lines and others and was especially interested in promoting a gravity water system for Catskill . . . .

Having delved into photography, Grandpa and Grandma and 17-year-old son, Arthur, made a Stereopticon Lecture Tour in 1890-91. First they visited relatives and other early pioneers who had gone "West." "West" meant central New York and going by oxcart or the Erie Canal. Then the trio followed the burgeoning industrial revolution, historic places and scenery through Ohio, Kentucky, and Alabama. They arrived in New Orleans during flood waters, just as the Mafia Gang had murdered Chief of Police Hennessy and bribed the jury, expecting to walk out free men the next day.

Highly respected city fathers called for action and crowds gathered and watched quietly while the proven murderers were lynched except for an 18-year-old boy and another with scanty evidence against him. Then all returned as quietly to their homes. No Italian vendor was molested. But there was high praise and extreme censure from the press across the whole country. Grandpa took pictures. One was printed in **Leslie's Weekly** which I found carefully preserved among all the memorabilia. Research revealed the Mafia was in control there for years. New Orleans was even its headquarters in the United States.

Another surprise developed from a letter written by Arthur to his sister back in Catskill. He had met a couple who had come across the Staked Plains of Texas in a "To Kansas or Bust" wagon. They reported desolation, rattlesnakes; they killed 30 in the first twenty days. Antelope were thick — sometimes 75 to 100 in a herd.

The Van Gelders only skirted the western part of this area which is really the Panhandle of Texas. Research revealed surprising facts of this comparatively small area. It was actually a microcosm of all I had ever heard of the Wild West. Famous in the region had been Coronado, Carson, Billy the Kid, the cattle wars, and much, much more.

After the scenic treasures of Colorado, the Van Gelders ended their lecture tour in Kansas where Grandma's brother, Smith Pine, had pioneered years before. Rebecca recalled her first visit just after Smith's wife had been burned to death, leaving two children. Rebecca had slept under a wagon on the prairie disturbed all night by "dogs barking." They were wolves and not far away.

Back home Arthur finished his senior year in high school and his father, Grandpa, interested himself in community affairs. Grandpa and Grandma went to New York City to do research and lecture at the same time that Arthur entered the College of Mines at Columbia. Carrie and her husband, Charles Wardle, again managed the properties and Grandpa gave some lectures and researched three branches of the Van Gelder families, some of whom had arrived in New Amsterdam as early as 1630.

Back in Catskill, the Water Works promotion continued. Grandpa was still at it when I was old enough to feel his keen disappointments when Carnegie and Rockefeller and many others were not interested *in* *backing it.*

Most exciting and charming of all to me were the letters from Francis R. Wardle, oldest brother of my father, Charles. I still have a cut glass perfume bottle that he brought from Paris in the 1890s. But in 1898 he and Aunt Isabel wrote of cliff-hanging trips on horseback up the Siskayun Mountains of Oregon to the Jupiter Gold Mines that he managed for two years. Sometimes they had to tunnel out of the cabin when it was completely buried in snow. Aunt Isabel invited all the miners for such a Christmas dinner as they had never had before. *Always take along a red tablecloth,* she wrote. *It helps, especially the first few days.*

To recoup losses from the mine and repay investors, Uncle Frank signed up with the Portland Lumber Company and sailed for the Far East. They left San Francisco just as the infamous Boxer Rebellion broke out in China in 1900. They reached Japan nineteen days later. The news was not good. His well-researched articles were printed in the **Portland Oregonian.** But their personal experiences in these lands that were then still very strange indeed filled fascinating letters that all the families, including Grandpa, in the States, shared.

In Nikko, Japan's loveliest summer resort still visited by the King, Aunt Isabel stayed in safety while her husband made business trips to Tiensin, Port Arthur, and other coast cities. She tells of

charming Japanese children bowing deeply from the waist as they passed. Boys and girls bowed to each other. Mothers and daughters were dressed alike in bright kimonos and brighter obis. Little people carried lesser people strapped to their backs. I wish I could put windows in my letter so you could see what I am seeing and can never tell you.

Shanghai became another headquarters. They rented two rooms from an English family and had a Chinese boy to wait on them. Like the coolie class he spoke pigeon English. The only bit I remember learning was "Catchee Chow Chow Chop Chop" — get dinner, quickly.

They took a three-day sail to Hong Kong, another three days on to Manila, and then to Singapore. Swarms of boat people choked the waterways. At Calcutta, India, they cut short their planned sightseeing trip throughout India and left behind all the dirt and weary train rides.

A fat little envelope among the letters was labelled, "Pressed violets from the secret garden of the Dowager Empress in the Forbidden City." Peking had been hard to reach safely, but the Dowager Empress fled Peking just in time for their visit.

All these charming, enriching, and informative letters ceased when they set sail for San Francisco in April, 1902. A quick vacation in the Olympic Mountains of Washington, and they were soon settled in an apartment in San Francisco. Uncle Frank continued to manage his company's business there.

It is the family's good fortune that Uncle Frank compiled a Wardle Genealogy before his death in 1904. He went back to ancestors on his mother's side who were co-workers with the Wesleys. Grandpa Wardle at 18 years had come over in 1848 with his father, Hugh Wardle, a pharmacist, and put himself through medical school. But he had Wesleyan blood, too, and gave up a good medical practice in New York City, where my father had been born, to become a Methodist minister. He was very good at healing sick churches. When he served the Catskill church, Grandpa Van Gelder sat in the pews. Some years later, his daughter Carrie Van Gelder married the minister's son. Charles Athow Wardle was only 13 when his father was assigned by the bishop to another place, but Charles stayed on in Catskill. He slept on the counter of the drygoods store where he worked. My father's mother had died when he was only two and a half years old. His father remarried, but none of the first family of children were happy with the stepmother. It could hardly have been easy for her either to take over a family of six children.

The terrible San Francisco earthquake of 1906 forced Aunt Isabel to hurriedly pack a little bag with a change of underwear, a picture of her husband, and her Bible. She fled across the Bay to Berkeley, where cousins lived. Later she stretched out a slender income and enriched her life by living in Florence, Italy. I practiced my high school French on her, and remember especially a postcard of the quaint Ponte Vecchio that spans the Arno River. It is barnacled from end to end with shops hanging to its sides, It became my Mecca in 1953 when I left a tour group to Europe and headed for Rome to visit an Italian family.

All branches of the family had roots in this stony but beautiful Greene County. And so did my husband's ancestors. I lived for eight years in the old Fiero homestead. There was an old Dutch door opening into the "cellar kitchen" with its enormous fireplace. One could keep the lower half closed to keep out the farm animals, I suppose. I could not stand in the living room to play my violin without hitting the hand-hewn beams in the ceiling. A parchment deed dated 1774 shows it was part of the old Loveridge Patent. Valentine Fiero, a French Huguenot, came over with our own Palatine ancestors in 1710. Some descendants still worship in the old Catsbaan Church where Van Gelder ancestors also attended.

The letters tell of happenings far afield and among the hills and valleys, mountains and streams, villages and farms, churches and schools. And always there were the stones and more stones. Many were long since gathered one by one from the fields and made into picturesque stone walls between fields and roads in order that fields could be plowed.

The shallow stony soil of this whole area had meant back-breaking toil for farmers to be able to plow and raise crops. The picturesqueness of the stone walls only added to the beauty of the mountains and river. The Catskill Mountain House — visited by celebrities from all over the world — and other famous boarding houses began to attract so many that the less affluent were soon sharing the butter and cream, the fresh vegetables and eggs at many a farmers' table. Boarders became the farmer's crop. Grandpa Van Gelder's Cherry Hill House was built to attract visitors from far and near.

Then came the time when the lovely stone walls were shovelled into the maws of giant machines that ground them up for the good roads we seemed to value more. So we made the circle and have gradually come back to building beautiful retaining walls of field stone, patios and rock gardens, stone by stone.

Copy of map showing the Fiero Farm, which was part of the Loveridge Patent

PART II
SCHOOL AND HOME LIFE

Squirreled away so long in Grandpa Van Gelder's old pine chest, the letters are well rested and able to speak for themselves. The earliest has a postmark of 1854. James Harvey Van Gelder was at Charlotteville Seminary to get the education a one-room school could not provide. There was no road over the Catskill Mountains to his destination. One had to go to Albany by boat or stage and then southwest by stagecoach.

His next older brother, William Myer, wrote the early letter. It was from Ashland Seminary which had just been built. It was his first school session away from home. Because the salutation is so stilted, I imagine him at his table in his small room with a school book open at a chapter on "How To Write Letters." It is practically the only letter in those early years at school when punctuation was fairly carefully followed. Most letters ignored capitals except for a few interesting categories, and punctuation was punctiliously ignored. The handwriting was small but finely formed. This is how he addressed the brother he was so close to:

William Myer Van Gelder, brother of James Harvey Van Gelder.

Dear Sir: *Ashland, 1854*
I have neglected to write to you before, I shall improve the opportunity by informing you of this place. We arrived here Wednesday after quite a pleasant drive. The Seminary was dedicated Thursday. On Monday my classes commenced. Studying hours are from eight o'clock to twelve from two to five and seven to nine in the evening. We have exercises in the chapel in the morning and in the evening at five there is reading a chapter from the Bible and a prayer
I suppose there is about two hundred students here already. Every two students have a room furnished with a bed a stove wash stand table and three chairs and a pail. The rooms are not very large each room has a small clothes press. We have good board Ashland is a pleasant place but I do not like it as well as Windham Center five miles further east. We have to carry our water and wood. The wood is already cut they intend to lead water into the building soon.
No student may leave the seminary unless they have a written request from the parents until the end of the quarter or term. Please send me the Tribune or Greene County Whig. Write soon as convenient correct all my mistakes so goodby for this time
        William Myer Van Gelder

In sharp contrast I prefer a later more natural letter written from the farm. Peter had given his two young-

est sons land and stock so that they could earn money for their tuition. Sometimes they took turns at school and at other times they were at school together. Grandpa was now at Ashland in the mountains. It was much more convenient to reach and closer to home. William wrote,

. . . I will bring a seamstress tomorrow to make your pants and coat and Mother is getting a pair of stockings ready so you wont have to go barefooted. I have bad news for you I had three fine roosters they were very promising and I expected a lot from them but day before yesterday our gobler struck the largest one with his wing and knocked him into kingdom come and so he went to pot I have received the first number of the Great Republic Magazine it is got up in fine style Jacob sent some books . . .
I would like to visit Ashland during the winter but I fear I shall not have time I paint some on stormy days. There are many scenes I desire to paint. I must close it is getting late the south wind howls without like an evil spirit wandering over the earth The folks are asleep The hens are on the roost the cats are gone on a general rat hunt or to a cat fight this has been the coldest day of the year
        William

Unlike later letters and especially the charming informative ones from Uncle Frank Wardle from China, punctuation is generally ignored and capitals practically non-existent in the letters of many of the friends and fellow students. One writer calls his letter *a gabble of pen and ink.* There was also a garble of the alphabet in most spelling. I garnered a few choice spellings. *Blessud immortality* for *rhiteous peopple* whose *elecution* may have had *Parasing* effect on any who came in *seckond*. One would be *busiere* than a centipede trying to put on his rubbers if he *excepted* all the *difrent nuse* he *herd* from *Coxacie* (Coxsackie) to *Callifernia*. You would find it *tegeous* and he would be *wearrying your patience*. *Go-aheadativeness* is not *rong* even if one breaks a *fieu* rules of *ediquet* as long as he tries to *speak more propper*. At *preasant* the *prise* is too high and might *bruse* your feeling, especially in a cold *whinter*. One of the worst spellers in the letters put an *h* after every *w* and left the final *e* off every word.

David, the oldest of Peter's four sons, still used the old-fashioned *s* which looks like an emotionally disturbed *f*, the upper part fooling us that it is a quite normal member of the alphabet, but the lower half twisted backwards and seemingly beset with some kind of schizophrenic caper.

William complained to James Harvey in one early letter of this oldest brother's criticism.

Dear Brother,
I was very glad to hear from you   David criticized my composition by examining my letters which were written carelessly and no definate subject. He also spoke of my being homesick now he does not know my thoughts and if I did get homesick it is no wonder as we are penned up here in a little room with no pleasure but study and no physical activity except the pleasure of eating when we have a good dinner or when we manage to get some pie in our room   The declamations and reading compositions on Saturday night are very interesting. I am much delighted with your conumdrums   Suppose you write some more
                    William

Other chit chat and seriousness afford fun and understanding unless you are looking for good composition and complete explanations of all the goings-on at home and school. To try to pick out the puzzle pieces from the letters and fit them together in a well designed picture or arrange them topically is practically impossible. The letters might lose much of their charm. I like it when William writes, *David has the walls of the octagon house half up   mother is making you some drawers   we are going to plow the south field tomorrow.*

The more I learned about the Van Gelder boys, the more curious I became about my great grandfather, Peter Van Gelder, the father of those four dirt farmers. Today they would be called entrepreneurs. Peter's letters written to the younger boys at school are scarce and to the point. One said little more than "You're spending too much money." He certainly was not a hard-headed old Dutchman who tried to keep them "down on the farm," though they all did their bit there. He let Grandpa take that rosewood melodeon way over to Charlotteville so he could learn to play it.

The newspaper, **The Catskill Mountain Star,** which printed a History of the Van Gelder Family wrote,

Peter Van Gelder was born May 20, 1800, in Catskill (the farm on the Old King's Road), and was educated in the district schools of the neighborhood, gaining a fair knowledge of the elementary branches, which he added to by extensive

Peter Van Gelder, my great-grandfather

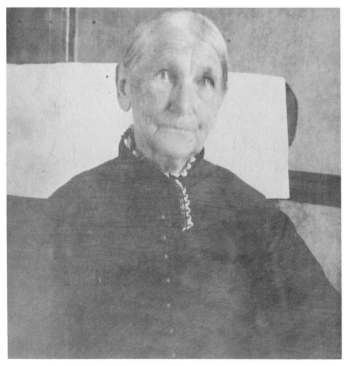

Sarah Myer Van Gelder, my great-grandmother.

reading becoming a well informed man. He had a good farm, and added to it from time to time until it became a valuable property. He was self-made man, of strong character possessing excellent business ability and was successful in anything he undertook. He was progressive in his methods for that day and being energetic and active, easily became a leader both in business circles and in politics. He was an old line Whig and was so popular with his fellow citizens that he could have had any office within their gift; but preferring to attend his private business and refusing many propositions looking to such an end. However he served for a time as assessor and road commissioner. He was a member of the Reformed Church of Katsbaan, in which he was an elder and a deacon (later moving to Catskill he was a member of the First Reformed Church). In affairs that had for their object public welfare he took an active part and was deeply interested in educational matters.

When Peter moved to the village, he turned over the running of the farm to his oldest son, David Henry Van Gelder, who was soon building an Octagon house not far from his father's house in town. It is the only Octagon house in Greene County and has been called "one of the purest examples of that unusual concept, now existing." It is a handsome red brick building still in good condition with some of the Norway spruce he planted still towering over it. The house could be seen from the Wardle's front porch.

J.C. Haviland, special correspondent for the **Times Union** of Albany wrote recently, "a handful of eight-sided dwellings scattered throughout the Hudson Valley and adjacent counties are graphic reminders of an architectural craze that swept the country." They were very popular during the 1850s when David's brothers, William Myer and James Harvey were away at Ashland Seminary. The man who promoted them was not even an architect but a phrenologist, Orson Squire Fowler. He was the author of many books. Letters tell of a phrenology course available at the school.

The main rooms in most octagon houses are not shaped like pieces of pie, as one might suppose. Instead they were usually square, with the leftover triangular space serving as closets, bathrooms and stair space. A nice touch in the grander octagons was a circular stairway leading all the way to the glassed in eight-sided cupolo on top of the house. Orson Fowler made the octagon house popular for ten years until 1850. They were roomier, brighter, cheaper to build, cleaner than their four-sided houses

Phrenology, a pseudo-science, read character from the shape of the head. Fowler lectured on phrenology and wrote manuals on marriage and health. In one of the lists of books and magazines that the Van Gelder boys were frequently buying and selling is one

with the title **Marriage.** But no author is given. There is also one on **Midwifery.** Did Fowler write them? How many light years were they away from our **Everything You Wanted to Know about Sex and Were Afraid to Ask?**

David was the husband of three wives, a record for our family. His also was the first divorce, rare in those days. Letters seem to justify the drastic action. His first wife, Mary C. Person, died in 1854, the year James Harvey, the youngest son went away to school. David's two daughters, Rebecca, seven, and Belle, often called Mary, five years of age, probably stayed with their grandparents when David went to Cleveland and into the grocery business. Contrary to the Van Gelder Genealogy, letters prove he was back in Greene County by November 23, 1856, when he "took hay down to Saugerties," and even earlier when he married Margaret Christiana Myers on April 2, 1856. Letters also show she did not get on well with her stepchildren or her in-laws. This marriage ended "between 1870-75."

Jacob wrote from his home in Saugerties to James at school, January 21, 1859:

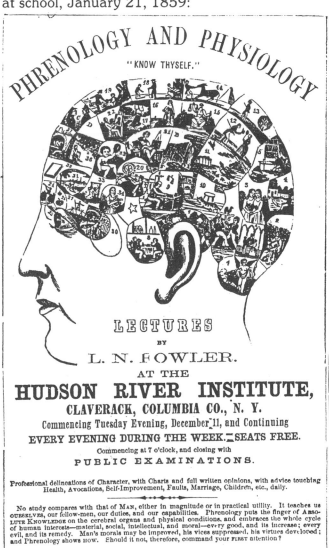

Phrenological Examinations Daily at the Institute.

Dear Brother,
As I have not received a line from you this winter I thought I would write to you and wake you up or are you absorbed or perhaps corresponding with [a picture of a pine tree referred to Rebecca Pine]. We are waking people up on the Water Cure journal and I have ordered some half dozen encyclopedias   Mr Silverchild had the croup very severely and he treated it with entire success on the watercure principle and . . . doctors losing every case they treated.

David told me you wanted him to run the farm now are you in favor of bringing his wife there and driving father and mother and all of us away now I will tell you what his plan is   he is doing all he can to induce father to go and live in Catskill and he has induced him to buy the old brick yard and build there and then have Rebecca and Belle live with our folks and have them educate them and he have the farm and all that is there and he knows mother never wanted to leave the farm but he is determined to have the farm and have them go away   our folks wanted him to buy John Haswell's place and then work part of the farm but he is determined to have the house and David's wife has been there and taken possession of all Mary's things and locked them up and carries the key around in her pocket and when she is up there she is just as independent and imposes on mother and the rest of them shamefully   Mother and Margaret Young even have to clean her room and wash for her young one and for her now are you in favor of having such a mistress in that house that our folks and all of us have worked so hard for   I could have no objections to David working the farm providing they did not live in that house because you and I could never go there

David has not the least feeling or respect for our folks or he would not have brought his whole family there this winter and made a slave of mother   I will expect to hear from you soon
Jacob Van Gelder

In August of that same year William wrote to James, still at Ashland Seminary,

Matters are not very amiable between mother and , well you know who   we have a supreme lord and Master in Petticoats, selfish, unreasonable, and ugly as the devil.

The home was enjoyed by a constant stream of friends and relatives and workers. But the die was cast, and by the next winter Peter was living in his new home in Catskill. David lost interest in the farm home and soon bought a part of the "farm in town" and started the Octagon house.

Aunt Ellen, the third wife, was a music teacher when I knew her. She was included in all our holiday dinners. Her one son, Howard, was an electrical engineer, very distinguished in a Van Dyke beard.

David was the last to be buried in the Van Gelder family burial plot. Cousin Lily from Saugerties took us there after I was married and pointed out where the slaves were buried with only wooden crosses, which had long since disintegrated. Then she added hastily and *very* defensively, *But Grandpa **freed** his slaves.* Only one slave is listed belonging to Van Gelder in the 1810 census acording to Beers' **History of Greene County, New York.** My husband could remember a colored man named Peter Van Gelder who used to walk past the Fiero farm on his way to Catskill. The deed to the cemetery was retained by the family, and the plot is protected by a thicket of blackberry bushes.

Jacob was five years younger than David. I remember him when my sister and I took the train to Saugerties to take violin and cello lessons from Ford Hummel, well-known violin teacher and father of two fine musicians, Earle Hummel, violinist, and Sanley, who is still giving concerts and teaching piano in the Albany area.

But as a young man, Jacob lived on his father's farm. When he was twenty-one, he became a school teacher. Later he moved to Saugerties where he devoted himself to horticulture and farming, chiefly as a dealer and trader. He also settled many estates and became well versed in commercial law. In 1877, he was elected director and later vice president of the First National Bank of Saugerties. He was an excellent debater and life member of the Pomological Society. A letter to James, then at Charlotteville in December, 1856, says:

Dear Brother,
I meant to write to you when I got back from New York, but Myer was down and said he was going there to school so he has told you that we have a Melodeon. I was their for Thanksgiving   Cousin Maria had the dinner and a party the next day I went to different Melodeons in the city and chose Mason and Hamlin   Jane Leifkin wants to give me lessons   I suppose you have Life Illustrated now.   I sent a subscription to Myer for six months direct to Charlotteville. I have not any business yet   I could have had a school if I wanted it but I did not like to go away from home   Julie is getting to be quite playful and mischievous   She begins to play the Melodeon. This winter I have a ticket to attend the lectures here   I have just attended the first one   it was by Prof. J.W. Fowler   he spoke two hours   the river is nearly closed   the Steamboat went down for the last time this evening
from your brother Jacob

In January, 1861, he wrote to James in his first year at Yale College:

Dear Brother
Our family has again been afflicted with the terrible disease of the brain and our little Willie is the

one   we had hopes for him until Saturday   but since Saturday evening he has had spasms almost continuously and is failing very fast now. 10½ A.M. our Willie is dying and he will soon breathe his last   the funeral will probably be on Wednesday parhaps at 1 oclock

Jacob Van Gelder

Like so many families, the children died young; Jacob lost three of his six children, ages one to four. Letters from other students spoke often of deaths, most often of the young. The young grown-ups died often from consumption or inflammation of the lungs as it was called. There was never the slightest suggestion that it was contagious.

Jacob's oldest living daughter, Annie, married her brother-in-law, Capt. Albert Thomas, who had been around the world three times as captain of a whaling ship. His last voyage is recorded in the log of the sloop Merlin in New Bedford, Massachusetts, in the Marina Museum. He was a spiritualist, we were told without comment, and that made him even more intriguing. Cousin Annie wrote quite intelligent but often wacky articles on nutrition and other hobbies for the local press. When my sister, Constance, wanted to borrow some money to study voice in Italy, Cousin Annie wrote back, "I'm trying for the Nobel Prize. If I win I'll help you."

Cousin Lily, Jacob's youngest daughter, was almost tragically short. She was sweet and mild but spunky enough to break away from her dominating sister, Annie, taking but few of a house full of antiques. She visited us often. When she missed her piano on which she could play simple hymns, I asked Stanley Hummel to help her pick out a miniature grand Steinway. A few years later when she moved to the home of her chauffeur's mother, she surprised me with the piano. Sometimes after our lessons Lily would walk the mile to the station with us. I was very tall and carried my violin case. Constance had her awkward cello. And when Lily tagged along with an old violin which Uncle Jacob gave us, we looked like a side-show troupe from the circus.

Peter's two youngest sons, William or Myer, as he was more often called, born 1836, and James Harvey called Harvey, born in 1838, were very close. Most of this group of letters saved in the old pine chest were written by William. He died at twenty-five years of age after being married just two years to a fellow artist.

In December, William closed a letter, sent to the farm, *We want to come home for Christmas if we can. If you would come up and fetch Willie and me on Friday before Christmas we should like to start from here Friday morning. Mr. Person will fetch us back.*

It is hoped the weather cooperated. Earlier in December Willie Person had written:

David Person came after James last night to

Cousin Lily Van Gelder seeing Constance Wardle off to Milan, Italy, where she would study voice.

attend the funeral of his sister Mary   he said snow had drifted so at Cairo that he had to leave his horse and come afoot up the mountain   he saw two stages drifted in the snow coming up the mountain and then he hired a man to fetch him up here   they started away from here at eight oclock last night   they werent going further than the top of the mountain last night.

James Harvey was home between terms when William wrote from Ashland, January 16, 1855:

you wrote such a short letter   inform me about the school at Charlotteville and of all the folks at home and what you study   I am more anxious to hear from home than you from me   you are only separated from one   I am separated from all the folks at home   send me some newspapers   I sent you some postage stamps in my last letter   I have received but one solitary paper from you since I have been here   I think that I shall not stay here more than the next half quarter if I do not like it better than I do now   write soon   as much as you can

Wm. Van Gelder

As mentioned previously, Peter had given his two youngest sons land and stock to work in order to earn money for their tuition. Once William wrote:

I've been pressing hay all day and took one load down this afternoon and will take another in the morning   Jacob is here evry week   as to company business I would say money comes in slowly and goes out fast   we received about 50¢ for our apples and cider   I have just paid father 25 on the grain and we have forty left   John Myer is here building a shed   Peter timmerman has been *here a few days we have commenced plowing the clover lot we have a piece in the vly to plow yet — that corner by the nut trees the nuts are all picked we sold some at $1.25 per bushel and can spare a few more*

Later when Peter was building his house in the village, he wrote to William and James at Ashland,

Do you want to work the farm this summer You need not work for wages. The chance I give you is after paying taxes and all necessary expenses and repairs you can give me one third of what the farm clears I will leave you all the farming utensils and team — that is three horses and other stock. If you take the form I should like to have a yoke of oxen. If you are not willing to work the farm let me know soon as you can as I must hire help or let it out. If I let it out you must expect to see it run down. Remember the loss will be yours more than mine. Write oftener than you have of late. David sent $50.

Your father

Happenings at school as at home are told best by the letters themselves. R. Edsall's long letter from Dixon, Illinois, was dated June 7, 1859:

Thank you for the information concerning our good old Philomantic League. I thought those fine who first joined hands in fellowship, having as their object self culture and the attainment of knowledge. I think I shall comply with your request and write some for your paper. I thought I would attend the Collegiate Institute here but it had commenced so I decided not to this term. My brother has a young law student. I recite Latin and Greek to him. I read history and other reading. From this source I believe we derive more than half of our education. I have good sources, the City library, my brother's books, my own library. It all remains for me to bring out the dormant faculties if there are any in my cranium. The "Word of God" I also consider to be very important. It demands our strictest attention in that we are taught the kind of knowledge which will prepare us for life and a blessed immortality.

Four months later, Peter Myers wrote in December, with the keen appreciation so many of the students showed for the Philomantic Society. Many willingly took part in the exhibitions and wrote articles for the paper they had.

I had the pleasure of speaking to your brother William Saturday he gave me much hopes of the Society I am glad, very glad that the Society is flourishing — a condition the other Society has long been boasting of their noble intellects and master exhibitions and harboured such ill feelings toward this Philomantic that it appears that the Society which has so long been persecuted and scoffed at by a larger and older Society shall at last become superior.

Debating was popular in school as well as in the community. James' father-in-law to be, Walter Pine of Kiskatom, a pillar of the Methodist Church, debated the Dutch Dominie of Kiskatom on Predestination in 1855. And they were *of the same opinion still* when they finished. William wrote James in March, 1859,

In your debating when they bring up an argument against something that does not exist you may say it reminds you of an Irishman who went hunting for the first time he saw a bird in the top of a tree and thinking he would kill it if he only pointed his gun toward the tree he blazed away and then went searching under the tree for his game and picking up a toad he exclaimed Arrah what a pretty bird you was before I shot all the feathers off you.

Astronomy also intrigued the students. An Atlas I found, bought, I'm sure, for school use, names two planets, Hershel and LeVerrier. They are now called Uranus and Neptune.

Willie Post asked:

Do you study astronomy? If you do give a night to Howard's telescope he made it I seen Jupiter and the moons around it and I seen the moon it looked very rugged and places that you cant see any stars with the naked eye you see hundreds of them. This is what I call a nasty day down here It will spoil the wheeling we have had splendid wheeling for the last few days.

When I rode my first bicycle over fifty years later, I too called it my "wheel."

Books and a lot of magazine subscriptions were sold by all the Van Gelder boys at home and in school. William wrote James at Ashland, December 20, 1858:

I send these books Jacob left 4 almanacs in the package which you dispose of as you think best I have not the bill yet but I will make it right with Jacob and charge your account.

The list is intriguing:

Bill 1858	James Harvey Van Gelder to Jacob Van Gelder, Dr.	
Dec. 16	1 Moral and Intellectual Science	$1.90
"	1 Combs Infancy	.45
"	1 Hereditary Descent	.45
"	1 Marriage	.36
"	1 Delia's Doctors in paper, no muslin	.37
"	1 Curiosities	.60
"	1 Midwifery	.60
"	1 Self Culture	1.45
"	1 Fruits and Farmacia	.60
	1 Syringe #1	2.00

The ladies were special, always. William Person, then at Claverack, New York, wrote to James Harvey at Ashland:

The school is a good deal larger than . . . Ashland rooms and they are furnished with the same as

your school is and the same kind of Ladies and we have pie and **pudden** *every dinner and apples and that is more than you have*

There was always vying to get students to come to their particular choice of school. J.W.W. wrote from Malden:

I have waited for you to write until I am tired now ill write to you and get rested . . . I suppose you have a fine time withe the Ladays as usual. Write soon.

Big news was the organization of a ladies' branch of the Society. Mulligan wrote from Palenville, December 4, 1859:

Your success in organizing a ladies branch of our Society and in gaining new members to fill our Hall has gone far beyond my most sanguine expectations. You can better imagine than I can describe the pleasure afforded me to learn of your success. And I hope those who have joined will be Philomantheans indeed. The Society Hall must present quite an appearance after having $10 or more spent on it fitting it up.

You requested to know how I got along teaching school. Well, I have 31 mischief loving urchins to exhaust my patience. However, I have succeeded very well so far. At first, I thought I would get along without a whip but before the close of the first week I became fully convinced of the truthfulness of Solomon's proverb, — If you spare the rod you spoil the child. It was with emotions of thankfulness to the author of all good that I received through you the intelligence of a glorious display of the power of God in awakening and I trust happy conversion of immortal Souls among those with whom I have been acquainted. I rejoice that the power of God unto salvation is being felt in your prayer meetings and hope it may be so general that all now within those spacious walls of learning may become savingly acquainted with him who hath power on earth to forgive sins. . . my time is so taken up in and out of school that I doubt I can send any pieces for the paper. I do not feel very well. Goodbye for the present
Bartholomew Mulligan

There was a special lady that was noted often in the letters — Rebecca Pine who married James Harvey Van Gelder when he graduated from Yale in 1864. She and her brother, Andrew, are both listed as students at Ashland. He was one of the many young persons who died at an early age of consumption. Rebecca continued to paint most of her life. Her easel was often around as I grew up.

Nostalgia was expressed in many letters when students were away from the school. It was especially poignant after the Seminary burned. Among the memories was *sitting around the stove with the Van Gelder carpet bag full of nuts and apples.*

Student preaching and prayer meetings were a part of the Ashland happenings, as well as back home. Many letters mentioned their own and others' spiritual health as naturally and as often as their physical condition. They *enjoyed religion*. It was accepted that one had to make a definite commitment to God, *born again,* some would say, in order to have a better life here and certainty of a blessed future for eternity. Were the more lavish expressions of religious convictions from those of the Methodist persuasion? But Beekman Van Gelder out in Seneca Falls took his religion, Dutch Reformed, just as seriously and yearned to go to the missionary field as a teacher. Even after he was married he speaks of a fine Sunday School class of boys that he enjoys, but wishes he were *teaching those who had never heard of Christianity.*

It is clear James Harvey *kept up the prayer meetings* at school, according to other students' letters. He was one of those who preached and had a reputation for being the *ablest of the student preachers* and was admired by the Ashland professors. Many letters attest to the fact that James Harvey entered Yale expecting to become a minister. Except for James' letter to William shortly before his death, the Van Gelder writers make no mention of their religious experiences or beliefs. They attend church, prayer meetings, and discuss sermons they hear. Is this the more reserved attitude of the Dutch and their denomination's greater emphasis in those earlier days on a well-educated ministry in addition to being converted and receiving a *call* to the ministry? Ashland Seminary was part of the

rapid growth of Methodism in New York just before the Civil War era. It spread like a belt from Amenia in Dutchess County to Cooperstown, New York. Although never officially under the control of the Methodist Church, including the one at Ashland, they were closely affiliated with

Rebecca Pine Van Gelder

that denomination . . . *The Methodist affiliation was further enhanced by the employment of ministers as principals. Faculty members were recruited from the same source.*

(Ashland Academy, by Flora Tompkins)

No words of a religious nature appeared in ink, but William comes across as a man who lives his religion without talking too much about it. On June 13, 1860, he wrote to James, who continued at Ashland all summer until he entered Yale, presumably polishing up his Greek. After telling of painting some photographs for Mr. Van Loan, who would give William and his wife Lizzie *all the work he can get, however without orders yet,* of progress on David's house, of having papered their new house, of a number of calls from Mrs. Cole, (widow of Thomas Cole, Hudson River painter), and her daughter as well as others, he says they returned the Cole call and *enjoyed it very much.*

I heard an excellent sermon Sunday evening at our church. it was on the spread of Christianity by the extension of civilization. he said, wherever civilization goes, there Christianity is steadily working its way never to be subdued all the Powers on earth cannot subdue it although an evil is nevertheless extending the influence of Christianity and all are working out the design of the Creator.

Slavery, that giant evil is more cornered in a small portion of the globe its grave is dug the knell of its departure is sounding France and England have abolished it and Russia is following their example. Caste is being abolished in India. China by her prejudices and intolerance which are ten times more formidable than her wall has tried to keep out Christianity but its subtle power will work its way through any barrier and that far off secluded people the Japanese Ah, they are among us he ended by a most earnest appeal to all to acknowledge the God of infinite power.

The minister was from the Trinity School, New York We expect our new minister Mr Chadwell of Maine this week. Lizzie intended to write this time but will do so next time. The locusts render the air vocal by their incessant music. Mr. Bennett is in Burlington Vt he will visit us this fall He says he is glad you're studying for the ministry and hopes you make a progressive one.

    William

On the home front everyday farm work continued to be interlaced with trips here and there, more frequent no doubt after the harvest was in.

In November, 1855, William wrote to James at Charlotteville:

Jacob went to New York with some sheep I went down Monday night and arrived 9 oclock Tuesday. Jacob met me and we boarded at DeGralls We had excellent board Went to the fair at the American Institute I think it equals the

World's Fair The Crystal Palace is as beautiful as ever it is a monument to Industry this immense light and airy structure was crowded with visitors. We went to Fowlers and Wells and got some books and a bust Last night we took the boat and came up to Saugerties we reached home this afternoon I think I shall go to Catskill tomorrow and next Monday start school you must not get homesick

On November 10, 1858, William wrote;

Yours rec'd. Bennett [art professor and friend] is coming next week David is in Kingston buying up fruit and nuts and so forth and sends them to New York I think I shall go down there next Saturday and he will come up with me. Jacob and Eliza were there last Saturday The horn is blowing for dinner Jacob came here this afternoon he is going with me to Catskill I shall carry forty chickens down you did not send enough old ones off last summer I dont like to spare young hens the old ones are full of pin feathers we will finish plowing the orchard today I was to Saugerties last Saturday I have pressed no hay nor sent any off since you left.

For another angle on the home front, Willie Post contributed his confession,

I was thinking if it was best to write this morning or not I can tell you my hand is not very steady I'll tell you why . . . I was to a party last Eve and they had wine and we all got gay as you make them you may think I ought not to drink any but it was in a private house Of course I wouldent go to a saloon and drink They was about 20 couples went to Saugerties on a Sleighride I think they had a fine time I expect Jim down this afternoon to go to your house and stay until tomorrow I want to go see David I havent seen him since he came back from the West I think you must be good at composing compositions the way you composed my letter I think you have improved very much Oh by the way I have a compliment for you the young gentleman that was down with you said you was the smartest student their and the best 20 degrees below zero this morning I thought I was like to froze my nose off If I had froze half my nose I would still have a decent nose yet As you know I have a walliper Please answer soon.

William wrote his brother at school that a letter had come from their cousin in Seneca Castle saying he no longer considered going to California.

In January, they took ship timber to Athens but *we cannot get any money until March.*

we will furnish you all the money we can we have some on hand If you can get subscribers I send a circular of the Great Republic Magazine they cost me .16 a number of 2.00 a year and 10 per cent off on clubs.

Father has bought 12 acres at $1.25 per acre and building lots along the turnpike   Wilson will sell his house for $2250. I would like to teach soon but have heard nothing from Kings on   If I do not go there I will try to get a painting class in Catskill   Just received my paints from Boston   we have sold all our sheep and expect to sell oxen in a few days . . . Am going to sing now with Angeline and Kate — the nightengales and the bull frog.

Singing schools were very popular and were often held once or twice a week in the schoolhouse. Prayer meetings were held, according to one letter, only every two weeks. Elections were of great interest. William told James, then in Charlotteville, November 5, 1856:

We have finished husking corn. Alonzo is plowing   Ann went home Sunday   Hannah Myer is here now. I was to election yesterday   it seemed to go pretty strong for Fillmore but I guess it was all in vain   there was very few Buchanan men   I think there was more for Fremont than others   it rained a little in the afternnon but the voters most all turned out. I heard no news of election yet   I intended to go to New York but cannot   we have too much to do

>   *Your affectionate brother*

It must have been an interesting time with the beginnings of the Republican Party which was founded in 1854. It opposed the extension of slavery. James Buchanan, the Democratic candidate, won the election. His attempts to keep the pro-slavery and anti-slavery factions in balance were admired, and his constitutional views were considered sound.

Abraham Lincoln, candidate in 1860, won the election for the Republicans. Millard Fillmore had succeeded to the presidency on the death of Zachary Taylor. Fillmore unsuccessfully tried to make the Whigs a national party to conciliate sectional strife. He joined the Know-Nothing Movement in 1854, hoping to unite the North and South and was its presidential candidate in 1856. John Charles Fremont, American explorer, was the Republican candidate for president in 1856.

Grandpa's cousin, Beekman Van Gelder wrote:
Our people are much entangled in the Political Question since the Pennsylvania election the news is Buchanan had 2000 majority   I call to mind hours of enjoyment we spent together in our strolls in the mountains   I often think of my visit to your house   I dont know if I ever enjoyed myself more   I have been busy everyday gathering fall harvest   we just finished husking corn   we have commenced plowing which I like very much this time of year   I suppose you are thinking of going to school if you have not already gone   Have you attended any lectures this fall   Sarah sends regards   James I have not seen your likeness yet   I want your and William's likeness.

At that time there were daguerreotypes, tin types, and photographs. Daguerreotypes became known in 1839. Coloring them was probably practiced by 1840. Tin Types also became popular in the 19th century. By 1850 photography began to be developed into an art. Stereoscopic photography was popular in the second half of the 19th century with the use of cameras with twin lenses.

The next month Beekman said:
Our presidential strife is over and many a political man's blood that was boiling has cooled down and we will dream away another year.

By the next presidential election it was all about Lincoln, John Brown, and slavery.

Changes — big ones — took place in the lives of the Van Gelders in Catskill during the years 1859, 1860, and 1861.

The big change for Peter, father of the clan, was in 1859. He bought land and built a red brick house in the village of Catskill. There was sufficient land for a farm in town. The property ran along West Bridge Street from Division to the south end of Railroad Avenue, now Maple Avenue, at the apartment house which was formerly the Cutglass Factory. It followed up Railroad Avenue, which perhaps was not yet so named, and ran north to the subsequently completed Division Street, not yet cut through that far. Then it turned down the hill on Division Street about halfway, jogged down toward the Washburn brickyard, now the site of Catskill's junior and senior high schools. This was at about the end of Dumond Street but included land along there up to Division and took in the Knickerbocker, one of two apartment houses built by Grandpa in the 1880s. From there it joined the West Bridge Street boundary which took in the land on the West of Division. Some part of the land between George Holdrige's current home on West Bridge and the old Peter Van Gelder House was part of an old brick yard shown on an old map in the Bagley-Chadderdon-Pulver law offices in Catskill. There was plenty of clay and sand in this area.

While the new house was being built in the village, William wrote to James at Yale:
Father had an accident at the new house. Some timber fell on his leg, breaking small bones above the ankle. He has but little pain   Now he walks with a crutch   I suppose I will help him for a few weeks. The walls are up to the middle of the second story and will be finished in a few days.

A month later he wrote:
We are making hay in Catskill and will finish this week. Father's leg is most well. He only stayed in the house two days. He has been at work ever since. Today he has been casting brick

This is the only mention made of brickmaking. I doubt if he made many. There was the large brickyard working when I was young. The land was finally sold for the new high school built in my son's senior year. The old "Academy" burned and he went "through the mill" — Wiley's mill, now Oren's Furniture Store. He attended this temporary schoolhouse, graduating in 1936.

Barges continued to carry brick from this brickyard above the currently named "Uncle Sam Bridge," on down the Hudson in my memory. One loaded barge broke loose during a freshet and took the bridge with it. Half the bridge was turned by a crank in the middle of the span to let boats through. Once I managed to get a ride on it as it turned. The replacement was mechanized and the span lifted with the help of a heavy concrete block. That still hangs unused, except for occasional graffitti, over the east end of the span.

By September William wrote James Harvey, who had just entered at Yale,

The carpenter has just finished the steps in front of the veranda. It looks well. We have a coal stove in the east room and my room is carpetted.

It was not long before the newcomers were receiving callers. They started attending the First Dutch Reformed Church of Catskill on Main Street. Trees were planted, among them many beautiful Norway spruce. I remember them towering over the house. Some are still standing. Fruit trees and berries were added. Later all the Wardle children picked cherries and berries. Grandpa was still planting trees when he was quite feeble, trees he would never see come to fruition.

The big change came for David a few months later. He lost interest in the farm home he was so determined to have and bought land from his father in the village. Preparations were under way by April, 1861, to build an Octagon house.

David himself wrote to James in May, 1861:

Have a quantity of work to do . . . I sowed oats on Friday on the upper side of the road. The lower side in front is not yet plowed. The drain in the Ensign lot nearly half had to be relaid before we could sow it. I will plow the garden north of the house tomorrow. I have the hill west of the house all planted and half the sand bank plowed. I went to the farm and made that fence around the garden, I have got the house done and the railing up. All quiet. No secession.

Father and Mother have started a tour of Malden, Saugerties and Plattekill, The garden is good. I am digging and grading the street and making fence. Father sold dry wood in New York for $4. [David wrote this on June 10.]

By June they were running up the walls for the second story. William tells James,

David's house is most finished. His children are still all here now but he may keep house in a few weeks.

It is never clear from the letters where his second wife, "the Lord and Master in Petticoats" was staying. Rebecca and Belle, her stepchildren, were often

mentioned as being with the grandparents, but probably her own daughter, little Minerva, called Minnie, was included in William's mention of *all the children* at this time. The divorce did not take place until the seventies according to the Genealogy. A letter to James at Yale on November 18 says:

The Hudson River still ebbs and flows as usual despite Democratic predictions. Our town went Republican although the county dident

The Genealogy mentions going into the grocery business in Catskill. Also that Peter deeded the farm to David and Jacob in 1872. Jacob subsequently bought out David's share. David built four covered bridges that I know about, all of wood with wooden pegs. The only date I have is for the High Falls Bridge. Elsie and Barbara Van Orden wrote in the **Quarterly Journal** of the Greene County Historical Society, for the summer of 1980,

In 1857 a great freshet damaged many mills and bridges along the Cauterskill. The covered bridge at High Falls was erected a short time afterward to replace the earlier span; David Van Gelder was the builder.

A photo of the bridge by James Harvey Van Gelder is printed with the article. I do not remember this bridge, although we often drove to High Falls in Grandpa's four-seater on a Sunday afternoon. The Van Ordens continued,

On one occasion Rufus (Smith) was shingling the bridge roof without a scaffold, lost his toehold, and nearly fell into the deep rocky gorge below. Fortunately another carpenter on the bridge caught Rufus by his thick head of hair and saved his life.

Another freshet in the spring of 1865 took smaller bridges away again, including a footbridge the Smiths used frequently. They replaced it right away. In 1921 the town took the covered bridge down and erected the present metal structure. At Asbury the covered bridge was replaced in 1908, while the one at Uncle Bob Smith's, near La Rive Restaurant, lasted into the 1920's.

This last bridge was one of three built. I remember driving over it and being told Uncle David built it. It was at the northwest corner of the Van Gelder farm on the Old King's road. I also remember in the 1920s that Frederick Fiero, my husband, helped take down covered bridges and replace them. Especially I remember the one by the Natural Dam. The Town Tool House was built on part of the Fiero farm, and he liked to work with the men. Anything in the building or mechanical field intrigued him more than farming, and he was excellent at it.

The question of how one gets to be a *leading local master builder of covered bridges* as the Genealogy says, is perhaps answered by the fact that David was a carpenter as well as a farmer. **The Covered Bridges of the Northeast,** a book by Richard Sanders

Covered bridge built by David Van Gelder near Van Gelder
farm on Old King's Road.

Octagon House, redbrick, built by David Van Gelder in 1860.

Allen, lists no Greene County bridges, but does tell of the Italian Architect Andrea Palladio of the post Renaissance period. He had a great deal of influence over our covered bridges and came to be called the grandfather of American covered bridges. In 1570 his four-volume **Treatise on Architecture** shows four different applications of the truss system to bridge building. He put plans on paper for others to follow. In 1764, two decades after his designs appeared in an English edition, the first application of the truss system to bridges in America is supposed to have occurred. The big timbers that went into the pioneer bridges took considerable manpower to put together. There was a crying need for a substantial bridge that could be built by a common carpenter's gang. Thiel Town devised an entirely new type of bridge truss. Copies of his pamphlets with his patented method were spread far and wide. Rival bridge promoters exchanged polite notes via the press. Much information was available for local bridge builders.

Meanwhile, Jacob remained in Saugerties and did well in several areas of business and agriculture. He married Eliza Van Etten, June 24, 1854. He had six children, of which three died when they were very young. Three daughters lived to adulthood, but he had no grandchildren.

The **Catskill Mountain Star** of Saugerties continues the Van Gelder Family History,

Jacob acquired a good education in the district schools and was especially proficient in mathematics ... After making his home in Saugerties he devoted himself to horticulture and farming and became widely known as an authority on fruit culture ... He had thoroughly mastered the science of pomology, and was eminently successful ... Much of his time was occupied settling estates ... and in real estate and banking business ... becoming vice president of the First National Bank. He was always a popular man and a leader in all movements tending to the public welfare. In politics he was a Republican, and while not taking a very active part in political matters, endeavoured to see that good men were put into office.

The big change for William was his marriage to a fellow art student, Eliza Taylor of Glastonbury, Connecticut. He wrote New Year's Day, 1859, to James, still in Ashland for his final year. William was at the new home in Catskill village.

I expect to be made very happy on January 25. It would be pleasant if we could go together to Conn. They want me there the Sunday before.

William had advised his brother that he would need a new coat and hat. He had bought the material for James in Saugerties and said Mr. Lyons, the tailor, thought he *could make it fit even without measurements.*

Shall I get a necktie for you   they make them of

ribbon and have them about ¾ of an inch wide they cost but little   I have two standing collars you may have one ... the marriage will take place in the church about 10 or 11 A.M. on the 25th then we will start for Hartford immediately after   there will be two bridesmaids and two

Jacob Van Gelder, brother of James Harvey

groomsmen   You and Jane will enter first and we will follow and the other groomsman and bridesmaid will bring up the rear   You and Jane will stand on our right   the bride will wear a travelling dress and hat.

I will go up to Catskill, Saturday if I can   I have seven pupils commenced here in Saugerties but I will have to work hard to finish them and I do not think I can collect all the bills immediately   it will be hard to get money enough   there is still about 28 dollars in the pocketbook proceeds of the sale of one steer   the other is not yet sold   I suppose the money in the pocketbook belongs mostly to me and father   If I cannot collect enough I suppose I must borrow a little   Mother has not been very well but is better   write soon

William

In January, before the wedding, William took time to arrange to have printed in the Saugerties paper, an article written by James describing a visit to Thomas Cole's studio. At the same time he put an ad in the paper, **SCHOOL OF DESIGN.** As usual, William was always busy those months before the wedding. He worked on the land and helped with the new house and grounds. One day Jacob came up with 500 plants, and *we put them in.* Callers came to welcome the new residents. William painted, and even more important at this time, he tried to start painting classes. Besides the nearby towns, he went as far as Princeton, New Jersey, but found there was little money around for art lessons.

After they were married William and Lizzie apparently made his father's new home their headquarters. They got some coloring work from Walton Van Loan, cartographer, well known for his maps, panorama of the Catskill Mountains, and as author of the annual **Catskill Mountain Guide.** Although Van Loan promised them all the coloring work he got, very little seems to have been forthcoming. They continued to travel around to start painting classes. On October 5, 1860, William wrote to his brother,

I feel considerably better. David and I went to the fair at Cairo, Tuesday and Wednesday. I took a collection of apples and some chickens. Lizzie sent some photographs and that little landscape of mine, the scene in New Hampshire.

A leaflet about his paintings includes a list of paintings from the Adirondacks and New England states, besides the copies of Thomas Cole's Voyage of Life series, Childhood, Youth, Manhood, and Old Age. When he made trips to the Adirondacks, there is no clue.

I received a $2 premium at the fair for the best and greatest variety of apples. I had 14 varieties and I received second premium of the Volume, Transactions, on fowls   a lot of Shanghais took the first premium because they were a little larger   they were old ones and mine were chickens   Lizzie took a premium — that little landscape of $2.00 and a Volume on Transactions as a discretionary on the Photographs as there was no premium offered on painted photographs. David received no premium on his colt although he thought it was the best   it certainly did not look as slick as the others. My expenses at the Fair were $2.00   the fair was quite creditable   That note for the heifers has been paid $34.00 to whom does the money belong   the Company or you or I? There is nothing in the books about it   has father paid for the straw cutter? It is not down in the book   Everything that the Company sold ought to be in the cash book   i remember nothing about that note but thought it belonged to the Company.

Lizzie's father and mother are coming to visit us soon   we are picking our winter apples   [These must have been from out on the farm.] Apples are from 75 cts to $1.50 per bbl. We have Rainy weather most of the time.

Write soon, Yours etc.   W.M. Van Gelder

William had begun for the first time to mention his health in these letters. A little earlier in August, 1860, before that trip to the Cairo Fair, he had spent some time at the Water Cure in New York City. He wrote James, at home.

. . . I think I am improving slowly. I am feeling better and have a good appetite, but do not feel very strong, especially those warm days this I think is the warmest day we have had   My expenses

here are $10.50 a week as I room alone and do not find my own bathing sheets, blankets and comforter   this is the only way I could do this week   Next week I could get a room with someone else and it would cost me $8 per week

They have a man here to give the movement cure   he exercises the patients for an hour each day by moving their limbs in every direction and they use their strength to draw them back   in that way he exercises all the muscles in the body   one patient says he has doubled his strength in two weeks   the man charges a dollar a week to give the movements   I have not tried it yet   I am tired of the city and wish I were home   I may possibly come Monday with the dayboat instead of Wednesday but I suppose it would be better to stay until Wednesday   if I can get money enough   If I come Monday I shall want $12 and if I stay until Wednesday I shall need $3 more   It would be best to send me the money yet this week   I expect Lizzie Saturday morning   She wants to make some visits here.

I saw George Fox day before yesterday and today again that first barrel sold for $2.50   he thinks he will sell tomorrow for $2 or $2.25 for sweet and $1.75 for sour   so you can judge what they come to and know what balance to send me.

Yours truly   William

The Water Cure seems to have been quite popular. In earlier letters Jacob and his brothers mention selling subscriptions to the **Water Cure** magazine. Andrew Pine, whose sister Rebecca became my grandmother Van Gelder, took the cure. At one time his health was reported very much better. But he died very young in 1859, after a long illness — consumption which was rampant throughout the area. William wrote James at Yale, November 20, 1860, after the fair,

I intend to go back to the Water Cure in about four weeks. My health does not seem to improve as much as I desire   my cough is no better   I have appropriated $11.88 of yours which I hope you can spare till I receive some from pupils. Lizzie and I are forming a class in painting   I cannot speak of success yet. I expect Mr. Bennett here in about two weeks.

Back in New York for another Water Cure, he wrote on December 29, 1860,

We have now decided to go to Wilmington, Del. tomorrow at 7 A.M.   I bought here some packing clothes (for the Water Cure) that I do not use, viz 2 comforters and a woolen blanket   I will send them to you by Express Yours in haste
*   Wm.*

The only letter I have which was written by James Harvey himself is dated December 30, 1860. James was at Yale and William and Lizzie had decided to go to the warmer climate for his health.

New Haven, Dec. 30, 1860

Dear Brother,

I received yours one day after I sent my last to you. I am sorry that you feel your health is such that it will be necessary for you to do another Watercure.

Try to keep your courage and look to the source of all strength and support.

In case of sickness as in everything else we should do all in our power for ourselves while we leave the result to God. He knoweth what is best for us better than we ourselves.

Then let no gloomy thoughts and discouragements oppress you but resign yourself wholly to the will of Christ, who knoweth our infirmities and who has promised never to leave us or forsake us. If you can live thus resigned feeling you have done all in your power, that trust and consequent cheerfulness which you enjoy, will tend to hasten your recovery, while if the worst must come, it will be your passport to a fairer land than this.

JHVG

Two weeks later, still striving to improve his health while attempting to start painting classes in Wilmington, William wrote his brother on January 14, 1861,

I am as well as usual and we like it here very much. It is not so cold here and I can go out every day   I like it at Dr. Craig's   We alone board there   It seems much like home and we have excellent board which suits us   have plenty of sweet potatoes and it cost us $11 per week   We would like to stay here until the latter part of March   We dont do much teaching as there are hard times here   there is much manufacturing for the South market and the hands are either discharged or on half pay.

I shall try to introduce the Art in some of the schools in a few days   Perhaps I can do something there   If I cannot pay my expenses I will borrow money and stay for my health demands it. I cannot go to a cheaper Cure   I wrote home Friday morning   I have not heard from home in some time   I am entirely out of money at present
Yours,

Direct c/o Dr. Craig   William M Van Gelder

About three weeks later on February 5, 1861, William wrote,

I have had a severe cold for more than a week past and have been kept indoors but am better now   I walk out every day   It is warm and pleasant.

I could not get money to stay more than the middle of this month and we had decided to go home then but Dr. Craig came to my room this morning and said he was afraid to let me go home   It would be too cold for me   that I would run much risk so rather than let me go I might stay three weeks longer and he would take pictures to pay That will be the 7th of March. I think I will stay the river may be open then and we could go $4

cheaper.

Lizzie has gone out in the country this week to visit a friend about three miles from here   She is going to give the girl lessons in painting   She has given the doctor's wife lessons in painting   That is all that we have done down here   The times is too hard   Mr. Bennett has given up teaching and gone to Charlotteville with his wife   He took supper with father last week

People is mostly for the union here   I thought if I went home I would send you what money I have left when I get home   I dont know when I can spare any more   Write soon.

William died twelve days later, at the age of 25 years. He was game until the end though finding it harder and harder to make both ends meet during the hard times and with increasing poor health.

On Christmas Day 1860 Donald Brown wrote from South Amenia, Dutchess County, N.Y.

Dear friend Van Gelder,

A thousand merry hearts are in New Haven today, I hope you are one of them. A merry Christmas to you. I am having a happy time of it. I lectured on Sunday evening to a full house and succeeded well. I lecture again next Sunday morning. I shall probably lecture at Amenia, 7 miles north of here before a Literary Society connected with the Academy. Also on Sunday afternoon and evening on Mission. Of course I am the lion of the place here. They have an idea that a student from Yale is almost a supernatural being. I have been invited to parties, to make calls in various places and to perform many other outlandish things. Indeed I went so far the other night as to go home with a pretty young lady. Of course, I did not tell her that I was conditioned in Euclid. But I did tell her many things of Yale. I shall leave here next Tuesday and be in New Haven on Wednesday. Do not forget to send me immediately any letters. I am confident that I can make at least $25 here before I leave.

But James' heart was hardly merry. It was on December 30, 1860, that he wrote to William. The letter must have been returned to him after William's death so soon after. The letter is evidence that he knew how serious William's condition was at that time.

Professor C.C. Bennett was not only his art teacher, but a close friend, who visited often at the Van Gelder home. His obituary for William in **The Examiner** is surely one of the choicest of its kind for that era and no less sincere for all its flowery phrases. It is impossible to choose what could be left out. If the reader can skip some of it, more power to him. I relish every word. It tops everything in this book for this type of writing. If Bennett painted as lavishly as he wrote this ode to William, he must have outrainbowed Van Gogh's brilliant third period.

The Late Wm. M. Van Gelder
by Prof. C.C. Bennett

One more gone — one more faithful and beloved friend departed — **PROFESSOR WILLIAM MYER VAN GELDER IS NO MORE!** — "Gone" sings the blue-bird, waking the spring with a sadder tone — and the trees that were hastening to put forth their leaves to gladden his sight again, shiver through all their fibres. "Departed" sob the waters just bursting their winter chains, and in whose depths he loved to see the reflections of the soft landscape around. "No more!" groan the grand old Catskills, that had lifted their tremendous figures of sublimity before his rapt vision for nearly a quarter of a century. "No more!" I heard that sound in its deep monotone roll along the lonely mountain lakes, leap, and wail, and murmur through the cavernous abysses and ravines of the now desolate Kaaterskill! Hear the voice of the woods and waters, "Who now," they ask, "will perpetuate our forms of beauty in living colors — who now shall study us with fond admiration and draw from us the wonderful lessons taught through us by the Great Creator?" and wind answers to wave, and wave to mountain solitude — "Lo! he has left us, and who shall fill his place on earth?"

Ah, I remember the quiet unobtrusive face, the first day I saw it — how it won upon me with the gentleness — how it's influence strengthened, on and on, with the years! Then I went to his mountain home, in the year of the great comet — all will remember the autumnal beauty of that year: to me it was one of peculiar interest. Their happy home among the hills; it rises before me now in all the richness of its surroundings of well cultivated fields, and fine old forests, and magnificent views, afar and near. We strolled and sketched together, days and days in that autumn sunlight so golden, till the foliage, at first green, changing little by little into a gorgeous glory that gradually fell, leaving the bare arms of the trees against the hazy sky. How often have I thought of his musical laugh then — the out gush of his genial nature. I remarked it as vieing with the low cadence of the rippling streams playing over the pebbly beds, by whose side we wandered and wove the web of passing time. His fair young wife! now **alone!** How well I remember **that** summer — that to her never-to-be forgotten summer, in that most beautiful City of Elms — ancient trees that whisper through all their over-arching branches the true tales of the long ago, echo upon wavelets borne through all the summer air. It was there and then they saw each other for the first time — she in the full bloom of her girlhood, he in the maturity of his strength. I was at their Catskill home in December last, when they left for the South. I saw the unusual lingering radiance of the last sunset before his departure — heard the winds roar through the passes of the echoing mountains, and listened to the pine-trees moan, but I did not know that it was because he was leaving them forever. I saw that Mother part with her sick son for the last time, while her eyes with tears were brimming o'er. Who can know how deeply her heart is crushed! A few weeks since she said to me, "O, I feel that there is no hope of his recovery by man — no one now can restore him but his Saviour." About the day he was expected home the angels took him — the lamp of life had burned to its socket — it flickered — then suddenly all was dark — he was dead! That light now irradiates a more blissful sphere: one more tie is severed that bound me to earth — one more attraction is set that draws us towards heaven.

Williamstown, Massachusetts,
2nd March, 1861

Four paintings known to me of William's are still in existence. Two are from the allegorical Voyage of Life series by Thomas Cole which William copied when was in New Haven. It seems logical that he studied art from C.C. Bennett at New Haven, possibly knowing him first from the Charlotteville Seminary. It is possible also that he met his wife there as a fellow art student. She came from Glastonbury, near Hartford, Connecticut. These two copies, now hanging with Thomas Cole mementoes in the Bronck House, were in my possession for many years and hung on my wall, even though the Hudson River School of Art was not as popular then as it is now. It seems to have made a comeback. The ones I had were "Childhood Emerging from a Dark Cave" and "Old Age," headed for great unearthly "castles in the sky." Another landscape of William's was given to the Catskill Public Library and hangs in the front reading room almost opposite "Prometheus Bound," the smaller one Cole painted, which is hanging over the mantle in the back reading room. I remember the immense painting of "Prometheus Bound" of Thomas Cole's that hung over the mantle in the Cole home, where our Monday Club met one day.

I have one of William's own landscapes — very delicate work. It is keeping watch over my shoulder while I'm writing about this talented and cultured young man.

William's widow stayed in Catskill. She wrote James at Yale on April 5, 1861,

Dear Harvey,

. . . I am pleased that you will meet me in New York. I will wait for you Tuesday morning on the Catskill boat. I know if I should stay a few weeks longer it would be much pleasanter traveling but it is always pleasant at home and I so long to go. I know that you will be very lonely there now that Myer is taken away but you will find so much to

Grandfather clock case made by Frederick C. Fiero at 15 years of age. It encloses "old wag on the wall clock." Sawfish caught by James Harvey Van Gelder at New Orleans during Stereopticon Lecture Tour. Painting by his brother, William Myer Van Gelder, who did copies of Thomas Cole's Voyage of Life paintings which are in the Bronck House Museum, Coxsackie, New York. Fiero rocker. *Photograph by Winifred J. Clark.*

take your time and attention that you will enjoy your vacation. All are well at home. Your mother is busying herself with preparations for your return.

 I hope to see you Tuesday morning. I remain
   Truly yours, E.T.V.G.

From South Glastonbury, her parents' home she wrote July 16, 1861,

Harvey,

My dear Brother . . . We will be most happy to see you. I was on the point of writing to beg that you would come and stay for a few days. I feared that you would think you had to hurry home as soon as possible and not come to us. I intend to return home with you. Jennie may go with us. She wishes to and I wish to have her. I shall not think of telling you more until I see you . . . Henry will meet you in Hartford at the West Thompson's Store at 3 P.M. I shall ask a favor of you if you please and it is convenient. We would like you to go to Mr. Person's and get a package. It is a dress Uncle Henry

was to get for Jennie. If you can bring it with you, you will be doing Jennie a great favor.
   Yours truly,
   Sister Lizzie

James was still home for the summer when Lizzie wrote on August 17, 1861, from Brighton, Pennsylvania, at the Kenwood School:

Probably this letter will find you at home or somewhere in the neighborhood of Kiskatom where you are enjoying yourself quite as much as at home. Give my love and best wishes to Miss Pine. I hope to see you in Catskill in a few weeks.

I have come to the conclusion that it is not best for me to remain here through the winter . . . That is my selfish opinion. I cannot give up the study of Art and wish to improve myself in it. I cannot give it up . . . I have written this in confidence. You will not mention it to the family at home. If you could advance a sufficient amount of money to pay my fare home by disposing of the Melodeon it would oblige me greatly. I regret exceedingly the necessity of speaking of it but if I have a share in the Melodeon I can feel perfectly right in doing so . . . I would not ask if I had any other way of possessing the means of defraying my expenses home. I do not feel that I can ask father. There are others that depend on him for everything. Do not think it strange for me to ask this favor. It is the only way of easing the small need that I have at my command.

Remember me with much love to all. Write me as soon as you can.
   Yours with sisterly regard, ETVG

Two years had passed before another letter to James, still in Yale, managed to get itself saved for posterity. William's widow wrote from Kenwood in Pennsylvania on June 8, 1863,

Dear Brother,

You will be somewhat surprised to hear that I am really in Brighton. I have been here two weeks and feel quite at home. The scenery is picturesque and charming and I have commenced making sketches. I feel encouraged as my uncle is quite a critic and does not consider my poor attempts without merit . . . I am very sorry to disappoint the people at Catskill, but will hope to see them at no very distant date. I did not know that I should come here until a few days before I left home.

Mrs. Taylor is an invalid, extremely ladylike, and somewhat haughty and formal in her manners. She has been accustomed to the best society that Washington can afford, a southerner by birth and sympathy. I would not think of calling her anything but Mrs. Taylor although she is very friendly to me . . . My uncle is extremely kind and thoughtful for my happiness. Both Mr. and Mrs. Taylor will not allow me to do anything that Mrs. Taylor would not do. I trust the pleasure of hearing from me will

make you overlook all that is amiss in this letter.
I remain truly your sister,
E.T. Van Gelder

Still in Kenwood, Lizzie wrote some weeks later, on August 28, 1863,

Dear Brother,
You must have thought when you read my last letter that I was in a great fret to get away from Kenwood. So I was and I am not anxious to remain after thinking about it. I was quite ashamed of my letter. I was very much distressed about something that occurred at that time, and which I will explain when I see you. I cannot feel quite happy here although Kenwood is a lovely place. Give Father many thanks for the present he sent me. I hope to see you some time next month.
Remember me with love to all,
Sister Lizzie

The final letter from his brother's widow found among the letters in the chest in the attic is dated December 22, 1863. She was at Hartford at her parents.

You have probably heard of my return home before now . . . I hope that our invitation for you to spend Christmas with us in Glastonbury will not be too late. As this is your last year in college we cannot expect to have you visit very often when you have left the state. Mother is very anxious that you should come and speaks of it nearly every day. I have so many things to tell you about that I dont know where to begin, so I shall not attempt to tell you anything until you come. Hoping to see you very soon, I remain with love,
Sister Lizzie

The big change for James Harvey Van Gelder, the youngest of the four sons of Peter Van Gelder and Sarah Myer, came when he went to Yale College in New Haven, Connecticut, in the fall of 1860.

All during 1859, he had continued to be very active in Ashland Seminary. Letters from fellow students attest to the fact that he was a moving spirit in the Philomantic Society, the students' self-culture organization. James started a Ladies branch. Letters ask, *Do you still keep up the prayer meetings?* Rev. Howard wrote, *I hear your sermons are spoken of as the ablest among the young preachers. Dominie Hal esteemed it highly. So did Miss Beard.* In fact when this professor wrote to him in November after he had entered Yale, he addressed the letter to the Rev. James H. Van Gelder. This seems a little previous just because he had preached some good sermons and made up his mind to enter Yale as a Divinity student.

He had continued in Ashland right through the summer of 1860 to improve his Greek. There had been some criticism of the quality of the teaching of this subject at Ashland. Some students went into it quite thoroughly and injured the professor's feelings.

By the time James was in Yale the Rev. Howard wrote,

Your letter was perfectly satisfactory regarding the points to which I called your attention. Did you ever meet with difficulty in Greek which was not satisfactorily disposed of between us?
I am glad to ascribe to you uncommon perseverance in research. When a scholar digs out that which I did not correctly perceive at a hasty glance, nothing gives me more pleasure than to ascribe to him all the merit. I have seen college professors who have to back down from assumed positions. Meanwhile, if I can succeed in awakening a spirit of inquiry I am satisfied however it might put myself to the test . . .I have appeared in the October number of the "Ladies' Repository"
Yours fraternally, R.H. Howard

There were bound volumes of this magazine with Rebecca Pine's name and also some with her mother's name on them. Copies were given to the Bronck Museum Library to complete their set. One marked Rebecca Pine was given to Grandma's great grandchild, Rebecca Pine Daniels, my brother Charles' granddaughter.

Although the ties with the farm had shifted to the new home in Catskill village, Grandpa and William continued to mention their "company business" at the farm. Jacob Lasher was to work the farm. David would still have part of it during the summer.

Two bits of news showed up in letters at this time. Beekman Van Gelder, Grandpa's cousin, had married in June, 1860. He had built a house. They talked of visiting Catskill on their honeymoon, but the outcome of the plans is unknown. A letter about an unknown person said, *Ann P was married so Mary must dance in the pig's dish.* It takes a little imagination to try to figure out what that colloquialism meant, but a fair guess would be that Mary was the older sister and had been left in the lurch by available swains.

Just one letter from Rebecca Pine, James' fiancée, had been found many years later. She was attending the Charlotteville Seminary from which she graduated in 1862 as valedictorian. During that last summer she wrote in June, 1860, when James was still in Ashland before entering Yale in the fall.

Dear Harvey,
Your last I received Wednesday. I must say to you it was welcome. They always are; so also would your presence be on the great fourth so near at hand . . . I should be so happy to see you then; you know it is Leap Year. I am taking advantages.
I am in the room of a dear sister Weslyan. She is just now assisting another one of our noble band, when that is done her Latin books are ready for her   She likes it very much, and so do I but I think it would have been better to read Caesar before Virgil.

The spirit of writing seems to have left me; I thought when I commenced that I was blessed with the presence of such a spirit, but never mind it may fly this way again.

How I would like to be at Conesville tomorrow to hear that young Dominie, but wishes are vain, so I will pray for your success: you say that you are glad to hear that I am enjoying myself so much in religion . . . I am glad too and secretly wish I had a great deal more   there is a lady here, a Miss Hill from Conn; the most devoted lady I have ever known: she has a good influence of course: I am sure I will never forget her . . .

Three weeks ago immediately after tea we had a short prayer meeting as is our custom in Miss Hill's room. It was not unusually interesting to me but Miss H seemed so perfectly happy I wished that I might feel so too. I thought I would stay and talk with her   Carrie stayed too   in a very short time it was proposed we have a kneeling again before the public one in the Chapel   It was perhaps nearly an hour before the bell rang all of which time we spent in prayer and such a blessing as we received I think cannot soon be forgotten   it seemed as though light came right down from heaven upon us. it was for pure and holy hearts that we were praying   Miss H received the blessing of sanctification two years ago: she is so happy always   O, that I might always live in possession of this perfect peace: God is so willing to give it to us and always so ready to aid in our endeavours to do good: We should be more careful of our daily influence and avoid the very appearance of evil: our minister this morning spoke of the strange inconsistencies in the lives of some who prayed so earnestly . . . all our good desires unless put into practice every hour will avail nothing . . .

I do not know that I need apologize for writing so much about religion for it surely concerns us more than anything else . . . There are some men here who seem inclined to carelessness and wickedness in their daily lives but I was completely surprised a few mornings since to learn that one young man, not more than sixteen who seemed so devoted last term, and who is preparing for missionary work, to learn that he was found drunk this morning. I feel I dare put confidence in no man. I was so much pleased with him and thought he was so good then to find myself so mistaken, but my thoughts quickly turned to one in whom I had confidence, one who I believe to be virtuous and free from the many cursed evils with which the lives of so many young men are bound . . . Purity of life, purity of thought and purity of purpose we must have to be happy here   My faith is strong tonight . . . You know I have sometimes dreaded to become old for fear I should not be so happy as I am now, yet I do my duty I shall be happy, and

*why not   I have friends to love me and **one** that I feel **is** and **will** be true to me, sharing all my life, one than can overlook my faults and love me still though so unworthy: But here I have been scribbling and near the bottom of the seventh page with a miserable pen, if you do not get a little out of patience reading it, I shall almost wonder **Please** to answer this with your presence. I wish so much to see you and to hear among other things how the young dominie succeeded today at Conesville.*

From your "Lulu"
[Rebecca Pine]

It would be four years later before they were married soon after Grandpa's graduation from Yale. Meanwhile, a letter from a fellow student who had gone to Concord to study for the ministry clearly depicted activities in the churches at that time.

We have to study hard here from morning till night yet I am enjoying it and in fine spirits. I preached in the chapel about four weeks ago and had the best time I ever had. The Lord was with me. I did not use any notes. We have established a Preachers' Association here for preaching to the southern part of the city. The Association has hired a hall for the purpose of preaching Sunday evenings. The most of the seniors have preaching places.

I suppose you are rejoicing over the election of Lincoln. Although I have not turned Republican yet I dont know as I have much against his being president. Certainly I wish for prosperity for our country whether the government is in the hands of the republicans or democrats. There may be some disorder in the South yet I hope that everything may move quietly and peace and harmony reign throughout our borders. I believe this is the sentiment of every true-hearted democrat.

Am now taking lessons in elecution from Prof. Roe of Vermont   We pay him $60 for twelve lessons, (forty of us). He understands the art well. I think I have already profited much. I suppose you are making your mark in college.

About four weeks before William died, on January 15, he had written, *Is it true that Ashland burned?* The best description of that catastrophe which I found among the letters was from A. Coons. He wrote,

Dear Friend,   January 17, 1861
I write these lines to inform you the Ashland Seminary is no more. On Tuesday, Jan. 5, 1861, at one o'clock PM that noble edifice was crumbling to the earth under the effect of that terrible element, fire. At 3 o'clock it was a heap of ruins. The way the fire originated no one exactly knows. It is conjectured however that it started from the chimney. It was first seen from the fifth floor right at the belfry. We were at dinner when the alarm was given. From there you may easily expect that there

was a rush however not much confusion. The students saved nearly all their things. Prof. Henry J lost considerable many things as did Otto. The pianos were saved except one, as was also the Library. The philosophical apperatus, the beds in all the students' rooms, the stoves, tables, chairs were nearly all burned. Prof. J. Fox expects to rent in the village until Spring then go into other business. He feels very bad. I am feeling very well and expect to go to Claverack to school ere long. Maybe not till the commencement of next term. I think at any rate this change will keep me from college this fall. I have sometimes thought I would wait another year and come to Yale.

> Yours with regards   Write soon
> A. Coons

Other letters mourned happy times at Ashland.
> Burlington, Jan. 30, 1861
> Dear Brother Van Gelder
> You have of course heard of the sad fate of the Ashland Collegiate Institute, that beautiful edifice in which we have spent so many happy days, which you saved indeed from being consumed by fire, exists now only in the memories of those who loved her . . . Her place is now marked only by a dreary and ignoble heap of ashes. . . Had the catastrophe come upon us in the night many lives might have been lost.
> In two days the students had all scattered and Ashland was as desolate almost as before the woodsman ax was heard in the woods and glens. There is no resurrection for this school. On my way home I stopped and had a visit with our boys at Troy University. I am now at home and at leisure. I am not certain what I will do next but have pretty nearly made up my mind to join the New York Conference next Spring and go into the regular work of preaching. I was much pleased with your last letter particularly with your account of Hadley's method of teaching Greek. It trains students to use their store of knowledge. Our school this last winter had been a particularly pleasant and harmonious one . . . How I hate to give up my boys I was preparing for college. Did you see my article in the Advocate a few weeks ago?
> Goodbye.
> Yours truly,   R.H. Howard

In April, Rev. Howard wrote,
> I was pained to hear of your brother's death. He never looked long to me for this world. I am glad you are getting on so well at Yale. I doubt if they are as thourough at Troy as at Yale. In fact in nearly all schools they are too mechanical, they awaken comparatively no interest in their pursuit, stimulate no healthful development and arouse no elemental energies. Their work is cold, dry, heartless oppressive drudgery. Everything is done at arm's length. I have an idea that Yale is an exception and does more to stimulate and develop original, independent powers. I do very much desire an old-fashioned visit with you.

An earlier letter had said,
> Since you left, I have had no one to speculate with . . . no congenial mind. Prof. Ruland is no more like me as far as intellectual habits are concerned than light is like darkness. When I was in New York last I went to Springler's Institute with Bro. Saxe to see the original "Voyage of Life" of Cole's.
> Write soon.   R.H. Howard

Other letters mourned the happy times at Ashland, also. Hollenbeck at Preston Hollow wrote,
> There will never be any more happy or sorrowful times in Ashland which I hold sacred. I did wish to see it once again and once more wind through its halls and dream of other days, live them over again . . . As I think of the old reception room, the glorious times experienced in the chapel, of old Philomantic Hall, there are tears in my eyes . . . As I live over again the life in this hallowed spot, my heart is softened. Many are the green spots in that page of my life's history on which memory loves fondly to linger and gathers around it delights of other days by which to refresh the spirit. I think I am becoming morbid. Sometimes I am weary and dust-covered but usually my spirits are more vivacious than yours.

Mrs. Smith, the widow of a professor at Ashland, wrote often to James. She too recalled *sitting around the stove with the Van Gelder nut bag also containing apples.* She recalled *the many kind things you did for me* and urged him to visit her at Haverstraw where she had started a school.

A typical response to William's death was a letter from a fellow student then in college in Troy,

> May 14, 1861
> I was shocked when I heard of your brother's death. Sad it is indeed to see a young man of talent cut down in the bloom of life, and when first he enters upon the realization of his bright dreams and fondest hopes long cherished and purchased only by long weary hours of toil. Alas! How fleeting is life. I can deeply sympathize with you in your loss: and fain would impart a word of consolation and whisper words of joy about the bright land above, where the redeemed spirit of your noble brother has found rest. I too have ties in that spirit land which are drawing me thither and exerting a benign influence upon my daily life. Let us feel the responsiblity resting upon us in preparing for so holy a calling as that of the ministry. You have my prayers and best wishes for success.
> We are just beginning review. Soon we shall be sophomores. The exhilerating morn is beginning

to dawn. The shadows of approbrious "Freshman" are fast leaving.

Less is known about James' life at Yale before graduating than at Ashland and home. His second year James was in the dorm, and he had given up the idea of becoming a minister. In pencil on the back of a letter was a list of furniture for his room.

Bedstead	3.00
Mattress	1.50
Chair	1.25
Washstand	1.37
Glass	1.00
2 Chairs	1.00
Cushion	.75
Table	4.00
Stove	3.00
Pitcher & B	1.00
	Carpet 62 per yard

A bill, dated December 17, 1861, from the college *for the term ending this day* comes to $25.33. A rebate is listed at 14.00 leaving a balance due of 11.23, plus from a preceding bill 6.12, totaling 17.43. A note mentions *monitor's pay for you.*

He became a member of Gamma Nu, took first prize for Solution of Mathematical problems in his senior year, and received an Oration at Commencement. He was listed as a Phi Beta Kappa. A copy of the **Yale Banner** for September 21, 1860, lists many Societies as well as names of faculty, instructors, and students. There are two freshmen from Greene County — J.W. Teal of East Durham, living at 14 Grove Street, and J.H. Van Gelder, Catskill, with a room at 25 High Street. A Program called POW-WOW, Class of '64, Yale, June 19, 1861,

shows college humor at that time. There were Latin sons, and at the end outlined in black, the following: *The remains of the class of '62 will be removed the 20th of June, from then late resting place to the South Aisle. The Bishop, pastor, and entire parish will participate in the ceremony.*

Amid all the doings at Yale of which we know little, the burning of the Ashland Seminary, William's death, there was much talk of national problems. In fact a letter from William a year before his death indicated this.

I know the invasion of Brown has aroused the South against the North. But the North can now see the reigning tyranny that darkens the South. The scales have fallen from the Northern Democrats and the whole American people can see the evil of slavery the crisis must soon come when slave power shall lose the ascendency in the American Republic and the crisis has been hastened by John Brown.

Months later military training was going on even in the schools. By September, 1861, Hollenbeck reports study hours but,

I am an orderly sergeant so I have good a deal of military business to perform, but my health is better . . . Until midsummer I was troubled somewhat with my old trouble of the stomach. I believe now I am almost rid of it I have not had such an appetite or my food digest so well for a long time. Besides military drill I have two good walks a day so I think I shall not suffer from lack of exercise. Our school is doing better than was hoped by the most sanguine. We will come up to 180 boarders and 30 day scholars in another week. Almost

VOL. 17—No. 1. YALE COLLEGE, SEPTEMBER, 21st, 1860. Price 6 Cents.

LITERARY SOCIETIES.

Linonia.

S. ARTHUR BENT, President.
WILLIAM E. SIMS, Vice President.
ARTHUR W. WRIGHT, Librarian.
WILLIAM H. H. MURRAY, Secretary.
GEORGE S. HAMLIN, Vice Secretary.

Orators for Statement of Facts.

S. ARTHUR BENT, President.
GEORGE M. TOWLE, of the Senior Class.
D. H. CHAMBERLAIN, of the Junior Class.

SENIOR SOCIETIES.

Skull and Bones.

JUNIOR SOCIETIES.

Alpha Delta Phi.

Seniors.

Delta Kappa Epsilon.

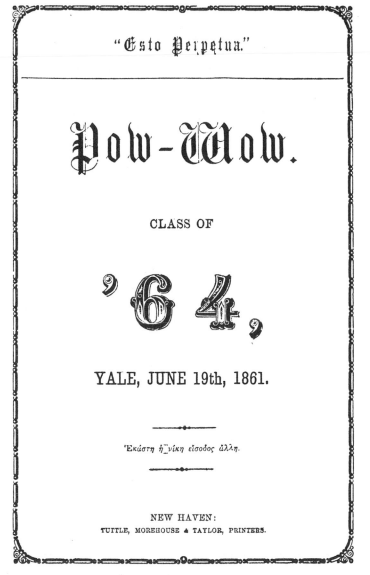

"Esto Perpetua."

Pow-Wow.

CLASS OF

'64,

YALE, JUNE 19th, 1861.

Ἑκάστη ἥ νίκη εἴσοδος ἄλλη.

NEW HAVEN:
TUTTLE, MOREHOUSE & TAYLOR, PRINTERS.

Mementos of Yale.

every other boarding school has fallen off one third to one half. Half of them around here must shut down in six months more. The times is growing worse and worse so far as I know.

I believe the federal cause looks gloomier than ever before nor can I see what we are coming to. We can only trust to a loving Providence for success of right. Many have faith that all will turn out right that we as a nation will be gainers, but I cant see it. I see no bright future for our country   My country is not the beauty and the pride of my heart that she once was. Well, Van, how are you getting along?

Sarah Smith, widowed while at Ashland wrote from Haverstraw.

We have two young ladies from Staten Island and 30 day students. God is very good to us. He indeed is the widow's God and Father of the fatherless.

I remember with gratitude without any drawbacks to chill its warmth, my friend, yourself. We have heard from Hollenbeck and some of the others of the old friends. Miss Woodruff says the Capitol is surrounded with armed troops constantly. Is the tocsin of War sounding in your land of steady habits? Troops have been raised here ready to go at short warning. Have any of the students left Yale? Many have resigned at West Point and gone home to serve their native states.

We remember you with great gratitude, for a year ago at this time we were suffering and your kindness will never be forgotten. If you came here now you would find us in circumstances to return some of the nice treats of apples and so forth. You remember how we served you and Mr. Hollenbeck to apples in my room out of your carpet bag, dont you? Please write again and receive the regards of the children.

  Sarah V. Smith

On January 6, 1862, Sarah Smith wrote again of the school prospering and but for the war and hard times consequent might even hope for more success.

My son at the west is married and gone to war and is now near Fairfax Seminary. He belongs to Major Farnsworth Illinois Cavalry. One week ago Fannie married and went to Washington. She has now returned to Fort Hamilton where Mr. Ferris is now stationed on recruiting service for the 8th regiment. He is quartermaster at present   She is not far from home now but he may be ordered away. We do not know   My eldest daughter has returned from the west and takes Fannie's place in school and I expect Miss Woodruff to teach music. You can hardly imagine how Emily has grown and improved in her studies.

An earlier letter had said, *Emily has at last given up and sits at Jesus' feet.*

The war was real! Bartholomew Mulligan wrote James Harvey, who was living in the college dorm, of the rigors of war.

  October 2, 1862

I was glad to hear you had arrived safely in your rooms in college and although confusion rules the hour I hope you have things all to your mind by this time.

As regards myself, I am doing picket duty and fortunately I am on the reserves. There is therefore no great danger of the approach of the enemy. I improve the leisure hours by writing letters, the first being to you. Since I wrote last we have moved to a different camp. It is not as clean but it is a very good situation within about 1½ miles from Alexandria City, which I have visited twice. As a city Alexandria will compare very well with Hudson in point of members but is very inferior in regard to buildings and general improvements. I saw the house in which Colonel Ellsworth lost his

29

life and also the flag which he raised in place of the miserable secession rag. It has been floating on the breeze since he raised it and it is destined to float much longer. There is a great business being done in Alexandria now due to the great number of troops stationed within a few miles.

I learned on good authority that 50,000 troops took passage on steamboats there yesterday on their way to Maryland. I hope they will soon render a good account of themselves.

There has been some hard fought battles since I wrote you, but though Madam Rumor has reported us badly cut up and nearly destroyed I have not been nearer than to hear the last rumbling of the distant canon warning. I was glad to hear through your letter that the good people of Catskill remember me in their approaches to the throne of grace, for I am admonished day after day that I need more of the grace of God to keep me faithful to the discharge of my duties to my comrades in arms and my God. The wickedness in the army is terrible. Officers and privates alike seen to have forgotten (with few exceptions) the influences that surrounded them at home, and what little regard they have had for the commands in God's word and are striving with one another apparently to see which can do most that is wicked. I hope that

God will let the influence of His spirit so work on the hearts of men in Government service that they will see their true condition and be led to make their calling and election sure.

All the men in Sickles' division are reviewed today at 3 o'clock; being that I am on picket duty I will escape the tiresome performance. Our camp is within a mile and a half of Fairfax Seminary. It is now being used as a hospital and there are nearly 2000 sick and wounded cared for in that institution. There are barracks connected to it.

I must close and please write soon. If all those to whom I write could know how much pleasure and comfort I derive from receiving prompt replies they would not keep me waiting so long. Remember me in your prayers and I will you.

> *Yours etc.*
> *B. Mulligan*

Mulligan was stationed at Headquarters #120 Regiment Pickets, Alexandria, Virginia, in the eastern theater while Harry Augustus Pelham wrote from the 110th Regiment in the western theater. Mulligan writes of battles, including the famous battles of Chancellorsville and Fredericksburg while the Pelham letters describe both the home front and the war front.

PART III
THE CIVIL WAR

Fredericksburg and Chancellorsville were only names to me until I examined **The Picture History of the Civil War** by Richard M. Ketcham, published by American Heritage. These battles were in the Spring of 1863, the same year that the Civil War letters were written by and to Augustus Pelham, Jr., of the 110th Regiment from Oswego, New York. Pelham was at New Orleans and tells of orders to leave camp and head for Baton Rouge and to attack Port Hudson. If successful they would go on to Vicksburg. These two compaigns were interrelated. A little orientation will do for both. **The American Picture History** says,

In the spring of 1863 the Northern grip on the Confederacy was slowly tightening; yet there was still a chance for the South to upset everything, and for a few unendurable tense weeks that chance seemed very good. With Rosecrans inactive in Tennessee and with Grant seemingly bogged down hopelessly in the steaming low country north of Vicksburg, attention shifts to the East and it appeared that a Southern victory here might restore the bright prospects that had gone so dim the preceding September. Robert E. Lee set out to provide that victory; winning it, he then made his supreme effort to win one final unattainable triumph that would bring the new nation independence. He never came quite as close to success as men supposed at that time but he did give the war its most memorable hour of drama (at Chancellorsville).

Joe Hooker, who replaced Burnside of the side whiskers, had done admirably in repairing the Army of the Potomac . . . He turned his cavalry corps into an outfit that could fight Job Stuart's boys on something like equal terms, and he restored the weary army's confidence in itself. When Hooker began to move, Lee's army in and around Fredericksburg numbered hardly more than 60,000 men of all arms. Hooker had more than twice that number and he was handling them with strategic insight. He would not repeat Burnside's mistake of butting head-on against stout Confederate forces at Fredericksburg. It might have worked except for two things. At the critical moment Hooker lost his nerve — and Lee refused to act by the script Hooker had written.

Mulligan took up the story from there in his letter of Fredericksburg and Chancellorsville.

Camp of the 120th Regiment at Potomac Creek Station, Va. June 7th, 1863

Dear Friend,

I was glad you enjoyed yourself so well during the holidays. How could it be otherwise in the society of an intelligent, sociable, lovely young lady. [Rebecca Pine]

When I read your letter and learned of the meetings, donations, sleigh rides and all the holiday good times you had, I would have been homesick but for the noble cause in which I was and am still engaged. The satisfaction I realize in doing my duty more than compensates me for all the sacrifices I have made and will continue to make, how long, the Great Disposer of events only knows. I can and do believe that the secret of my continual good health is that our Heavenly Father has in answer to the united prayers of my friends, remembered me in mercy. . . . Since the receipt of your letter our Regt has made many and fatiguing marches, marches through violent storms of snow and rain, mud and dust and always I have enjoyed health good enough to go with the Regt. If I should write you a detailed account of all our marches and other duties I would either exhaust your patience or cause you to neglect your studies . . . Suffice it to say that I have tried to perform all my duties with a conscience void of offense . . . You say you have found consolation in not finding accounts of our Regt in the papers . . . for my part I wish that our employment had been such as be mentioned in papers as I think we would not have lost so many men as we have. I think it doubtful that any Regt that has been through all the Battles fought for the last 5 months has been reduced as much as ours was in that line.

During the recent Battles of Fredericksburg and Chancellorville our Corps, (the 3rd) our Division the 2nd Berry's, distinguished themselves rending great service to the Country and punishing the Audacious Rebels very severely.

When the advance was first ordered April 28th our Corps was assigned the position of the Grand Reserve. In that capacity we took our position about two miles from Fredericksburg and awaited orders which were received on the 30th at about 11 o'clock and were in effect for us to march to the Right and cross the Rappahonnoch at U S ford, a distance of about 15 miles by the road we traveled That night we marched till after 12 o'clock when we halted and slept soundly in the open air. Next day we crossed the River on pontoon bridges and continued our line of march toward the front where we arrived at about sun down and were received by the enemy in not the most friendly manner possible. After spending another night in the open air we cooked and ate a light breakfast then held ourselves in readiness to fight at any moment

The engagement did not become general until about 3 o'clock in the afternoon when the enemy attacked our left, then for awhile the din of Battle and shouts of the foemen was awfully grand. The Rebs finding themselves unable to break our lines at this point changed their positions from Left to Right (under cover of a dense forest) and at sunset made an attack on our right where the 11th Corps was stationed. No sooner had the engagement commenced on the right than we were ordered to leave our knapsacks in a pile and march to participate in the fight.

The Battle was raging with even greater fierceness than early in the afternoon and the order double quick march having been given we fixed bayonets and rushed forward to the scene of action. Imagine if you can, our surprise and disappointment in striking the plank road to find the 11th Corps in full retreat and the enemy in hot pursuit. Thank God we had a Division Commander Berry that comprehended the whole thing at a glance and he immediately formed his line of battle so as to check the enemy's advance.

No sooner had the broken and huddled ranks of the 11th Corps passed our lines than the enemy flushed with its success in dislodging the 11th Corps rushed boldly forward expecting to achieve more and possibly greater victories. Our Artillery then opened on the advancing columns of the Rebs with murderous precision and many a Rebel bit the dust when least expecting to and advanced to within easy musket range. Our boys poured into their ranks volley after volley with murderous effect. So emboldened had they become by the advantage gained that they rushed forward still, regardless of dead and dying that were falling by the score on their every hand.

When so close that our noble boys had no time to reload and fire they sprang forward with a shout and drove the audacious Rebels back at the point of the bayonet. By this time the enemy found their opponents to be made of very different metal than the 11th Corps and finding all efforts at breaking our rank futile they wisely withdrew from the attack for the night.

I wish you could have been near enough to have witnessed the fight that night. The full moon was shining with all its mild splendor making sufficient light for active opperations. In addition to the light of the moon the constant blaze bursting forth from the mouths of numerous cannon and the flash of thousands of muskets made a scene magnificently awful.

As the Battles were stopped we set about con-structing breast works of logs the better to enable us to resist the attack which we knew would come with early morning. After finishing the breast-works we lay behind them and slept some. With the early dawn we were arroused, ate a light breakfast and took our position to await the onslaught nor did we have to wait long for the enemy had occupied the night in reconstructing their forces for the final attack. Soon the skirmishes became engaged and in a few minutes the whole line was hard at it and unfortunately at the commencement of the fight Berry was killed and our Brigadier General being little more than a coward we were left almost entirely without orders and so we fought on our own responsibility and punished the Rebels most severely. The Rebs came down on our left wing with such a rush and such overwhelming numbers (for they had massed their forces for the purpose) that they succeeded in turning our left flank. Then it was that such a man as Berry was needed to maneuver the troops in such a way as to foil the enemy, but Berry was not there so that the line commenced to retire slowly from the left till it came up to our position which was on the Right and after stubborn resistance the whole line retired.

The Battle Sunday morning was the hottest of the series but resulted in the enemy attaining possession of the plank road from Chancellorville to Fredericksburg when their main force marched down to operate against Sedgwick who was fighting his way up to join Hooker on the Right.

My time and space will not permit of a longer letter this time but I will try to write again soon, If we remain in our present camp I will have more time than I have had in some time. In my neyt letter I will state some of the facts relative to our retreat that I know by experience. As I expect soon to go on guard . . .

Thanking you for your good wishes and prayers, I remain truly your friend.

              Bartholomew Mulligan

There were 17,000 Union soldiers and 12,000 Southern men who died at Chancellorsville, nearly 30,000 in three days. Further Union reverses were suffered at Fredericksburg.

Meanwhile others in Greene County played their part. On the home front Beers says in his **History of Greene County,**

When the war clouds of 1861 began to darken the political horizon, the patriotic blood of Greene County was fired to take part in the contest. In the latter part of May Company A of the old 20th Regiment of militia and the Catskill Engineer Corps took up their line of march to join the regiment at Kingston, and thence to the seat of war.

Beers also gives accounts of war meetings, liberty poles raised, and stars and stripes floating over every village and hamlet. During the summer enlistments were numerous. Provisions were made to raise the county's share of the $20,000,000 war tax Congress had levied. Committees were appointed and money raised for payment of bounties by voluntary subscription. According to Beers,

> The ladies, with true womanly instinct had taken earnest hold of the work of preparing materials for the relief of the suffering soldiers. Refreshment, blankets, articles of clothing and knick knacks were provided and forwarded through the different channels. Their work sent joy to hundreds of those who received their gifts. In May, 1863, the Legislature offered a bounty of $75 for each enlistment of three year men. In July the terrible draft riots occurred in New York. But the draft in this district was quietly consumated. Men were mustered out in 1865 and 1866.

Several letters are also included in Beer's **History of Greene County, New York.** Official records are incomplete but all Greene County soldiers serving in the Civil War by townships are listed. The letters from fellow students to James Harvey Van Gelder refer to the war, slavery, John Brown, troops, and draft.

The final letter from Mulligan written after he came home wounded to Palenville reads,

> I suppose that you are not sure of my whereabouts. I have not heard from you in a long time. I am at Palenville where I enjoy myself very much. With few exceptions I find my friends very well. Truly our heavenly father is very merciful to permit us to enjoy each other's society again. Surely James, the goodness and mercy of God toward me has been magnified by my spiritual eyes a hundred fold since I have been home.
> I must tell you that my wound is improving very rapidly. Two large pieces of bone have been taken out since I have been home. I think there is one other piece to come out yet.
> When at Catskill I had the pleasure of having many friends call upon me and among the rest were your mother and father. I was glad to see them looking so well.
> I have not seen Miss Rebecca yet but have heard she is quite well as usual, but of course, you are always well informed on that subject.
> I feel the Lord is doing a great and good work in this place since I was here 10 months ago. And many who were travelling broad road are now walking the narrow way. Hoping to hear from you,
>
> I remain,   Your   B. Mulligan

Bartholomew Mulligan, who made the Chancellorsville battle so real, may not have known Harry Augustus Pelham, who fought for the Union with the 110th Regiment of New York since that Regiment was largely from the Oswego area of Central and Western Central New York State.

Nevertheless, the letters of Harry Augustus Pelham, Jr., slept for over a hundred years, bedded down in the same old pine chest with the Van Gelder letters of 1854-64. Yet there is no hint that he could by any monkey business have climbed our family tree. Only a slender thread connects the two groups. Pelham's name is mentioned just once in a letter to James Harvey Van Gelder away at school. There was also a chest marked **Pelham** in my cellar which must have arrived there with all the other things cleared from the Van Gelder Cherry Hill House. Grandpa surely knew him well or the trunk would not have been stored there. These letters claim attention chiefly because of what they reveal about the home front during the Civil War.

The Civil War had begun in 1861 with the Southern attack on Fort Sumter. Our soldier boy wrote his mother, Mariette Pelham, in March, 1863. His regiment had just been moved up the Mississippi from camp at New Orleans to Baton Rouge. Both East and West, the war was in a stalemate. The second Battle of Bull Run in 1862 had been a severe defeat for the North. The same year New Orleans was lost to the South confining its hold on the great river to the Vicksburg area. In March of 1862 the most famous naval battle of the War had been fought. The Southern Merrimac finally retired and the famous Northern Monitor remained intact. Knowledge of the campaigns and battles, the juggling of generals, and all the ups and downs of the opposing armies is easily acquired from such books as the colorful **Picture History of the Civil War** with concise narrative by the famous Bruce Catton.

The first letter is from Harry Augustus Pelham, Jr., himself. It is his only letter and plunges us right into the War.

> Baton Rouge Camp
> March 9, 1863
>
> Dear Mother,
> I sit down to write a few lines to let you know that I am well. We have changed our Camp. We got orders to move the 4th, went on board the Steamer New Brunswick the 5th, started out for Baton Rouge the 6th, landed and went into Camp here the 7th. This morning we received orders to be ready   Six days rations cooked   60 rounds of Cartridges to go in light marching order at a moments warning   We expect we will be sent forward to attack Fort Hudson and if we succeed in driving the rebels there we will go to Vicksburg   We are now 15 miles from Fort Hudson by land and 23 by water   2 miles from the Rebel Pickets   I received your two letters and answered them directly and have written as often as once a fortnight
> It has been very sickly since we arrived at New Orleans   We buried 16 men since but we are in hopes it will be more healthy now as the land is

higher and water better. There is only 400 for duty in our regt   There is 30 to 40 thousand men here now to go forward. We do not get much news here. We expect a mail tomorrow. So I will close. Hoping this may find you well

To All My Best Respects

H.A. Pelham

Lack of punctuation rarely interferes with the clarity of what is written. The paucity of periods and commas is sometimes over compensated for by the promiscuous use of capitals. The sister Levera, whose name is seldom spelled the same, writes her soldier "Brother Gufs" using the *ʃ* shaped *s*. She had been sick with the *diphtheria* but was again *Feeling real Smart.*

. . . We had a great funeral here yesterday   it was a Soldier that was brought home   his name is talor   the firemen were out and the Band played the dead march   it was held in the Babtist Church   then Gen Sumner was burried in Syracuse yesterday   Mr Pruyne went up   Gen Fremont was there   also an Italian general   he said there was a great crowd there   soldiers from a number of places   his horse was lead just back of the hearse with the Saddle and Briddle all on and his boots and spurs fastened on   all was there except Sumner himself   Mother was here yesterday   Mr. Pruynes folks get there butter of her

Her letter reports the weather — *not much sleighing* and the inability to deliver his letter to their Mother because of *such awful going that we couldent get there.* Sometimes weeks went by. News included a surprise party at Mexico, a little village nearby.

Two carryall loads from here and some from Fulton   had a splendid time   went to George Pruynes   got home the next day about noon   Jute and Aunt Orpha are at our house and Celestia [Livia's younger sister] has left Wellingtons and is living to Curly Pruynes to work. The Soldiers at the Fort are gone away   wee miss there music they had a fine band   Father is to work yet on that job at red crick   Has any of your company died   how are the stanton boys and Jeff Perkins and William Henry Darrow . . . Big Bater brought home a coloured man from the south and he and two whites had a fight and the black man was killed the other two are in jail . . . Do you get anough to eat down there or are you half starved   do you like living in the sunny south   is it as pleasant as you expected. The 24th will soon be home   they expect to be discharged in May Dont you wish it was the 110th

It is awful dull times here in Oswego   The dullest I ever knew it to be   Gufs did you know that Lucy Buffington is married   last night two or three got married and tonight Bill Druerys sister is to be married

Gufs I will close this   Mr and Mrs Pruyne and

Lydia and Sime send their best respects   write soon

Livera

Letters opened mainly with statements and questions regarding *your health*, the *Family's health*, friends' health and one's own. Benjamin Bowen, Co. I, 100th Regiment, wrote from Glouster Point, Virginia, on April 21, 1863:

Dear friend Harry,

. . . and I am glad you are well and Sckiber is well we have left Morris Island and are now at Glouster Point . . . a letter from our folks in the last mail says there has some of the boys enlisted from our place   the names are Paul Pilky Babcock   Aron Mackmullen Syrus frailich and Mark Ostrander they are at Washington   I havent learned what regt they are in yet   Gust, pa is a going to michigan this spring to buy a farm   I am glad to hear that Hick is going to live with him out west   Well Gust we dident have the fun of taking Charleston but I hope that we shall take Richmond this time . . . I heard from Stephen he was in Albany in school and he is as usual . . . so good bye and God prosper you all

By May 19, 1863, this Benjamin Bowen was at Camp Holly, 7 miles from Charleston and writes that he has at last learned that Pelham is a *solger* in the 110th and stationed at New Orleans . . .

I saw the regiment that you are in at Baltimore but I dident see you   but I saw George hubard and saw bracket and mister sage   mister sage was the first one I saw that I new and he told me whare to find the phoenix boys and I saw them but I dident see you.

The family had written him that all the boys at the lock were well and in great spirits and all the girls *as lively as ever.*

. . . Gust our regiment has been paid off   they were paid last month I sent $50 home to my father   Gust this regt is giving out furlos   four of each company each month   my turn will come in 4 or 5 months   then I shall see my native home once more   Charleston is not taken yet nor wont be very soon for our ironclads isent enuff for old fort sumpter and all the rest of the forts at this place we are now 7 miles from the sitty of Charleston . . . I think there wont be any fighting very soon we can see the sitty of Charleston quite plain   we can see also fort sumpter . . . and castel pickney with the naked eye   everything is quiet here the monties are at fort royal . . . I had a letter from Andrew Betts   he is well and at aqua crick va

Several things had gone wrong on the Western battlefront. Never again was the South to be so near victory or to hold the initiative in every major theater of war but then the tide began to ebb. The Federals would begin a new campaign against Richmond and, in the West, continue the drive to open the whole Mississippi Valley.

Two more letters were written to Pelham during that summer, but no battles are mentioned. It is home front news. From Granby, New York, on July 10, 1863, Pelham's aunt, Helen Willcox wrote:

Dear Nephew,

. . . When I got your last letter Stephen had been staying home about a month, he was elected assessor of this town this year, and his office will hold three years, so he had to stay at home to attend to his business,   he went away a week yesterday   Luke and Mary were married in March and went on the boat this spring, but Mary was sick all the time, so she came off last week and they have a soldier's wife on now. We live in the room we did last summer on our own place,   Mother is about as she was last summer. she takes a considerable care of Elmer

I hope she will live to see you again. Elmer has grown to be a fine boy, he is almost ten months old and is about as large as Freddy when he died. I will now inform you of the loss in Charles family, the great destroyer has been in there family and claimed one of its infants as his own, on the twenty fifth of April   Harriet died of spotted fever, she was confined to her bed only about two days   all feel the loss greatly, yet we hope they mourn not as one dead, but that she liveth forever in that celestial home where there is no parting. Harry has gone to California again. I do not know what started him   I havent seen his wife since he went so you will have to wait for particulars untill next time. I will now tell you about the neighbors Charley Allen is at home this summer   he was to a chopping bee when he cut his foot very badly. William works at the stave machine the one Will Stevens sold. it is out on the road now on the corner opposite both Mr. Lees houses. they have an engine instead of horses to run the machine Ruben Johnson has got home   you recollect he went in the twenty fourth regiment   their time is out and they are at liberty.   he lives in one of Mr Lees houses   Mary Ann Hill is married   she married a soldier his name is Streeter   he came from down east   he is a cousin of her step mother . . . I guess all the house is asleep I have to get up early for I am going to Fulton tomorrow with Mrs. Hill to mail this letter . . .

> *from your affectionate aunt*
> *Helen M. Willcox*

This last letter is almost unique in the using of commas and periods profusely. Capitals are unusually scarce. The next letter needs to be seen to be appreciated. Mr. Pruyne and his son "Sime" not only have unusually fine penmanship, but what signatures! They should have been wasted on nothing less than the Declaration of Independence, the Magna Carta, or the Emancipation Proclamation. One from the elder Pruyne has long been safe in the Bronck Museum Library. The whole letter is one grand spread of calligraphy. The son only manages a signature and with lesser expertise. Once before he wrote to tell Pelham that his father had received from him ten dollars at one time and twenty at another. This time he says:

Father got the money from Kingsford and wants to know what kind of bills you sent   Whether it was green backs or other bills   for green backs is a little scarce and if you sent them he kept them and paid father in something else . . . they have drafted here and it went off very quiet   they had a guard here from the Invalid Corps and that kinder scairt the boys so that they did not want to make a fuss   the most men that are drafted will pay there $300 and let them go   one of the boys in the shop was drafted but he got his papers from the British Consul showing him to be a British subject

> *write soon*
> *Yours*

Pelham received a letter from his older sister dated September 13 from Oswego. It was also signed by the two Pruyne young people, Lydia and "Sime." The former, Livia, says *sits here on the floor munching pumpkin pie   I wish we could send you some.* She explained that when Uncle Harry went to California   *He started for the canal boat and went to California instead. Harriet Dutcher is dead and burried. Father is on the same place yet.*

Gufs do you see Jeff Perkins   tell him for me we would like to hear from him   he has not written to us since he left and I do not think it is right Have you been in any battles yet   if so write and let us know all about everything for we are ancious to hear   you have not written in a long time. We had a great funeral here the other day   it was Major Underwood   the the funeral was at the fort   he was burried in Riverside Cemetary there was a long procefsion all the soldiers and the Band   The Murry Black got afire yesterday afternoon but it was put out before much damage was done   it would have been a good thing if it had burned to the ground . . so goodbye now write soon   Father has a new horse

> *Leave and Lydia and Sime*

December arrived and on the fifth Harry Pelham, the father, wrote to *his ever dear son.* He says he has *waited with patience since last July the 22nd to hear You must be ungrateful not to write a few lines to console the grieved heart of a Poor Father and Mother. Likewise your dear Brothers and Sisters.*

He talks of 200 acres of tamarack swamp. He got out 600 *knees and had two years left to get the timber off . . . I still work on the farm and probably will for 3 or 4 years.* He closes his letter with *Wishes for every good health and hapnes shall be the constant prayer of your loving Father.   Harry Pelham*

Oswego Aug 12th 1863

Mr A A Pelham
   Sir
        Father wishes
me to write you a few lines to let
you know that he got the money from
Kingsford and wants to know what king of bills
you sent whether it was green backs or other bills
for green backs are a little scarce and if you sent
them he kept them and paid him in some thing
els Out enough of that for now they have
drafted here and it went off very quiet they
had a guard here from the Invilid Corps
and that kinder scart the boys so that they
did not want to make a fuss the most
of the men that are drafted will pay there
$9,00 and let them go one of the boys in
the shop was drafted but has got papers from
the British Consel shewing him to be a British
subject but I can think of no more so
I will close by telling you that the
folks are all well and send their best
respects

        write soon
        Yours &c
        Simon T Pruyne

Letter to Pelham from Simon T. Pruyne.

(Boat knees, referred to sometimes just as knees, are, according to the dictionary, *A crook in a tree branch; a piece of timber naturally bent for use in supporting structures coming together at an angle as framing and deck beams of a ship.*)

The soldier son wrote the family on December 10th and on the 22nd enclosing a *likeness*, a paper, and two confederate notes. This was the first time they had heard in six months. The Mother writes:

When Capt Doyl was here last August I sent a package of 8 papers   a long letter   four sheets of paper   four envelopes and four 3 cts postage stamps, 1 military sheet   1 large gilt edge, 2 military envelopes, 1 yellow one, one white   one of the papers were the Commercial Times with such reading matter as I wished you to see and thought would be interesting to you. I bought a Harpers Weekly and sent it to you that day. I think you have not received the package as you have not mentioned it as you had left the Regt the 1st of Sept and Capt Doyl left here the 20th of August so of course you had left before he arrived   I would not have had you miss the package for money; for I think it would have been interesting to you and many others which have perhaps gone to their long home as we thought you had, or taken by guerrillas

His mother goes on and on with details that get rather boring but are representative of the home life, so that the soldier may appreciate every word including the constant criticism of receiving no letters and no detailed acknowledgment of everything they sent him. Life was drab. There was lots of drudgery and penny pinching. Health was always too important not to detail and also the weather. In quoting from the letters, much of that will be skipped.

When Col Page was home your father was very anxious to go see him as he thought you were dead or taken prisner . . . your father is still in suspense about your whereabouts for he left home this morning before Livia fetched the letters. Your father and Bill Thompson has a job of making hoops himself besides separate from the Boat Knees   he wishes you were home to be in that business   it is such a money making business Abe Aviell dug knees enough to come to forty dollars in six days

. . . it has been severe cold everywhere; people have frozen in a great many places, frozen to death by the side of the road and dozens of people freezing in Canada; and snow where it has never been before in North Carolina, so the papers stated

John Pek has enlisted for six hundred seventy seven dollars bounty   his winter quarters is in Auburn   Benny Tallman has enlisted for $300   I told you last summer Ben Botter went as a substitute

Uncle Harry wrote from California that he was three hundred and sixty feet under ground at work for three dollars   Eugene [16 years] talks daily of enlisting.

General Butler had asked for a million men for ninety days to go liberate the Richmond prisoners. This must refer to Libby Prison in Richmond, Virginia, used for captured Union officers in the Civil War. It was formerly a tobacco warehouse. Living conditions were notoriously bad, causing deaths of thousands.

She had not had time to have Merritt's and Fred's likenesses taken to send this brother. Fred had gotten in the first reader. His father had hired a post office box so letters could now be sent to her instead of in care of Pruyne, *for its weeks before we get them sometimes. The city is alive with soldiers, more than ever this winter. Write soon* is his mother's closing to a long letter stretched over many days.

Sixteen-year-old Eugene does enlist and life is never the same for the Pelham family though the daily grind is humdrum as usual. This letter written by the mother tells of Eugene's first days in the army.

Oswego, New York, March 1st, 64
Well, Augustus, I received your letter and was glad you were well. you stated "we are in the circle" but you did not say who we were. your Father has not been well this winter
. . . Eugene has gone; he enlisted Jan 25th mustered in   went to Fort Ontario the 27th   left this fort the 15th of Feb for Elmira   I received a letter from him the 29th written the 26th   he stated he staid a week to Elmira   he was detailed for guard   stood guard   I dont know whether it was 2 or 3 hours and then orders came to march they started for Elmira about 2 o'clock   road 2 days and a ½ and 2 nights   went from Washington in the morning, got to the Regt about 6   about 5 miles from Washington across the Potomac, in a pleasant place, they have good quarters, good feed   he liked it very well   he sent a hundred and eight dollars by express to Mr. Pruyne   he left his bounty with him   he had 677 dollars   we are very sorry he went, after he had sworn himself in and received bounty money we could not do anything with him   that is the law   I hope he will do well   he had no person he had ever seen to go with him   he enlisted in the 2nd heavy NY Artillery Co . . . Your advice came too late   I think if it had been sooner he would not have gone
your uncle Charles enlisted in the Scotts 9th cavalry so Eugene said.

A new paper was printed in Oswego and his mother planned to send him a copy with the list of enlisted men of the 2nd NY Artillery. It included Eugene. The day was beautiful but so cold she was afraid *the little calf would freeze to death. It was 2 years old.*

Last fall he sold it for twenty dollars   to sell hay your father got rid of the old horse the first October after you left.   last July he bought Mr Stevens old Dun with colt ten days old and we are raising it.

The next day she continues the letter with a plea to tell her all about the place he is in and all about his voyage. She urged him to tell of everyone of their acquaintants,

Mr. Nightengale, H Darrow, John Harrigan, and his brother William who enlisted, the Stanton boys, Geo. Lee and all that were with him, that little Dutch that came from Canada and Mr Morg.

Here is the first use of the word photograph. In both groups of letters they were always exchanging "Likenesses." His mother wrote:

If Eugene had had some photographs taken I would have sent one to you, but he and Celestia went to the Gallery and had four dagueriotypes taken   two sitting and two standing and paid three dollars for them   then there was so much dissatisfaction about it   Mrs Pruyne told Eugene she should think he might give her his likeness he spent 25 dollars so quick Mr Pruyne told him he should not spend any more money for likenesses   therefore he did not get any taken your father saw Ben Perkins   he said Harvey Tracy had enlisted   Austin Tracy was in Washington this winter a breaking horses   he came down on the cars with your father   he was quite noisy   they had to speak to him to be still   he was on his way home from Washington   hes since gone back   Michael and May Lyon have an heir   mice has bought a place of Mr. Lewis George Holenbeck and Ellen Clofs were married a year ago last fall and they have an heir   Mr Henry Miller went in the 177th he has got his discharge and came home 2 weeks ago

March 4th/64

I want to write to Eugene today and take it down to the City tomorrow   The reenlisted men of the eighty-first is coming in tomorrow at four o'clock and I want to be there

Pelham's letter was held over to include 6 papers, a **Herald, New York Times,** an **Oswego Daily Commercial, Advertizer,** and 3 of the **Commercial Times.**

The speech is on the second page headed Facts For the People. The career of a demogogue in the New York Times you will see on the the 8th page . . . the condition of our prisoners at Richmond Col Streights account of his captivity.

Also she urged him to read that attentively. Your Father is home to attend the special election for to see if a vote will be carried in the State to have the soldiers vote at the next Presidential Election. He

said he would vote for that if he never voted again. Celestia went to the City yesterday and fetched the letters you sent to Livia   They quite disheartened me to find you felt so disconsolate about going to that Island   Mr. Brewster told your father where your regiment had gone. He said you would have plenty of fish and turtle to eat and also it was very healthy but very lonesome You mention in Dec the hollyday   We all wished you would come. we were prepared, besides the ducks and chicken pies   Martin Gray has moved his cooper shop on the corner and made a saloon of it   Your Father and Eugene went and they got 3 turkeys and 2 ducks   feed was so high we killed them all   That was at Thanksgiving and Christmas and then before New Year your Father and Bill Thompson went and raffled and got 3 geese   they were already dressed and we had plenty of apples and cider   I put up two pounds of apples (dried) on purpose for you, if you should come home . . . Since Eugene has left we have killed a hog   it weighed three hundred and sixty. We made thirty weight of sausage, had thirty pounds of lard, made a three gallon jar of sauce made mince pies of the head   Your Father got some beef to put with it   we are sorry you are neither of you with us to share them with us. Screenings are fifty-five and sixty cents a bushel, eggs are twenty cents a dozen, butter 28-30 cents a lb . . . I nearly forgot to tell you the Fort Eugene is in it is Fort Strong

From your Mother
Mariette L. Pelham

Four or five weeks later Pelham got a letter from Livia and Lydia Pruyn with the news of Eugene's death. It was not until May 10 that we find a letter from his mother about the tragic death. Livia's and Lydia's letter was from Oswego, dated April 12, 1864, and seems to have been written by Lydia rather than his sister.

Dear Brother and Friend
It is with a sad heart That I seat myself to write to you for I have sad news to tell you.
Last saturday we got a Telegraph Dispatch that Eugene was dead   he died last Saturday afternoon and was to be burried Sunday   your mother was here when we got the dispatch   she felt very bad indeed   poor woman. I felt sorry for her she stayed with us all night and the next day was taken home in the Carrage   Father was in Syracuse and she stayed to see him   they have concluded not to bring the body home for people say it is almost impossible to get the body after he is burried   poor fellow he will be just as well off but for his mother's sake I wish he could be buried here . . .

Lydia goes on to tell how Eugene had the measles

and probably left the hospital too soon for the last letter they got from him he said he was still very weak. The night before they had received a letter from him written by his Captain. It was written the morning of the day he died, the same day as the dispatch about his death. He had explained that his health was very poor and that he was to be discharged from the service. He wanted his Father who had his money to send him 30 dollars to pay his fare home.

He was in Camp Strong . . . poor fellow   I hope he is in a happier place than any of us where there is no Cruel War nor parting as death   Well we will change the subject . . . Gus we are alone now as far as men are concerned   we are going to Syracuse   the Shop is now in running order up there and we will go the first of May. Leave is going with us . . . our baby is the smartest Child that was   Leave says she will get a picture taken and send to you

The 81st Regt started for the south again yesterday   they have reenlisted for three years   Jule and her husband talk of going sailing this summer   Gus where is that Leah Parmington of yours   Leave got a letter from her awhile ago and that is the last we have heard

Do you ever see Sell Perkins   if so how is he   I wish he would write to me   Did you hear that Syrus Willcox is married he came home from California and married Martha Hall   where is Ben Bowen   you spoke of him in your letter to your mother and Leave wants to know where he is and if you see Uncle Charley again tell him to write to Leave . . . Well we dont think of any more to write so good by   write soon to your sister and friend
            Leave and Lydia

Names of enlisted men are the only ones reported in Ben Bowen's letter of April from Glouster Point, Virginia   *Enlisted from our place are Paul Pilky Babcock, Aron Mackmullen, Syrus frailich and Mark Ostrander.* They were at Washington but the regiment was unknown to Bowen. He was glad his father was going to Michigan in the Spring to buy a farm and that Hick was going to live with him *out west.*

A fellow soldier and uncle wrote from Donalsonville, Louisiana, May 10.

I was pretty sick last week. I had the diahreah but I went blackberrying and picked about 4 quarts and stewed them up et them and they curde me . . .

we left New Orleans the 31st of March   we are 76 miles up the river on what is called Governor Mannings plantations   There is 4000 acres and in it there is more plows and wagons on it than there is in the city of Oswego for sale   we arrived here on a friday and tuesday the same week guerillas come here and took 7 mules and 3 horses and tried to set fire to the barn but there was about 20 boys in it drove them away and shot one dead

and wounded one and the rest got away   we go scouting once a week   we generally bring in from 1 to 8   some is on mules and some is on mustangs   they are very sly   they keep in the woods almost all day and come out nights   3 weeks last Sunday morning we started about 2 o'clock   we got to Newriver about daybrake   there were 50 of our company and 50 of Co E   Captain Halleck in command of us   we on one side of the river and the woods on the other   when all at once 5 shots was fired out of the woods   3 taken affect   1 hit Captain Halleck in the head   1 hit a Sargeant in the shoulder   the Sargeant and a private is getting along well but the captain they say can never get well. The doctors say they can never get the ball out without killing him and it cant stay in his head without killing him   our Colonel says we have got to hunt them black hounds out - everyone that's around within 100 miles   so I guess we have all we want to do for this summer   it comes very hard for me to go on these Scouting trips for we have to take from 2 to 3 days raisions with us and it goes hard with me to eat hardtack
            Charles Dutcher

Regarding Eugene's death, the mother wrote from Oswego, May 2, 1864. She *seats herself to write* letting him know they are all well and *hoping you are the same.* This is par for the course in all letters. As usual also all recent letters are listed, the papers sent — seven this time — answers received or not received and the query *how you liked them.* Also did he receive the package sent by Capt Doyle. One had been sent to Eugene also.

In your letter of the 23rd of March was enclosed fifty cents to the little boys   they were much pleased with it   they have not spent it yet   I went down the 9th of April intending to get some paper to write to you and Eugene the next day, for we expected to move the next week and I did not know when I should get time again. I carried your letter to let Mr. Pruyn that they could read it   While I was there a telegraph dispatch was brought in stating that Eugene had died that afternoon and would be buried the next day. I wished him brought home   Mr Pruyne was in Syracuse   Lydia and Mrs. Hall went to the telegraph office and sent him a dispatch to tell him of Eugene's death and my wishes to have his remains brought home, but he did not understand or did not wish to and did not send an answer back. It was Saturday night and Mr Pruyne was coming home. Lydia told me to stay until her father came home. I staid. Mrs. Pruyne had gone to Syracuse that afternoon, it was ten o'clock in the evening when they got home, then Mr. Pryne said if I wanted him to go for Eugene he was ready to go. I told him I did and I thought we ought to telegraph the Capt. of the Company Eugene had been in, he went to the telegraph office   They had closed for the night   he came back then Mr. Pruyne said there must be some mistake they could not send a dispatch so quick. Ellen Dempsey and Wm. Sweetland said they could. To settle the dispute Mr. Pruyne went to the Boarding house of the telegraph operator to see him. He came back and the operator said it could not be done. there must be a mistake in the date   it must have been Friday he died and furthermore they did not telegraph on Sunday. I wanted them to telegraph to have him embalmed and not bury him until we could send for him, I went to the telegraph office at six o'clock and asked if they would send dispatches on Sunday   they said not, only in case of death. I staid there that night

The letter continues on and on in this vein. But one gets a sense of what each was going through. Mr. Pruyne tried to *preach* to her the next morning about the difficulty of bringing Eugene home for burial. He tried to get her to see how much better it would be to

let the money Eugene sent him to keep for three years and let his family have it. Let it stay where it is and draw ten or twelve for yourself. It cant do Eugene any good and but very little satisfaction to you.

She told him Eugene had lost his life by it and she would rather spend it for him than any other way.

I could never feel right in using it for myself unless he was brought home and buried here.
I went home. your Father, Celestia both said bring him home.
I sent your father down to Mr. Pruynes   there was another man there and they talked over the matter   Mr. Pruyne I suppose thinking of keeping the money for three years and not knowing at the time that your father was the main heir and could take it from him at any time concluded not to send for him when if we had money we should send for him. If I had telegraphed the same afternoon to the Capt. to have him embalmed and kept but Lydia offered to telegraph her father

And so on and on. It seems a sad sorry episode.

On Tuesday morning a young man came to their house with a letter his brother had written him. In it Eugene had requested his Father to come after him for he was not able to come home alone. This man, Wallace, belonged in the same company as Eugene did. The next morning when his father started after him, Mr. Pruyne would not let him have the money so he was not sent for. Eugene had written Mr. Pruyne to send him 30 dollars to come home as he was getting his discharge from the United States service.

But the poor boy died the same day   Oh if I had not let him gone   I wrote to the Capt to send his effects home to me   I received a letter yesterday that he had done so sent them by Adams Express

and stating Eugene was walking around the same day before he died and his advice and the Surgeons advice about having his remains brought home. The Capt advised that we let him remain where he was buried in a nice dry place   a Soldiers Cemetary   that he would have a nice headstone made with his name and Regt inserted on it but if I thought I must have him buried near me he would do all he could to assist me. The expense, after nearly three weeks would be very heavy, the Coffin alone costing from seventy-five to a hundred dollars we must have a metallic coffin . . .

It all seemed pretty depressing and gruesome and almost thoughtless to send this kind of letter to another soldier, expecially his brother. His mother promised to send paper and envelopes, postage stamps and some newspapers. She added that she was alone doing her work and had not time to write half she would like. *School is out for the afternoon and I am not ready to go   then supper to get   calf porage to make,* after she got home.

Your Uncle Steve brought a letter here last Friday from you with six dollars and two Confederate notes enclosed.
Mr. Pruynes have moved to Syracuse and Livia went with them Celestia lives down in the City with Mr Wentworth your Father send his best respects to you. Marriette and Fred send their love   give my respects to all who will accept them and receive my love yourself
*   Mariette Pelham*
PS I have sent a fine and course comb   6 sheets of paper   6 envelopes   6 postage stamps   1 Harpers Weekly   1 Commercial Advertizer   1 penholder   6 pens and several of the Commercial Times   it is seven o'clock and I am in the office

Life at home during the War is illustrated in his mother's letter of May 2. She had received a letter from him on May 16. It is hard to tell how many letters got written and of them how many got to their destination. His grandmother had died on the 18th. They thought it was the *erysipilas* combined with old age. Conflicting accounts told of Uncle Charles Dutcher being chosen for a Scouting party, being excused because he couldn't manage the hard tack and even that he was one of twelve chosen from the fort and shot by the rebels. At the grandmother's grave there was much catching up of family news. Aunt Octavia relayed the information that Uncle Harry was in California mining. She had insisted Livia come to the funeral since there *would not be near as many as at your grandfather's   the relatives are so scattered since his death.*

Livia called me away. All she wanted was about Eugene's money   she did not care one cent for anyone but the Pruyne family . . . Yesterday I saw John Post going down to the City   I ran down to

*the road fearing he was on his return to the Regt
. . . he thought he should get his furlough extended
I was relieved because I was intending to go to his
Father's a foot, fearing I should not get a chance
to send anything with anyone for I could not go to
Syracuse to send it in your box. I shall send 6 lbs,
¼ of dried apples 1 pint dried blackberrys   you
may think it small but it is nearly all I have   We
did not dry half as many as last year   last spring
I could have sent a sack full if I had had a chance
We had apple sauce on the table every meal until
berrys came there was not anyone but Eugene to
pear quarter and core and he had to run after
Steve's horses so much he was so tired and sleepy
it was only now and then an evening he done anything at it   Merritt strung them all   I did not have
any womankind to help me last fall so I did not get
time to work myself.*

*as for the berrys we did not have time to pick
them   I sent them all to you except some I
stewed today   if there is not any frost we shall
have several kinds. currents is getting quite
large   we shall have plenty of cherrys   Your
Aunt Orpha is here now making the little boys
some clothes   I shall send a paper of needles
they were eight cents   a piece of beeswax Aunt
Orpha sends that . . . I dident tell you I thought
John Peck cut that bee tree   your father thought
Mr moore cut it but I guess not . . . your Father
thought he would cut it in September and it was
already cut   there appeared to have been considerable honey   I shall send a ball of yarn*

> *June 3*

*Well my child I was called to the funeral of your
uncle Charles youngest child yesterday   I went
with your Uncle Stephen and staid at Steve's all
night   the three little boys staid alone at home
Frank milked   I made porage for the calf night
and morning   got breakfast   put up the boys
dinner   I got home about 2 o'clock   This morning your Aunt Helen had another letter from your
Uncle Charles Dutcher dated May 10th   he
received a letter from Aunt Helen and one stating
you were at Fort Jackson Florida*

*the news we had came very near being true   the
Capt and private were shot through the head
another through the shoulder but not killed   but
the Capt could not get well . . . your father went
to Syracuse Tuesday morning and has not
returned . . . the whistles are blowing   I wish you
were here to hear them   my boys have left the
sounds here at home   my poor dear Eugene
oh that I had not let him gone   but he was so
good natured about it I hoped for the best but if
they had not neglected him he now would be
home alive   it is that that makes me raving   he
had grown so large and smart for work anyone
would have given him a dollar or ten shilling a*

*day   the boatmen said he counted as much as
anyone on the boat and all your Father gave him
was a pair of boots, three dollars   one pair of
shirts   ninety six cents for all his summers work
and one pair of mittens for fall and winter work
until the fifteenth of February and that is another
thing that makes me distracted   oh that I could
bring back them four months and a half but I must
grieve on till death takes me away for I never can
be myself again*

Much can be read between the lines about their
lives. She closes with a description of a blue suit of
Garibaldi Zouaves pants in which little Merritt and
Fred had their *likenesses* taken with one for the soldier brother.

*The pants are trimmed . . . the outside seam with
red   The Garibaldis are trimmed with small metal butons about the size of a small pea across the
shoulders up and down the front   1 pocket on
the left side scalloped and trimmed with red so
that with a white handkerchief in the pocket and
their wrist bands turned over and their collar
make their suit red, white and blue. It was for last
fourth of July*

Another friend wrote from Hinmansville, July 3
1864:

*. . . I hope you will all have a pleasant fourth for we
are to have a big time in Oswego County   we
wont have no celebration at our place but we will
have a big dance   We got a new Hotel Gust
Pam keeps it   we trimb the hall yesterday and I
do wish you boys could be with us   No Gust,
Henry nor none of our boys have been in the
army   Henry belongs to the Home Gards . . . I
would like to be with you to go a little hunting for
I am great on the hunt and besides they are good
eating   I quit the steamboat and am to work on
the Dams   we are to work at Philipsville now
we will go to the Horse Shoe Dams   the hy water
raised the debel on the river this spring   I have to
close because they are making up the male Good
day from your friend   Wm. A Serrott*

The next several letters started July 22 are from
"Mother." They are repetitive and also fascinating in
revealing the drudgery of living without running
water, central heat, electricity, or telephones. Trans-
portation mostly on "shanks' ponies" can keep one's
life circumscribed and provincial. The virtues of the
situation may outweigh the difficulties, but it requires
effort to feel any empathy with some of it.

She told of his father's *bad spell again* with his leg.
He was taken very poorly and we thought he would die.
Doctor Gillette came and ordered horse radish leaves
put on his stomach and on the calves of his legs. It
drew a blister on one of them. When he was better
and the leg began to swell, she thought it was the *Ery-
sipelas*. Dr. Scott said it was dropsy. Doctor Gillette
said It would always set in and trouble him any time

anything ailed him. *he is better now and the same old Frank has earned two dollars and twenty-five cents   if your Father had been home he would not have let him went if he had taken him in the woods he would have said he did not earn anything   he shoveled shorts in the mill to load a boat by the hour and does all our chores   fed the cow and calf three times   watered them eight times   drew up tubs of water to water the garden and watered it and fetched ten pails of water for the house.*

July 25
I hardly know what to write   I am so confused it is six months ago today that Eugene enlisted   it was Monday then Oh that fatal day and he has been dead three months and a half, oh if I could be set back to that day and Eugene alive and know what I know now with all the rest of the children alive   how gladly I would live those days over when I see others with 6 or 8 children and hear them saying if they were all dead at once they could not mourn for them   I wonder why it could not have been one of them instead of mine for before I lost any I thought if I should lose one of mine I should be crazy and it did hurt my memory. Mrs. Powel has another boy and she wishes Mrs. Griffin would take it and she means it to   now they have six boys at home.

The theme switches easily to the *great drouth in these parts since last May, no rain in four weeks.* Another anniversary,

six months ago today Eugene put on his soldier cloths . . . Then Father was taken down again with his leg . . . Augustus those swellings did break however they are well now. I made salve of the balsom you saved in a teacup and saucer you fetched in when you dug boat knees before you left home it healed your father's leg   he and Frank have gone to making hoops   they are about five miles from here   they go through the City and board there

With the first of August there is a long tale of trying to get a package to him, but it failed either because there were too many dried apples, or maybe the Regt would go no further than New York and *what would he do with them* referring to whoever promised to deliver it.

I have begun to raise a calf for you of the brown cows   it was such a pretty creature   I could not bear to have it killed your Father is mad   I told him if I could not get along without it I would send to you for money   if it lives when you come home it will be a year old   if you happen to get married another year you may have a cow if it lives   if you do not approve of it let me know in your next letter   in haste
your Mother   Mariette Pelham

A postscript to a letter of Sept. 11 has enclosed in it five cents
such as we had to pass here this summer but now they will not pass, none only with the fish on it and that only in this City. So I sent them to you to look at and keep for pocket money . . . Celestia sent a piece of cloak she bought last fall, and a piece of her hat trimming   it is red velvet   her hat was black felt and a black plume. I have been particular in the description of her hat as she was sorry I had forgotten to tell you about it. she could not send a piece of her shawl she got the first fall after you left home. I will try to describe it   she paid six and a half dollars for it   it is plaid, black and white middle with blue in the border it is very fine and very heavy   now it could not be bought for less than ten dollars.

A later postscript ends with *my hands are aching with cold I have two caffs to see to.*

By the next day a box was on its way to him.
It was put aboard the cars at two o'clock   it weighed thirty-two pounds   there was a box of fishing tackle together with a paper of needles, some letters, an Ambrotype of Merritts and Freds [the two little boys] a three quart pail of butter two cans of spirits   some dried apples   a few dried cherrys a few black berrys and some reading I sent one of this month's Daily Times with the names for drafting men of different towns   I thought it might be interesting to you and some others to look over

Listed again are all the newspapers she sent and an answer requested concerning receiving each
Mrs. Boyer says she would not send any newspapers for the mail was so often heavy with letters that they would throw them away because the soldiers would rather have letters. It is Merritts birthday and he is ten years old   It is seven months tonight since Eugene slept at home last time   the next he left for the City   Poor boy he did not think he would go that day he bade Celestia and the little boys good by   poor little Freddie   he grieves today for him   he is all choked up talking about him of his own accord   When Eugene came home and said he enlisted Fred cried right out and cried a long time. It is so cold today my hands ache   I am baking and the fire feels comfortable.

It is incredible the number of attempts they made to send him the last box, through John Post; several times to Mr. Hammond's, and then they gave up the idea; 3 times to see W. Stevens all to no purpose; twice to Austin's; once to see his son that was expecting to go into the 110th Regt but was ordered to Rochester to the General Hospital as a medical assistant not a soldier; the father went three times to Capt. Jarrett of that regiment and the third time he saw him. He offered to call for it in New York if they would send it there, and he would probably be there in a week. So they sent it.

I heard later that the Capt was not directly from the Regt but he'd been to Key West. I hope he will prove himself more of a man than Capt Doyl did. I do not see why he did not send the package on to you or kept it for you   what authority did he have to undo it?

It was the third week in September when his mother wrote again with many of the same types of detail. His father and Frank were making hoops and planning a contract for fall. George Clause was working for him. Some of these names may be more meaningful than others; but if not, they still give a picture of everyday living during Civil War times. So many are mentioned as being involved with the war that it seems strange more historical matter is still unavailable in this area.

Celestia is home making a dress for me   She has got up to make some ginger snaps. She wanted to make some for your box but it needs the old strong molasses and we had none   Molasses is eleven shilling a gallon   Syrup two dollars   Sugar from 20 to 60 cents   cheese 25, butter from forty five to fifty, potatoes three dollars a bushel   onions and beans four dollars a bushel, three dollars and twenty cents a sack for flour mutton is 18 cents a pound, 18 cts for surlin steak, fourteen and sixteen for Tea and Coffee fifty cents a pound. Enough of this . . .

Your Father saw Harvey Bowen in the City   He came down to get some cloth cut   he is getting ready to go West and should send for his family next fall . . . they were very anxious for your Father to go with them . . .

Capt Davendorf's Mother in law said he would start for Tortugas Island the seventh of October   His furlough is extended to the 9th . . . Seven weeks from today Eugene would have been seventeen years old if he had lived

From your Mother   Marietta Pelham

George Hees told Marietta Pelham that the ink stand she was sending her son would not only last a life time but might save his life by shunning a bullet, and also he would always have it in memory of his mother. She suggested in this October 9 letter that with the supplies she was sending he could do mending.

Put a piece of cloth in the heels before they are fairly worn through thereby keeping the shape of the heel and making it easier to mend . . . I have sent you pieces of an old checked shirting for that purpose and you must first run the cloth on the inside and then darn it on the outside   do it before it gets as big as a shilling and save yourself some work for they are six shillings a pair   the inkstand was thirty cents   Celestia made a pin cushion and case for it and I filled it with four long

rows of pins . . . Merritt sent some chestnuts I sent cookies and fried cake.

I sent your military shirt   I dont know how you will like it   I thought you might as well have the good of it now as ever   the most I care for   I'm afraid you will spoil it from washing. I would not have sent it if I had had the money to buy cloth Celestia would make the cloth into shirts and then I should buy a box of collars and neckties for you . . . if I had money I would send a pair of slippers to you to put on to ease your feet from your shoes at times . . .

It is six months today since Eugene breathed his last

After more regrets and mourning she urges Augustus

be kind to all around you wherever you are   you can always think how our dear Eugene might have been saved for us thereby. I mean by kindness in season, do not let the chance slip by for it may be too late to do them any good and thereby death may come and a great grief must follow . . . It is so cold my hands ache and the children cant go chestnutting.

From your Mother

Well Augustus it is 9 days since I began this letter   If I had money I would have sent it a week ago . . . All the way I have to get money this summer is with eggs and now the hens are shedding their feathers and eggs are few   Perhaps you may think I have butter to sell but I will tell you I have not sold an ounce of butter only for you. We sold the old cow last April to George Kirk. That left us without any but the two year old and I was raising her calf for myself and took all the milk for it was very poor   I thought I would raise that so if we sold the brown cow I would have two left as your father sold the three year old last fall . . .

I said we had none but the two year old. The brown cow did not give milk until August and then I thought I would raise the calf for you it being a late calf   I give it better milk now . . . the first butter that we spared was to fill your pail, then I have sold some since to pay for letter paper and all such things and your socks

Next Marietta tells of the reactions of Juliet who had come from Jefferson County where they had moved and to which she was taking her furniture. Juliet liked Jefferson County more than his mother thought she herself would. It was good wheat country but without peaches and few apples. Even a twenty-year-old had never seen a peach or chestnuts.

A letter from Mr. Bowen seems to take it for granted that all of us, including you, Celestia and Livia should come there and each take a piece of land and have a homestead and get rich in ten years.

He is much mistaken if he thinks I will go there. If

Eugene were alive, but now I feel as though I never can leave this City where he has stood waiting for me, where I see so many places he has come with me. It is all fresh in my memory and I am afraid it may slip from me if I leave.

Oh I feel so awfully grieved when I am alone to think I must be surrounded with so many cares I cannot devote more time to mourning for the Dear Boy.

She is certainly possessed with grieving for Eugene and hugs it to her, being afraid that it may ease with time. She sacrifices to send things to Augustus and writes often, but priority is still placed on mourning for the sixteen-year-old who died so soon after enlisting.

Your Father has sent three election tickets for you to vote and instructions how you shall proceed to vote if you do it immediately in order to have your vote put in this election . . . it is eleven o'clock and I am writing by your lamp and all the family is asleep.

Time moves on. Important civilian reaction is revealed. A letter is written to H.A. Pelham, Co H 110th Regiment, N.Y. Volunteers, at Fort Jefferson via Key West. Anna Bowen writes from Hinmansville on October 30, 1864.

The last we heard from Benjamin two months ago he was before Petersburg right in the front we dont know but he has died a solger's death but I think and so does the rest that the reason he does not write is because the headman will not allow any of them to write on account of election if that is the case it is a shame and a disgrace I think it is bad enough for a poor solger to be in this bloody money making war without being deprived of writing his friends but never mind the white solgers but save the poor black and let this war continue so it may fill the rich man's pocket never mind the poor had ought to either starve or go to war and if they die they die in a good cause . . . James Bowen said he was willing to die for the negroes and shure enough he did for them poor fellows

he enlisted and went to war he and his brother William both and it was not but a short time after he and Bill was a going after a coffin to put another poor fellow in and James was shot dead by a sharp shooter

It is too bad as he was as good a fellow as ever lived in this world . . .

I must tell you Chansie has lost his Felice and Mary they have not got any children now they died with sore throats so poor aunt lectie haint got ainey thing to scold at but her cow now . . . Clance bought a steamboat it runs from Syracuse to Fulton every day or has all summer I believe it runs from Siracuse to Phoenix now

Write to us all Ben's directions if you wish to write are Benjamin Bowen Co 3 100th Regt NYS Vols Before Petersburg, Pa
Anna E Bowen

A good sample of the beginnings of most letters is as usual a succession of *We're well, hope you're well,* detailed accounts of letters sent and received, complaints when every message, stamp, cookie and newspaper is not acknowledged or worse, not received. For instance, *The one that had the election tickets you did not mention.*

Nov. 6, 1864

Dear Son,
. . . you did not tell if Dan Davendorf had arrived at the Regt or not and you did not tell me if the cookies were good, your Father said they were stringy I thought they were baked hard, if you have received all I sent, I wish you could let me know in your next letter there was two weeks you did not get the Weekly Oswego Times for when I called for them they had none but the 19th of Oct. I subscribed to the Times for you the man said they would send it to the office so it could go out with the letter, but you did not mention it. I had put the letter in the office and went directly to the Times office and subscribed. I had walked very fast down to have them go out on the 2 o'clock train and had got to go over the river, so I entrusted it to them as it was their business I hope you will get them regular I saw them put your name on the Book for one quarter it was thirty cents I paid it

Again for Eugene, *I have his knife and pocket book before me on the table he has been dead seven months tomorrow and the next day if he were living he would be seventeen.* Henry Wallace had been to see her and give correct information about Eugene. He died the eighth of April between six and seven o'clock in the evening. *Wallace and another young man by the name of Murray of this City laid him out.*

Murray was since killed by a shell instantly and Wallace was wounded with the same shell in the wrist. Aunt Adaline has a letter every week . . . he wrote home what a splendid dinner they had the fourth of July . . . all kinds of different Louisianna vegetables besides they killed a Crocadile the day before and skinned a part of its tail and he ate some of it and said it was as sweet fish as he ever ate.

Alone on November 10 at 4 o'clock she again tried to write, but
I have no help to do the work. I hope you will excuse all my mistakes I am baking and have to drop my pen quite often as I am one who attends strictly to baking . . . George Dutcher had been getting ten dollars a month all summer working on a farm.

In this letter I will enclose Merritt's and Fred's like-

nesses a standing   I was sorry they did not have their hats in their hands by their side so you could see how well they have kept those you gave me the money to buy before you went away   they are as good as ever only faded   they have worn them every Sunday to Sunday school and to all Hollidays and some to common school
Hercules Powell and his wife have come to town   Hiram's wife says Sylvia is so proud the ground is not good enough for her to walk on   Hercules is so scared all the time for fear she will be displeased   he is between hawk and buzzard   they went down to the City with Hiram and Mr Avery rode with them and Hercules said he wished he would not do or say anything to wound Sylvia's feelings. Mr Avery said no he would not do so for the world   Hercules did not hardly know what to do with himself   you know how bashful he looks   he has not outgrown that look   he worships his Sylvia. The wind has blown all day   I think we shall hear of shipwreck on the Lake.

That last sentence points up why some that seems mundane and repetitive has been included here. *I think we shall hear of shipwreck on the Lake.* This follows a weather report of wind blowing all day. One feels how the people live under such threats as many of their men work on the lake as well as the canal, the dams, and farms. It is an everyday fact of life.

In a letter of November 14 that she has been trying to write for days she says:

Do not send over five dollars to me in a letter Your Uncle Charlie does not send over that home nor do they send over that to him at one time   I think you do not wish to send any more to Mr Pruyne   you had better send it to your Uncle Stephen Willcox and have some understanding between you and him. I think that will be the most safe for you. do not hint of anything in your writing that I have said anything that your father can distrust   send word if your chestnuts were mouldy   your Father said they would mould.
I want you to practice writing yourself and not sign your mark   you can as well as Celestia   give my respects to all who accept them
From your Mother

This last paragraph is perplexing. Does it imply that Augustus did not get very far in school and doesn't write well? Many quit early to go to work and help out with finances. There is only one letter from him. Was it written for him? Our imaginations are left dangling, slowly turning in the mind.

His mother writes quite well, spells correctly almost always, and even uses punctuation more than most when she takes time. The letters indicate a hardworking family in meager circumstances. The father's letters are well written. He does demand that his wife read to him at length whether for the pleasant experience, eye trouble, or slow reading ability! There seems to have been a drinking problem with him from certain references to its not being best for him to get his hands on certain moneys because of it. Livia, the daughter who works for the Pruynes, says as much. The Pruynes seem to be among the richer people of the area. They have a home in Oswego and a shop in Syracuse where they also live at times. His signature and his son Simon's to a lesser extent outdo anything I have ever seen in calligraphy. But we are limited here to these letters. Many are missing and information lacking. In spite of this, they are a rich source indeed of much important history and indicate the mores of that time and place.

Here is a bit of history:

Cleveland   Dec. 18, 186-

Dear friend Pelham
I got my discharge last July On the 8th July   I embarked on the Christopher Pendleton for the North   The Capt and St.   were taken with yellow fever after they left Key West . . . I struck a bargain with the captain to take me North . . . we were eight days when we landed in Conecticutt   I had a plenty tough time of it since I got home   I was about gave up but under the pure and embracing air of the north I soon received I have been graguly recovering   I think if I had stayed in Key West a little longer I should never have got home   I was so wek that I could not have stood any attack of yellow fever but through the Providence of God I got hom alive
I suppose you are having a gay old time on that desolate island of the ocean   have you forgotten the good times we used to have in the city of New Orleans
. . . there was quite an exciting time hear during this election   I was surprized to find such strong opposition agance Mr Lincoln and the war   there are some hear who ar as big traitors as the Rebbles in arms . . .
Respecfully   John a Lane

December brought several family letters. His aunt M.A. Dutcher wrote that his Uncle Charley was in the Baton Rouge Hospital having been sick with a fever since September. When he got better of that he was *taken with the gravel and now has chills and fever. Now he says he is so poor he can reach around his arm anywhere above his elbow and he dont have any appetite to eat such food as they have there. He is going to try to get a furlow to come home if he dont get one I shall send him a box, but I am in hopes he gets a furlow. He hasn't drawed any pay since last April and it comes rather tough for both of us although I have got plenty of pancake timber and potatoes. I had about 20 bushels of buckwheat and fifty buschels of potatoes. The potatoes I hoed and dug myself and they are as nice* potatoes as you ever see. R took a load down and put them in his cellar and he has to show them to everyone that goes there.

The buckwheat Mr Albright got sowed on shares   Mrs Albright has got two or three brothers in your regiment   their names are Clarke   if you know them you can tell them the Albrights are well and likewise the Powel folks.

Orpha mad her home here this summer but I hope she comes back from sewing for Hellen and makes some clothes for your father's boys. I hope Orpha comes for if Charley dont get a furlow it is so lonesome when the children are all at school that I dont know what to do with myself since I got my outdoor work done and it comes pretty tough to be man, boy dog and fence and woman to boot   I have spun enough for fifteen yards of cloth and wove 45 yards but I suppose you will think I want to brag a little but I only want you to know what I have been up to

George has worked out the greater part of the season   he got ten dollars a month   if it hadn't been for him I guess we should have had to go to the poor house or somewhere else you wanted to know what Steve and Jim Garrett was adoing   Steve is boating and Jim has married him a wife and cant go as the old saying goes   he worked his father's farm this season   the old man started to go with Steve but didn't get very far before he drowned   they didn't know whether some one pushed him or he fell in himself

your aunt   Met Dutcher

Lievia (she likes an extra vowel) wrote her brother to find out about a box he had asked for.

Mr Pruyn said the largest size would be too big for you and to write back to you. He is not to blame because he said the money was ready anytime you wanted anything . . . But Father and Mother are down on Mr Pruyn about Eugene's money that he left with him but what he done was out of kindness for he tried to fix it so Father could not waist it or drink it up but all the thanks he gets was that they went to a lawyer to try to get it when they could have got it without trouble for if Mother had said she wanted it they could have got it but Mr Pruyn would not give it to Father if Mother did not say so   when Eugene first died Mr Pruyn talked with Mother   she said she wanted him to keep the money but next thing came up was this lawyer so I dont think Mr Pruyn was used well.

The tale from this other viewpoint continues:

Father came up to Syracuse and to Mr Pruyns and wanted money to go to Washington after Eugenes remains   he said that Mother sent him but he had been drinking and Mr Pruyn did not believe him so he got on the cars and went to Oswego to explain and got a livery horse and took me and wee went to see Mother and she seemed to join

in with Mr Pruyn in thinking it was not safe to trust so much money with him and told him he had better send Father home which he did but they have got it all now because they got it by way of the lawyer but what they have done with it I cant tell for I have not been home since I came to Syracuse but enough of that   I am tired of it and sorry there was any trouble

But what will I write about now   I am getting so I like Syracuse very well, better if anything than Oswego   I think the flowers you sent is splendid and I wish you would send me a box of shells and Mr Pruyn wants some too   I will send a book with this letter and if you get it do answer soon and tell me what you think of the proceeding   Mr Pruyn heard our folks was setting you up to send for your money but I must close   goodbye from your sister. In my next I will send a picture   the folks all send love

Lievia

No mention is made of Christmas day except a date on a letter from his Mother in Oswego.

Dec. 25, 1864

Dear Son,

I received your letter under date of the ninth and you may rest assured we were glad to get it for we had called a great many times and met with disappointments   we conjectured a great many things   I was thankful to learn you had been well . . . It is eleven months today since Eugene enlisted, and it is eight months and 17 days he has been dead. I little thought a year ago today I should soon be deprived of him   he had never said a word about soldiering in anyway whatever and I shall always think he never would have if it had not been for Bill Thompson and Celestia   Bill kept constantly at him and so did Celestia.

A fortnight later the letter is continued. She says on January 8 that they have moved and the weather has been the coldest in many years. Another delay and she takes up her pen on February 22. She has had

so much to do. You may think I can write Sunday, but there is no chance Sunday for I must read to your Father   he is so selfish and willful he would have me do to suit him if everyone and everything else died and then he would not be pleased   And I spent a great deal of time grieving for Eugene   I cannot help it   I think it was so wrong for us to let him go

She finally winds up with I suppose you have had enough of this while I could dwell upon it.

A registered letter arrived. It was late so she went to Mr. Brewster the next day

to get his advice on the note in it. I told him I was ignorant as to how I should proceed for I wanted to do the best for you and your Father was not at home so I could not ask him (but in fact he was in the City and I was anxious to have the business done before he got home). Mr Brewster said his advice was to keep it myself, but Augustus, he said states in his letter I could draw the money and give it to Uncle Steve or keep it just as I Choose and he said he believed any of the Banks would be willing to pay the money on it but if he was in my place he should keep it. It was as safe in my possession as it could be anywhere   It was drawing interest wherever it laid and his advice was to keep it myself so I thought I would fetch it home and lock it in your trunk and it would be there safe when you come home.

I went to the Post Office and found a letter advertized the 13th. It had a five dollar bill in it and Frank had called for one several times and they told him none. You say I must tell about getting the money from Livia. She came home the 29th and said Gust wrote to her to fetch $25 to Celestia   She started from Syracuse with the money she staid in the city that night and she traded so she had seventeen dollars then, then I gave ten dollars to Celestea and there was a five dollar bill and two dollars Livia said it cost her one dollar twenty cents and it would cost her the same to go back. If I could give her twenty cents she would leave one dollar with Mrs. Clark in the City When she come to look over her portmanteau she found ten cents and I gave her ten cents currency and she left a dollar bill with Mrs. Clark and Celestia got it and used fifty cents of it and gave fifty cents to me. Livia has sent me five dollars since, 2 at one time and three at another in letters and stated she would send the rest of it if I would write and let her know if I had received it safe

Now do not give yourself any uneasiness about it   Livia will send it all to me . . . Celestia is at work for your Aunt Hellen   Frank has taken two letters out of the office for her since she has been there   they laid in the office two weeks   we did not pay for a box this quarter   I suppose they think they will get a penny now and then for advertizing   they asked fifty cents instead of twenty five

A minute description of shells and coral sent — how many prongs broken and how she placed them on again so they looked perfectly whole. Henry Miller saw it and was surprised it was so *splendid*. He had never seen anything like it. But she advises if he sends more to pack it in straw or something to make it solid.

Aunt Orpha went to Alexandria Bay to see Juliet. She brought news of Uncle Charley whom Marietta believes may have been taken prisoner and if so might be exchanged soon   I hope he may. He has about $400 worth of wine and tobacco that is not sold yet

William and Juliet wrote to your Father and said Frank enlisted yesterday   He passed his examinations and they were making out papers and had

got a horse and cutter and come out to see if his Father would consent. Your Father told them he guessed not they might take him if they would Frank looked rather down today   he has a hard cold   it affects his head rather bad   your Father thinks he may go yet   he says they have found he has padded his examinations   they may see him in the City and take him to Auburn   they did a boy one day this week in one of the northern counties   a man gave the boy five hundred dollars and took him to Auburn and got seven hundred   his father followed them to Auburn and got the boy and took him home but could not find the man   they do not enlist boys without their parents consent   I tell you now not to give any more money to the girls   they are as able to earn for themselves as any one   you will want it for yourself   I am very much obliged for what you have sent me

Marietta L Pelham

The year is now 1865, and it is January. Livia writes her brother that she has taken the $25 for Celestia, but she has not heard if Celestia has had *the bunch taken off her side* or not. She judged from appearances that their folks were getting along pretty well. Then she inquires of Gust's girl.

She came to see me once and since then I have not heard from her until lately and then I heard she was married. Is it so   Have you concluded to marry when the war is over   But cheer up   Your three years is nearly up and then hurah for home and a wife. . . . I will send you a book to day and more when I get more money to spare but I have hard work to keep myself clothed decently when everything is so high . . . I think that leaf you sent Celestia is real pretty and if it isent too much trouble I wish you would send me some.

I dreamed last night that you came home and enlisted again and if you do go soldiering again I'll bust your eye.

Met Dutcher wrote from Little Utica, January 6, 1865:

Dear Nephew

I havent had a letter from Charley in five weeks . . . Ware wrote home that he had been transported from the general hospital to New York   but it has baen long enough for him to get there   I should think and the news come in the papers that there had been a boat lost loaded with soldiers   sick soldiers   there was 300 on board and they was all lost but 60 and I am so afraid he was on that boat that I am just about crazy for it does seem as though if he was alive he would write or get someone to write for him if he isent well enough to write himself   but I live in hopes of him yet if I dont die in despair   sometimes I get almost discouraged then again I think perhaps he is among strangers and without money you are without friends as a general thing

I have been weaving since I wrote you   I have wove a piece of 23 yards and have got another piece of 11 yards in the loom now and have two more pieces engaged to weave

You wrote you was going to have a dish of oysters for Christmas well I will tell you what I had   Chaffee came up and took us both down there   we had chicken and everything else good but oh Gust it wasent a merry Christmas to us   there was too many of our number missing   I had a present of a 20 dollar greenback   Father and Mother sent it to me   they are down here now on a visit   they got here day before yesterday   they want me to go home with them and I would go if I only knew where Charley was for it wouldent cost me anything to live while I stayed there and they want me to stay until his time is out   but I dont want to go until I know where he is for if he should come home I want to be here   I do wish the war would come to a close for it has caused so many heart aches and made so many homes desolate   but I am afraid there will be a great many more before it is through with   the talk is here that they are going to draft the 15th of next month . . .

A Mr A Connell has moved to Bette Corners. tell Mr Morse Marvin Showers funeral sermon is to be preached next Sunday in the brick school house to the lock   He was buried within the rebel lines so they cant get his body
I remain your aunt and well wisher   Met Dutcher

John Lane who *spent two long years in the far off south suffering and struggling alike for those principles which form the basis of all our happiness* wrote to his *Respected Friend* Augustus from Cleveland on February 4, 1865. It was good he said to hear they were all well in their far off island home.

I hope that God who holds all destinies in his own hands may spare your lives to return to your respective homes . . .
You wuld perhaps like to know what effect the war has had on those who staid at home   you would be surprised to see the feeling that experience in regard to the war has made . . . the solger coming home from the war is hardly noticed except by his friends   business is good and very plenty but the price has changed so that you cannot make as much as in the old times   People find a great deal of fault about their taxes being so high . . . there are a great many people whose patriotism reaches only to the bottom of their pockets   they had much rather live under Rebel oppression than to use their means to help put down would be Rulers   Such is the feeling of a great many who are living under protection of our Government   All I have to say is that if the country were rid of them we should be better off . . .
Everything seems quiet on the Potomac   there

seems to be considerable talk about a peace since I believe there is already some Commission has been sent to Richmond and are about to talk the matter over with the authorities at Washington but I have little hope   there has been so many   I was quite surprised to hear of some of the promotions in the Regt and it is quite an honor to the Regt as well as to those who are thus honored   How has Seth Stevens got along   Please let me know

Another letter from the same friend adds more about those who

are now gone and some never to return   I dont know some of the names you mention but we had a representative in almost every branch of the Service. A big fire in Cleveland burned Foster's Tavern off 'clean as a whistle' The loss was heavy although he was inshured for several thousand dollars I suppose you are looking forward to shak off the military of Uncle Sam and again be a free man   I hope you will live to see this day . . .

Tidings of Uncle Charley had not been received yet Uncle Chaffee went out beyond Baldwinsville to see a man that was in that boat that was lost but he dident find out anything much   his sister was with him   she said there was a man on the boat that answered to that description but he went with two canes and the doctor said he had the dropsy but she did not know his name. But your Aunt Orpha dont think it was Charley   she thinks he's taken prisoner and I have a good deal of faith in her prophisies and I hope and trust it may be so rather than the other for while there is life there is hope.

Orpha was working at Aunt Em Coffins. She was going to make a coat for Chaffee and then go to Lutes. Orpha said it appeared that when Henry wrote he had not heard of his Mother's death or Charley's enlisting or Harriet's or Dallas' death or of Eugene's. She continues to weave.

If the folks dont keep me in work so I have something to busy my mind they will have to take me to the big house in Utica if I dont hear from Charley before long.

The "big house in Utica" refers to a state mental institution which is still in operation.

A nice winter, plenty of snow and sleigh bells are reported in Livia's next letter to her brother, *but poor I have not had a single sleigh ride Mr Pruyn does not keep a team this winter as he has no barn where he lives* A long explanation starts again about Mr. Pruyne and Eugene's money,

but now he has paid it all and I hope they are satisfied and Mother did not know it had all been paid until I was in Oswego   I dont know what Father done with it   I was in hopes Father would do better but I am afraid he does not and I dont know but he is worse . . . but we must all hope for the best perhaps sometime he will do better.

Oswego March 18, 1865

To H.A. Pelham
Fort Jefferson
Dear Son,
I recd your letter of the 17th . . .
In Oswego everything is very high   Hay is 37-38 Dollars pr ton   Potatoes one dollar a buscel, Pork at $40 pr barrel . . . everything eatable is up to the highest notch   Wood is from 8, 9 to 12 dollars pr cord, it is enough for some of us to fall in love with a good Maple Log . . . winter commenced in November and there has been no thaw to 16 March. Snow 3-6 feet deep on the level Now on the 17th of March a most tremendous Flood   the River was never known to be so high   The Coffer Dam in the River is all swept away a great deal of labor and money lost at our Charter Election   the Democrats elected the majority of their tickett   however the Republicans elected their Mayor and one Supervisor, one Collector, one Alderman and the Democrats elected the balance
The Oil Fever in Pennsylvania is raging thousands are making their fortunes and tens of thousands are a loosing, it is like a Lottery   your investment may turn out well and may not notwithstanding I think a good finance man might do well in the Oil Region   the Oswego men have two companys in Oswego who are doing a good business selling shares of stock in different parts of Pennsylvania.
Relative to my business the major part of the summer I was unable to work   Rheumatism was severe   I bought 3 threes on the Bank of the River between Monetto and the high dam   I got 3 Bow Stems out of it and I got $20 a piece on the ground the remainder part of the trees brought about the same   I bought 2 black ash trees and made 1300 hoops which I got 9-10 dollars pr thousand   I paid $20 for the two trees   I paid $6 a piece for the Oaks above spoken of
A. C. Morton has the contract for the Building the Coffer Dam which is now swept away   I have been getting out 2500 feet of timber for the Purpose   I have got out this winter 2800 feet of Plank at 30 dollars pr thousand   My business is now getting out Hay hoops   expect 5-6000 to make at 30 dollars pr thousand about the size of a tight barrell hoop . . .
We have not heard from your Uncle Charley One year ago I bought the knees of 100 acres in a tamarack swamp   I got out about 1400 feet . . . Geo Goble had the most of them   the next winter I went there with Bill Thompson   we had contract for 1000   we got out about 200 for boats and vessels   We drawed in 100 and could not sell any more   Vessell Business was dull

nothing doing but repairing. John Peck went to Anapolis and thinks he will get a discharge   He is in the Hospital at that place
Relative to your business with Mr Pruyn my advice is your affairs should be more secure and think if you are careful you would place your means in a more secure hands say to Stephen   Prine took the advantage of me and wronged me out of about 40 dollars and in fact he is not considered very trustworthy

From your old Father
Harvey Pelham

Mother writes next on the 20th of March telling her son she is home alone with three boys. Augustus is in the war. Eugene is dead and Livia and Celestia work out. The father was in Sterling making hay hoops for Mr. Willis

Your father said he wrote you about the freshet News spread that the dam broke and Sunday was like a Town Meeting all day on both sides of the river to see but they were disappointed because it was not broke   but it broke Monday morning and all the roads have been full all week and it keeps wearing away.
The Lock house slipped into the River last Thursday and went down   I have not heard from it since. The tow path is all gone away about half the length of it below the dam   there was about a dozen men at work last week to prevent it wearing any more
Please write home where the wreck was   I have not heard from your Uncle Charley. I fear he will never be seen in these parts again   A ship carrying sick from the hospital where he sank   only 60 saved, no word since   I think Charles R Dutcher was your uncle   It is very easy for a scratch from a P to be taken for an R
If he had been taken prisoner he would have written home before now if he were alive so it appears to me   when you write I wish you would please let me know where the wreck was and if you know if he went ashore and was buried or if he sunk in the water   Oh this war is murdering those at home as well as those in the Army

She adds comments on the fact that Celestia is at Uncle Stephen's and Aunt Hellen has a two-month old baby. However

Uncle Harry wrote Aunt Hellen and did not know of Mother's death, nor Charles' enlisting nor of Eugene poor boys all   Oh if he has a heart anything like mine the blow will be heavy on him there are strange things in this world.

The letter continues with *beautiful Spring weather.* It is seldom one gets a hopeful note. It is the 28th as she continues about the river falling but making a great surging below the dam. It seemed an awful sight to people who kept coming to see it daily. There was expectation the mill might go next.

Your Father said it will but I thought the heft of the water would go through the break and so it has Are the hammond boys alive   I thought Mrs. Hammond passed here with a mourning bonnet on.

News on other fronts continued the next day:
Edwin Powel was here today and said his father is sick and the children all had the mumps Hercules wrote them he was attending a mill down East   He said Mrs. Talman had bought the place of Mrs. Brewster where we lived and is moving today. I do not know if I told you Talman had enlisted last summer   he had not been in any battle but been building Railroads and bridges so she was in full swing as Father used to say with the use of James and Benny's Bounty money

Frank went to the city with a load of potatoes for your Uncle Stephen. I thought he might bring more news   But it is five o'clock and I have my chores to do and some of Frank's   He had to get feed over a mile up the river at the Brewery and did not get home untill 8 o'clock   Pigeons is flying a plenty and Frank has a hunting fever   He is so mad at his father for selling the old musket. I objected to the selling of the gun for the reason that you and Eugene both used it and Eugene had scoured the barrel as bright as steel and he said he was always going to keep it   so he had till he died and I wanted to keep it until you come home. Miller said Eugene was dead and could never use it you could bring your own gun and not want it Frank is going fishing this afternoon

Syracuse March 29, 1865

H.A. Pelham Esqr
Fort Jefferson Fortugas
via Key West   Flo
Enclosed please find ten dollars ($10) which your sister Livia gave me to send it to you   she has got a felon on her finger and is not able to write But you must excuse me from writing any more on two accounts the shop is so cold tonight I can hardly hold a pen and I am in a hurry to meet an engagement

G Pruyn

At last the bad news is out and accepted. Uncle Charley is dead. It is continuously amazing how a sentence or more can reveal in almost Biblical manner a whole situation or character. An author could seldom do better in giving a lot of background in such a few words, and character shows up also, to say nothing of normal pettiness and antagonisms. Charley's widow writes her nephew:

April 17, 1865

Dear Nephew,
Regarding your Uncle Charley who is no more I am unwillingly forced to believe he was lost on the North America off the coast of Florida

I have sold the place and moved down by Chafees   I think when I get things strait I shall go west on a visit for I dont feel content here

Probably West was Michigan or some place a little west of Central New York. "Going west" did not seem to mean California. That was something else again.

I guess I shant get ready to go before your time in the service shall expire but oh I hope you will have better luck in getting home than Uncle Charley for it seems a great deal worse to me than it would to go into the battlefield for one goes into it expecting that it may be their last but to start for home with all their hopes in the world and then had all their hopes dashed from them and know that they must meet a watery grave   what could their feelings have been   it makes me shudder when I think of it.

Well, Aunt Met and Mother, it makes me "shudder" as I copy so many messages like this last one. Why write to a soldier and dwell on all the gruesome things he faces daily connected with living and dying. Mother seemed to think chiefly of her reactions and "mourning" in which she so continuously engaged. So now Augustus can imagine how he may be put on a leaky old boat and get himself drowned on his way home.

Dear Nephew,
I have been waiting for Orpha to come home then I shall have a funeral sermon preached Frank says tell Gust we live down by the depot in an old house that haint got any bark on it but it is all covered with scales   That is his description of the house we live in   you know we have lived in good houses ever since he can remember until now and he thinks it is awful   the children thinks your pictures is very nice

your aunt
Met Dutcher

It was his mother who wrote
it is very strange all the crew was saved there ought to be a penalty for hiring such poor vessels   It seems from your letter you have heard they have caught the assassin of the President, but before this reaches you you will know they had to shoot him before they could take him   And they have taken Jeff Davis and confined him at Fortress Monroe and refused him light. I suppose you thought you would not get another letter while in the service . . . I will put in one of the new kind of three cent pieces so you can see what kind of money we have now days.

It was to be the first of August before Augustus got out of the army. We can only imagine what effect the assassination of Lincoln, the cessation of war, and all the returning soldiers has on everybody. The letters do not tell us. The same was true of the Van Gelder lettes. At this time James Harvey Van Gelder and

Rebecca Pine Van Gelder were completing a year of running a private academy in Catskill. Since it did not pay very well and Grandma was great with child (my mother, to be specific), they were moving to Drummond Falls near Palenville on a farm not too far from her parents. Palenville may have been the link between Pelham's letters being in Grandpa's pine chest and eventually in my attic. The last date was 1874 and that is about the time J. H. Van Gelder moved back to Catskill. Conscience doth make such a coward of me that I'll never have courage to use any time to hunt up the link or Pelham's lineage. A few more tidbits and then "Finis" to the letters as well as the War.

May 7, 1865

To Pelham

. . . Chene has been out west where John was and he said John was well when he left him and that was two weeks ago Chene took him one hundred and sixty achers of land right next to John's one hundred and 60 achers and they are going out on them in a couple of weeks if nothing happens the rest of us will start in the fall Benjamin is here he came home two months ago he is one of the boys that was taken prisoner he was first in libby prison and he went from there to Salsberry prison he was in prison about six months he came home on a pay role he is now going to go to Anapleas to try to get his discharge for he is not able to do duty if he went back to stay the talk is now that there will not be any more fighting Oh dear I hope that it is so for I for my part dont like this war for it is horable horable distressed wicked dishonest murder scandlas doings and how many a poor wife is widowed on account of this hart rending war all it is for is to fill the rich mens pockets
well now I will tell you of the marriages . . .
Mr Lewis Serotte to Miss Charlotte Dingman
Mr Nelson Dibble to Mrs Wallace
Mr Lewis Buglie to Miss Mary Chase
Mr Lewis Mullen to Miss Jane Norgrove
Mr Hurman Cook to Miss Rith McMellen
Mr George McMellen to Miss Mary Betts
That is all that has been married lately but there has been a hundred and one since you went away and there is many more that is ingaged to be married in a short time
well you wanted to know about the high water well it was sixteen inches in front of the old lock house it was all over the toe path and it came cleane in Dingmans grosery two or three days and then it fell so it only covered the doorstep it took out every Shince between here and Syracuse and between here and Oswego and it washed out the slow pall in a good many places it was so a purpose to make work for poor men for there isent

much work here to do well I must close for this time for I must get supper excuse all mistakes and bad writing for I am in a hury respects from all write soon Good by
Anna Bowen to H A Pelham

William A. Serratt was out in Pensilvany during the winter working in the woods lumbering. He wrote to Augustus on the 19th of May. He had a gay time out there. Tracy came home for the winter and now has gone boating, he said. Ben Bowen was home after having been taken prisoner and then Parold He came home and was very sick. But Tracy and Tom Collins inlisted and were sent to Austin. Sterratt said he was in the Steam boat and made a trip every day from Fulton to Syracuse and back. They started at five o'clock in the morning and got home at nine o'clock, but did not think it was hard work, even so.

Pelham's mother wrote.

Oswego May 21, 1865

Well Augustus it is a month since I received your last letter Adaline had your Uncle Charley's funeral sermon preached your Aunt Orpha and Hellen and your Father and myself were all that was there of his relations except his wife and children she received a letter from the Capt of your uncles company stating he was lost on the ill fated ship North America the 22nd of December last . . . it was hard for the poor dear soldiers to die such an awful untimely death Your Aunt thinks there was foul play I think it was strange the entire crew was saved and one hundred and ninety seven soldiers drowned there was a young lady and her brother on board the same ship that described your uncle and said he was walking the deck every day her brother was one of Scotts nine hundred he was very sick she had been to take care of him they were going to leave him aboard the North America and his sister refused to leave the vessel unless he could be taken aboard the Mary E Libby she would have the same fate and they took him on board but your Uncle Charles and the other poor soldiers were left to go down with the ill fated vessel the poor creatures had no one to plead for them. I think there ought to be a penalty punishment put upon those who hire such poor vessels to transport soldiers for it seems to me to die in that way is worse than it would be to be shot.

As so often, it was days later, May 28, before she finished the letter. News was that George Dutcher came home with his Aunt Hellen and worked for his uncle until his mother left for the west. She was going to stay with her father for a year. Then if she likes, she would come back.

It seems from the tone of your letters that you have not heard they had caught the assassin of the President and I suppose you will before this reaches you   they had to shoot him before they could take him   he was taken in the night and fired on through the barn   when asked where he was hurt he said in the head   you have punished me And they have taken Jefferson Davis and confined him to Fortress Monroe and refused him light

They are already speaking in the Times and Advertizer of soldiers coming home and giving them a hand   There is some reception in Oswego   Those who have the good luck to come home will feel proud of the pains that will be taken for them

We have had some work to do   we have had twelve boarders that worked on the high dam   we have five boys from Jefferson County   2 from Canada   Prosper Tracy wanted us to board him but we could not have him   We expect a man and his wife to come next Thursday   it is worth seeing the work on the dam   the citizens are constantly passing to and fro to see it   I wish all of you poor soldiers had the privelege and you could have it if it had not been for this cursed Rebellion such things as Jeff Davis and many others   but he is to be hung   but that will not bring back the others so we must live a life of mourning

They are having some doings in the City   2 of our boarders went down   they said the soldiers were out and when they were all on the bridge a man took them in a group   they have been playing the band. We could hear them all afternoon   Henry Willcox has been a prisoner and with the parold prisoners and come home and he was awful sick   I have not heard lately   Tom Keys was at Charles funeral   he had been to Canada   do write again if you can

Your Mother
from Hinmansville, June 13, 1865

A very well but very discontented Aunt Octavia wrote her nephew that Harry was still in California. He had been gone two years. And you wanted to know about Charles. He is dead. Adaline had had his funeral sermon preached and had gone West. Shells were still a big item, and everyone wanted more of them.

I would like to see Fort Jefferson with my naked eye but I never shall. Evert Barnes has got back he looked better than I ever see him before and he said that he had got enough of solger life . . . things are very dull here Boating is very poor and business very dull everywhere and will be for a while

if it is not too much trouble, I would like to have you send me a box of shells and coral. I think a great deal of sutch presents . . . I will pay the charges.

So Octavia begins the letter and ends with shells. A more intriguing subject came from a cousin, Mrs. Juliet H. Babcock in Alexandria a short time later. No letter ever informs us whether Augustus' girl whom he left behind ever married someone else as hinted, or whether he has another interest. But it is June and the war is practically over for all the soldiers and marriage is in the air.

Dear Cousin,
. . . It is almost the 4th . . . I want you to come and see us as soon as you get home   Bet says she sends her love to you and she wants you to hurry and get home   she is Willis sister   I want you to remember her name   we have gay times here   you can make up your mind   there is lots of girls   but they is getting married awful fast   three got married lately   but never mind there is lots left there is eight lives right in sight of our house and only four boys so there is 2 girls for each boy   Where is your girl Gust   I suppose we will have a new cousin when you get home   bring her down here [Alexandria is way up on the St. Lawrence River.] Bring her here for your wedding   have your wedding tour too   now I think that's a top bottom plan dont you . . . Just send word when you will come and we will meet you at the wharf

from your most affectionate cousin
Jute

July 4 in 1865 was a day for festivities. A friend writes.

we will have a big time   we wont have no selibration at our place but we will have a big dance wish you boys could be here. Henry nor none of our boys has been in the army Henry belongs to the home guard and was married this spring I would like to be with you and do a little hunting.

He said he quit the steamboat and is working on the dams, at Philipsville, and then on to the Horseshoe Dams.

Almost the last family letter is from Celestia, July 12, 1865. She is in Syracuse with her sister Livia, who works for the Pruyns.

Dear Brother,
I received your kind letter but worried that you are not coming home until the 1st of August . . . Mrs Pruyn says if you and Jeff Perkins and some of the other boys she knows will send her a box of small shells and some Coral and a pair of those largest shells such as you sent to Ma   now do send her some Gust for she will be glad to get them   If you do be shure to send mostly small shells to make ornaments of . . . she will pay the Expense herself. Gust I have had that lump taken off my side   it waid 4 pounds Dr. Livingston and a doctor from Fulton took it off   I took choraform and did not know anything about it until the Doctors were standing by my bed calling me by name   I was very sick for two weeks but am better now   I think I am going to work next week . . . my side is not well yet nor will it be in four weeks but I am well

otherways with the exception of being weak but I think I shall be stronger in a few days   My Doctor bill is now $41 dollars and I have got to work someway to pay that.

. . . I think them rings is very handsome. I saw Ma three days ago and she had not heard from you in a long time   Livia sets there a scolding me because I wont answer her and says tell Gust I am a big Rowdy and has the same excuse Sime has for not writing . . . excuse this short letter for I am very tiard   when I get home I will write you again

> *This from your sister*
> *Celestia*

Augustus is home at last when a friend, George Fowler, writes from Red Creek Creek, Wayne County, on November 19, 1865. He is so pleased and happy with his gift of shells and thanks Gust a thousand times, and wants to buy some. There is business about hoops he had made and not been able to sell to John Fernice. He asks Gust if he knows anyone that wants them; and if he has been to Syracuse, let him know what they are bringing there.

So life is settling back into the same ruts, even though business may not be very good yet. Two years later in April a letter in marvelous penmanship carries bad news and a signature that cannot be deciphered.

Sir:

You will please vacate the house now occupied by you to Wm. J. Dickinson to whom I have rented it.   Respectfully,

The war has petered out. The letters have petered out. Six years pass. Augustus Pelham gets a letter addressed to him at South Buttler. The date is September 15, 1873. It is from Frank and Ella in Granby. I tried my undeveloped skill at figuring who was who. Augustus Pelham, Sr., was now Grandpa to Johnny mentioned in the letter who was the son of Frank. Frank was a younger brother of Augustus, Jr., and of Eugene. There were also two *little boys*, Merritt and Fred, younger than Frank. Frank must have been in the middle — young enough not to be in the army and old enough to do chores and run lots of errands, according to many references in his mother's letters. He was hard working, dependable, and indispensable to his mother. He married Ella, who wrote this last letter, but no hint appears of Augustus getting married. He is living apparently with his parents and is admonished by his sister-in-law to *be a good boy*. As in modern novels and plays, our imaginations are left dangling and turning slowly in the mind.

Ella gives him the dates of the Fair — 23, 24, and 25, and remarks that Frank got home from Aunt Helen's at two o'clock in the morning. That hardly raises an eyebrow for horse and buggy days since one could not claim flat tires or being out of gas, even though oil had been discovered in *Pensylvany.*

I have been picking beans and corn today   we have lots of dried beans and lots of seed sweet corn   Frank has been to work on his hoops until fiveoclock then he husked and braided his sweet corn up   Johnny has gone to bed   he worked helping me pick beans and cucumbers

they have put up a new hall on the Fair grounds   it is one hundred by one hundred and twenty   it is forty feet square in the center and a wing on the East and the West forty feet and it is two or three stories high

Aunt Orpha stays in Kingslands yet Wednesday night Frank is going down to the falls   I am so hurried with work I dont have much time to write

Johnny says tell Grandpa and Grandma he will get onto him and hug him   You must write whenever you can and read in the Bible to Father and Mother and be a good boy and God will bless and guide you in the future

> *Our love to you all*
> *Frank and Ella*

If there are gaps in the letters that leave us wondering about many people and happenings on the home front, this is not true of the concurrent Civil War activities. These are well chronicled and never better than by Bruce Catton. Besides his many books his concise commentaries for the **Picture History of the Civil War** published by American Heritage make every phase of it real and interesting. Great changes had taken place since the first major clash of North and South at Bull Run when Catton wrote

There is nothing in American military history quite like the Battle of Bull Run. It was a momentous fight of the Amateurs, the battle where everything went wrong, the great day of awakening for the whole nation North and South together . . . It ended the rosy time in which man could dream that the war would be short, glorious and bloodless. After Bull Run the nation got down to business.

And it was after Bull Run that our Civil War letters enter the picture with their very different drama. But the home front and the battle fronts as revealed by their writers seem very separated. There are very few letters among those saved written from the front. Augustus Pelham, Jr., plunges us right into the war, telling us of moving their camp from New Orleans to the Vicksburg area on the Mississippi. At the same time on the East front the North and South were confronting each other in the Virginia area.

Much more was going on besides the humdrum of the home front and the drum-hum of the war front than we are told in the letters. The newspapers were read and sent on often to the soldiers. There was no instant news via satellite. The letters don't even mention Lincoln's assassination except in one that says his assassin had been caught. It was the press that told about the night scenes in New York City after election as the **New York Herald** performed the amazing feat of displaying the returns in calcium lights! Such happenings as Sherman's March to the Sea, Gettysburg, escaping slaves seem to have been off limits as far as the pen and ink of any letter writer was concerned.

Feelings have to be imagined when Lee surrendered at Appomattox Court House on April 9, 1865. Pelham did not arrive home until August, so the war petered out slowly for him.

Grant and Lee were both desirous of seeing this terrible war end with a good peace. Catton says that Grant believed the whole point of the war was to prove Northerners and Southerners would always be fellow citizens and the moment fighting stopped he believed they ought to begin behaving that way.

The terms were humane. Lincoln and Grant wanted no revenge. The Southerners could take home arms and horses and get working on their farms without disturbance from the government. When all was signed, the Union artillery began to fire salutes. Grant stopped it. "We do not wish to exult over their downfall," he said.

History does not tell us a pretty story after Lincoln's death and the end of his policies of reconciliation. Nor did Reconstruction materialize. But Catton says:

Nothing could be done rationally at that time because wars do not leave men in a rational mood. It may be many years before the ultimate consequences of the Civil War are fully comprehended. We understand today a little more than could be understood in 1865 but the whole truth remains dim.

Here was the greatest and most moving chapter in American History, a blending of meanness and greatness. An ending and a beginning. . . It did not go as man had planned it.

The Almighty had His own purposes.

PART IV
YEARS OF CHANGE

An old picture shows James Harvey Van Gelder in a pony tail when he was in one of the Seminaries preparing for Yale College over a hundred years ago. But he was not "Making a Statement" as some young men were doing here not so long ago with the same hirsute arrangement. Along with some long hair, it pleased their peers but caused conflict and raised eyebrows to a large degree. But it caused no comment back then. As my grandfather received his diploma cum laude in 1864 his beard as pictured in the Yale 1864 book is identical to recent beards that have caused family rifts but no doubt lots of satisfaction among peers. When fathers and uncles began to take over the fashion, younger men began to shave and cut theirs off. I have yet to understand what statement was being made aside from declaring their independence of current mores and their elders.

The Civil War continued to battle it out for some months before General Lee surrendered at Appomattox, in April, 1865. Grandpa married his sweetheart of many years, Rebecca Pine, August 2, 1864. Neighbors "talked" because they got married on her father's lawn, an unusual manner of tying the nuptial knot in those days.

The newlyweds opened a private school on the corner of Spring and William Streets, where today the Grammar School of St. Patrick's Church is located. I knew the location as the home of a Fiero family. Father Peter Van Gelder and mother Sarah Myer were living in the new brick home on Walnut Street in West Catskill where he had bought the "farm in town" after leaving the Van Gelder farm on the Old King's Road in 1859. Brother David was in his octagon house nearby. Jacob, next younger was married and living in Saugerties. Rebecca's father, Walter Pine, was farming out in the Kiskatom area. He had debated with the Dutch Dominie of the Kiskatom Dutch Church on Predestination, a doctrine accepted by most Calvinistic Dutch Reformed members. But the Methodist Pines with their Wesleyan English heritage challenged it, as do great grandchildren today. The debaters were both of the "same opinion still" when they finished as the printed debate clearly shows. In spite of my Dutch heritage also, I root for Great Grandpa Pine. Anyway in one denomination you can "fall from grace" and in the other you can't. So I figure belonging to both I have it made.

The attendance at the school was disappointing. Grandma and Grandpa went to a farm at Drummond Falls near her father. My mother was born in the old stone house on June 14, 1865. They had planned to name her Abraham Lincoln. I have Grandma's painting of the old stone house.

James Harvey Van Gelder — graduation from Yale — 1864.

Rebecca Pine ca1870-75.

Again neighbors disapproved; this time of some of James Harvey's contraptions that he rigged up. He had a bucket line from the falls to the fairly distant kitchen door. Neighbors said, "Van Gelder is too lazy to carry his own water," so reported to us as children by our grocerman, Charles Britt, who had lived in the area. The Centennial edition of the **Examiner**, 1896, says "When James Harvey Van Gelder hitched up some crude machinery to his own invented water wheel he had built nearby, they derided his laziness. He even had a cradle rocked by machinery. Merciful goodness how lazy he would make his wife" . . . I remember being told he had a churn and cradle hitched together so she could keep both going with one foot. Leila born 1867 and Alma in 1871 both died as babies. Arthur Pine, born July 13, 1873, was born in Peter's house after his parents moved back to Catskill in 1872.

The late 70s and early 80s were a potpourri of small happenings among the younger people. Carrie Van Gelder received many letters especially from her cousin Annie Van Gelder, one of Jacob's three daughters living in Saugerties.

Bits and pieces of information are sometimes interesting. Annie would tell that in 1877 there was a tunnel under the Chicago River and that she secretly wrote notes in school and got a mark of 95 in writing. *We had lots of fun in the snow walking in it up to our knees it's awful fun.* Lillie tells of a Temperance meeting. Twenty-four hundred had signed the pledge not to drink anything alcoholic. Lillie still wore the little white ribbon bow when I knew her, showing she was a loyal member of The Temperance Society. She wrote:

I must tell you of Pet chicken. I began his name with a capital because he was just like a person and we considered him so. Well, he has been cooked in the pot. He was killed a month before I knew it. I've been to Kingston this summer. You must come to Sagerties and hear Annie speak French.

Another summer Annie was visiting in Durham, Greenville, and Cornwallville.

What a beautiful country it is. I saw meteours last night and northern lights, a glorious rainbow especially seeing them against the mountains. But I must descend to the commonplace before I get going on the glen I visited. My health has been wretched, but I am putting on a few pounds. Now I'm getting to be quite a substantial shadow of my former self. I have gained 10 pounds.

Her occupations were berrying and driving the hay wagon, and she drove a team one night without upsetting anything.

She also gathered stones for a collection and was learning to shoot. She went riding every day and expected to have a saddle soon. Life was not all dull "down on the farm" for the village girl.

She wondered what had become of the boy across

Caroline Waldron Pine, great-grandmother, copied from an ambrotype ca1855-60.

Walter Pine, great-grandfather, copied from an ambrotype ca1855-60.

the street in Catskill who had come over the night of the Fourth of July *and helped us fire off our firecrackers.*

Another time she wrote,
Dear Carrie,
The Saugerties Institute had an Exhibition last Sunday evening. I figured in several pieces but

unfortunately I looked so different from my real self that nobody recognized me, not even Hattie and Pa.

I wonder how many buschels of poetry that Poetical Club of yours has masticated already. I've nearly finished the Deserted Village. I'm going to skip all verse I dont like. I can learn five or six pleasant verses in half an hour but an unpleasant one takes a half a month. I think I will learn a pretty French poem.

From your very affectionate
Cousin Annie

These young people seemed to be quite interested in mythology and discussed the story of the God Thor in the land of the enchanted giants.

I'd like to hear some of the other stories from your mythology book. I know the story of Philo stealing Ceres, about the courtship and marriage of Adriadne and Bacchus, the God of Wine. That's all I can think of. If you don't know them I'll tell you in a letter.

Hattie was nearly drowned last Friday. It has been in three different papers. They had an awful time getting her out. She was going down for the last time. If it had not been for Herman Rowe she would surely have been drowned, as she tumbled in head first.

Later she wrote:

Have splendid times with our nightgown parties in Hattie's dressing-room. Everybody took such a fancy to you, Carrie, you were so intelligent looking, etc. Hattie crimped my hair Sunday. Now she does it all the time.

Eliza Van Gelder, Jacob's first wife and Annie's mother wrote Carrie:

I've attended three Republican meetings, splendid ones. There is an Assembly speaker always makes me think of him as a masterful piece of stupidity and dullness. What a prodigious figurehead he would make. Wouldnt it have been fun if they had nominated him for vice president with Gen. Hancock? The Democrats would not have had to say a word about Military pomposities and the Republicans wouldn't have had any supurb Figure Head to adorn and illuminate their canvas. But we owe him some thanks for largely contributinhg to Grant's defeat for a 3rd term by his dense stupidity and blundering.

The railroad is progressing finely around here. I understand it dont go through yours or Uncle David's property in Catskill [It went a couple of blocks west but did cut into the source of a spring that filled a cistern on the hill and gave running water to all the Van Gelder houses. This I remember hearing about.]

The West Shore Railroad has bought the right-of-way in a few places just to delay the Wallkill Valley Railroad, and it is the managers of the Hudson River Railroad. That is the opinion of a gentleman who has large dealings with all classes of capitalists and railroad stock in New York. The company wanted to buy some land here right in front of his house on the river, one of the finest country seats around. He said he wasn't going to give them a deed for it until he was sure they were going through with it. He is in favor of railroads but there will be time enough to sell to them. They might build a soap factory in front of his house.

Aunt Maimie says when you go to the Prospect House to listen to the band you go right in on the piazza or in the parlor if you want to.

Have you seen my mystic album? You can let Charlie write in it. Give my love to Aunt Rebecca and Arthur and tell him his Aunt Eliza dont have a very good opinion of his correspondense.

Among the many letters was one quoting Jerusha Jenkins with advice for girls.

My dear young friend,

I have noticed your conduct with interest as I thought I saw in you something above the average class of girls. But a few facts coming to my knowledge have led me to write you a few words of advice. Permit me to say in the first place you have a very naturally sweet disposition capable of bringing you many friends, both male and female. Here then is one danger for you. Be careful what friends you make. Try each one with an impartial judgment and after you have fully analyzed their character decide whether there is enough good in them to cherish.

Then second, Do not let any sentimentality have any place in your mind. Make no male acquaintances [Carrie was 15 years old and Annie 8 years.] Write no letters nor receive any that you would not be willing for your parents to read.

Attend punctually to duty in whatever form it may come. It is good practical education and good to learn to express your thoughts in the prettiest and most concise manner.

And last, Be good and then you will be happy. Hope you will accept these few words of advice.
I am your friend,
Jerusha Jenkins
Johnstown, New Jersey

Annie continued corresponding. She said she liked to write letters and chose to do so rather than go to see Pinafore again as I have seen nearly all the pieces before I left school. She reported a road along the creek which was lovely for walks and driving. They try to get in one nice sail, she said.

Why cant you and your mother come down with the sleigh? We have no horse now. Mother has been very sick till a month ago. Pa was out at Prattsville. He likes it out there. Florence has a certificate to teach. Lillie says she is very smart in arithmetic. We have 200-300 tube roses. Two *crops.*

Alas, I remember their tube roses years later when my sister Constance and I went to Saugerties to meet our violin and cello teacher. We were always given tube roses and had to hold them for the long walk to the railroad station that cousin Lillie walked with us. We couldn't wait until the train pulled out, and we could throw them out the window. I never see them any more. They had such a heavy, heavy, sickishly sweet smell; it was almost unbearable, at least to us. They were quite a popular flower at funerals at that time, too.

News that Rev. John Knight Wardle, M.D. later my paternal grandfather, was to stay on at the church in Catskill was in an 1880 letter. A school friend, Emma Sweeney, who was very close, wrote from the Mountain House in the summer. I never could figure out exactly what she did there, but she was working and taught school in the winter. She said, *The colored people meet in the ironing room every Sunday night. One of the waiters is a colored minister, and exalts the people after the preaching is over.*

Years later my brothers, Philip and Francis, enjoyed running the great searchlight when they worked at the Mountain House one summer. We watched from Catskill as the night boat and the Mountain House crossed their lights in the sky over the Hudson River.

Innocuous girl and boy talk went on in the letters. Visits were made by Carrie to Brooklyn, where her dear friend Bertha Johnson lived. She often visited us when the Wardle children were little. She was then Editor of the Kindergarten Magazine.

Besides seeing a lot of Charles Wardle, son of the Methodist pastor, Carrie had letters from Asa Wyncoop, who was at Rutgers College. Bits of news from Asa include going to the Dutch Reformed Church at New Brunswick. He wrote of the intense earnestness

of Dr. Eaton. But he was beginning to think sermons were not going to do him any good. More pleasant and profitable were college literary societies, football, debates and orations, extemporaneously given. Their team wore white knee breeches, scarlet jerseys, and red stockings. He had three or four recitations a day in Rhetoric, Greek Prose, Latin Prose, Natural History, Solid Geometry. Wyncoop continued to write from Rutgers signing himself "Your affectionate classmate."

Carrie Van Gelder graduated from Catskill High School. Letters show that she wrote to several Musical Conservatories, but her career in music turned out to be mostly teaching her own and other children who remember it well, they tell me. Each of the Wardle children learned an instrument in addition to the piano so that later Carrie had a family orchestra of six that performed for visiting relatives.

During the summer Carrie was busy helping with the boarders at Cherry Hill House, enjoying all the picnics and mountain trips with the team and four-seater. Charades were a popular amusement at night.

The oldest brother, Francis R. Wardle, for whom one of my brothers was named, visited us many times. He ran away from home and stayed in Washington with relatives for some time, arriving home to a dying mother when she had become unconscious after calling for her oldest boy all day.

There are letters from him later in the 1890s when he traveled to Europe for a perfume company. We have cut glass perfume bottles that make beautiful carafes for wine. Some letters told of plans for the Jupiter Gold Mine. His two-year superintendency in the Siskayune Mountains of Oregon was a disaster financially but rich with letters from him and Aunt Isabel. The most charming and interesting of all the letters from the pine chest were from the Far East.

Teasing Carrie about Charlie Wardle was an active sport among her girlfriends. They married in 1885. He was for some years a teller in the Tanners National Bank and also set up an insurance office in the Oyster Bay House at the corner of Bridge and Main Streets on properties where the Court House now stands.

By the time all the buildings in the Court House block were removed Charles had put plate glass in the corner windows and put a Locomobile on show. This was the beginning of automobiles in Catskill. It was a steamer — looking like a carriage more than like the cars of today. Charles was soon selling Locomobiles and setting up agencies from Ohio to Texas to California; and the family moved to Oak Park, Illinois, for three years.

He and Carrie built a house on Van Gelder land in sight of Peter Van Gelder's brick house, David's Octagon house, and Grandpa's Cherry Hill House down the hill. Most of us Wardles were born there,

Carrie Van Gelder at graduation.

House built by Charles and Carrie Wardle in 1880s in sight of Peter Van Gelder's house, the Octagon House, and Cherry Hill House. Birthplace of most of the Wardle children. Home of J. Robert Fiero from 1923 to 1942.

and I lived there with my husband and son for many years after eight years on the Fiero farm. I finally sold the house after renting out an upstairs apartment made after my husband, Frederick, died in 1950. It was in that attic I made my difficult **Odyssey** through all the stuff and where these letters were stored in the chest. Grandpa's pine chest had been moved with much else up from the Cherry Hill House after Mother's death; and we moved there about 1923, when my son, Bob, was 4½ years old.

When, by the 1890s, Grandpa, Grandma, and Uncle Arthur went on the Stereopticon Lecture Tour, Charles and Carrie looked after their rental properties and land.

But in the 1880s Carrie's friends were still writing many letters. Bertha Johnson was away at school. Her father's home in Brooklyn was a great place to visit. They had so many friends among well-known persons, interesting soirees at the house, and plenty of museums and theatres to visit there. One later letter of Miss Bertha's, as we children called her, is one in which she argues against a belief in the Virgin Birth. Higher criticism was going at quite a pace then, too. Emma Sweeney taught school in several towns but *would gladly give it up if there was another way to earn a living.* A visit to Howe's Cave was very different than it is today. It was very primitive and slippery. Today there is an elevator and good walks.

Here is a "cutie."

June 8, 1882

Dear Carrie,
    We saw the Devil flying south
    With Emma Sweeney in his mouth
    And when he saw she was a fool
    He dropped her down to teach our school.

Raymond Beecher, dedicated Curator of the Bronck House Museum and now Librarian and publisher of the Greene County Historical Society's **Quarterly**, says in the 1978 Winter number under the heading, "James Van Gelder's Lake Kiskatom Pure Water and Cheap Electric Power,"

It was a well-conceived plan to supply to the village of Catskill and suburbs, and Athens, with an enormous amount of pure water; cheap electric power was to be an important by-product. The brain child of James Harvey Van Gelder, the water supply had first been proposed to the Catskill village trustees in 1880-81, when it became obvious that a more dependable source of water for household, public and fire-protection purposes was needed; the dug wells, springs and cisterns were no longer adequate. But the village had voted in favor of the less expensive plan, that of a pumping station from the Hudson River.

After the Deiper Hook pumping station on the Hudson was developed in 1883-4, Catskill did continue to grow; also the pollution of the river increased as indoor sanitary plumbing grew in popularity. The steam pumping system with its water from the Hudson, was not the bargain it first appeared to be — repairs of an extensive nature were already needed.

It was not until 1897, after his Stereopticon Lecture Tour that James Harvey again began promoting his idea, and those of engineers engaged to do something more practical, for Catskill household water supply. I remember those later attempts and discouragements well, though I was fairly young.

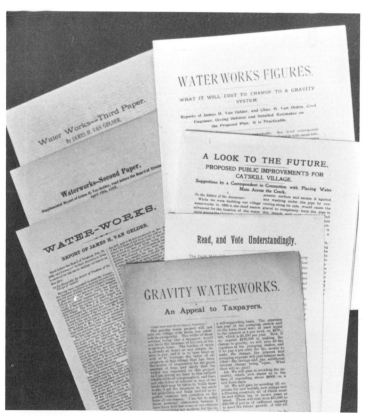

Flyers used by James Harvey Van Gelder to promote gravity waterworks for Catskill. *Photograph by Winifred J. Clark.*

But in December, 1890, James Harvey, took his wife and 17-year-old son, Arthur; and they started a several months' Stereopticon Lecture Tour. Charles and Carrie looked after the Catskill end of things. Carrie had a five-year-old boy, a very sick baby who seemed to be fading those months, and a new baby due in February. The letters back and forth tell their own story full of fascinating tour happenings in those earlier days.

Old Stone House painted by Rebecca Pine Van Gelder. My mother, Carrie, was born there, June 14, 1865. *Photograph by Winifred J. Clark.*

Osceola, French type apartment house built by J.H. Van Gelder. ca1880.

Knickerbocker Apartment House built by J.H. Van Gelder

PART V
HO! FOR TEXAS!

Ho! for Texas! is the upbeat beginning of an 1890-91 diary of adventures and happenings on an eight-month trip taken by three Van Gelders — James Harvey Van Gelder, my grandfather, Rebecca Pine, my grandmother, and their son, Arthur Pine Van Gelder. In Arthur's seventeen years he had stretched beyond the not inconsiderable height of his parents to over six feet. He acted as advance agent with surprising assurance and success for a high school junior, substituting travel for much of his school year of books. He often booked the illustrated lectures, went ahead and found lodgings, and got back in time to help his father assemble the paraphernalia for the Stereopticon Lectures. It was hoped this would finance the trip during which Harvey was *in search of health and pleasure.*

The peak of excitement came when they reached New Orleans after traveling through Western New York, studded with relatives, to Ohio, down through Kentucky and Tennessee, and then over thousands of acres of the flooded South. They reached New Orleans just as the Mafia who had murdered Chief of Police Henessey had succeeded in bribing the jury. To keep this Sicilian gang from regaining a stranglehold, a call went out to citizens from a group of sixty-one respected and influential men of the city. "Meet at Clay Statue at 10 A.M., March 14, 1890." This orderly group carried out what they believed to be their civic duty, without riots or disturbances of any kind. There was local and countywide condemnation and equal commendation about *taking the law into one's own hands.* That the Mafia even existed in New Orleans in 1890 came as a great surprise to me. More surprising, research revealed New Orleans was the Mafia headquarters in the United States from the first.

Briefing a great nephew, William Wardle, just graduated from Yale Law School, on his great, great grandfather, I mentioned the Lecture Tour. William queried, "Stereopticon? I never heard the word!" So soon do the wonders of one period sink into oblivion. In a Stereopticon two similar pictures are united to give an illusion of depth. Our eyes form a mental image which is a composite of what our two eyes see separately from slightly different positions. The same procedure is used in stereopticon equipment.

Probably more is known about the stereoscope still sought by antique hunters and once used by many of us. It combines two photographs, taken from positions related approximately as the position of a person's eyes, thus making a composite that has depth. With this once popular hand-held stereoscope, one

Mississippi Steamers at the Levees, New Orleans, 1891. *Photographed by J.H. Van Gelder, A.M.*

could look at the double picture, one green, one red, inserted in front of the lens and see a three-dimensional picture, as exciting to us as psychedelic marvels are today.

Rebecca added her own contributions to the trip. She wrote a Diary, and she kept her husband's and her son's clothes in order. All wrote letters home, but Rebecca wrote most of them. News of the family, which included two small children, and doings of friends in town were usually related by my mother, Carrie. Although my brother Francis was to arrive on this planet the middle of February, I did not even become a gleam in any eye for almost two more years.

Raymond Beecher, editor of the **Quarterly Journal** of the Greene County Historical Society and former Curator of the Bronck Museum, writes:

It was James Harvey Van Gelder's intention to seek bookings with pastors, superintendents of Sunday Schools, Y.M.C.A.s or public educational systems. His fee was low and sponsoring organizations would find a source of "money-raising" for supportive programs. To this purpose Van Gelder formulated a dignified sales broadside, which was distributed both before and while en route. In it he announced, "I am about to start on a lecture tour through the central portion of our country, and expect to go to Niagara Falls, then to Cleveland, and thence across Ohio, Kentucky, Tennessee. From thence to New Orleans and Texas returning through the Western states . . . I shall take my camera with me and make a point of photographing and noting any matters of interest along the route. In order to better study the country and acquaint myself with the communities through which I pass, I will give a series of illustrated lectures, with photographic views, shown in the highest style of art, with calcium light. . . [the best light available]

Favorable letters of endorsement were many. From W. A. Adams, Superintendent of Schools in Camibier, Ohio, Mr. Beecher reports:

I have seen the photographic Art Exhibition given by Prof. Van Gelder both nights and find them to be everything he represents them to be and more. It is pure, instructive, entertaining. The views are exceedingly fine and realistic and also very true to nature. No one need hesitate concerning the morality or the religious sentiment of his views. We had the entertainment under the auspices of the Public School and found nothing amiss in it. No one can say a word against the culture or refinement of it. I know anyone who engages Prof. Van Gelder will rejoice as I have at the opportunity of seeing so much for so little money.

"Pure," "moral," "cultural," and "refined" — hardly words used in public relations today.

Travel was by rail unless a rowboat or a ferry was needed. In towns they went by trolley, by horse and carriage, and on many fairly long walks by "shanks' ponies." With today's automotive travel, few except joggers are aware they have these so-called "shanks' ponies" or "shanks' mares" as they were also called.

Snow travelled with them and stayed the night as the three Van Gelders started from Catskill on Wednesday, December 3, 1890. Harvey and Rebecca remained overnight at Clyde in Central New York. Arthur continued on to Palmyra on his first booking trip and came back as far as Lyons where they all met the next day. In connection with the Exhibition that

Home of Beekman Van Gelder, second cousin of James Harvey Van Gelder. James Harvey and Rebecca visited him on the Stereopticon Lecture Tour.

evening, the Ladies Aid had prepared a supper. On Friday, the fifth, they were ,met in Newark by the Rev. Mr. Wright,who took them to his home for dinner. Rebecca writes in her Diary:

We visited a cousin, Mrs. Eliza Myer and her family who lived there, and found Cousin Angeline quite ill. The Presbyterian minister's wife came for tea, then we had the Exhibition at the Methodist Church in the evening. A Mrs. P.A. Vary called, also. She had spent the summer two years ago at the Sandwich Islands. [We would say Hawaii.] She had dined with the King and later visited Alaska, as she was interested in a mission there.

By noon, December 6th, we took the train to the town of Seneca Castle and found Cousin Beekman Van Gelder waiting at the station. We had a good dinner with him and his wife Ellen.

Beekman Van Gelder wrote some of the letters quoted in the first group of this **Attic Odyssey**. Beekman and James Harvey, second cousins, had spent many happy days together during school age, hiking in the Catskill Mountains when Beekman came to visit. His desire was to go away to school as his cousin had done, but he ended up buying a farm and building a house for his bride, Ellen. Here, thirty years later, the cousins would reminisce.

Beekman's father, Garret Beekman Van Gelder, whom they also visited, was born on the southern half of the Van Gelder farm on the Old King's Road, Catskill. James Harvey, son of Garret's first cousin Peter Van Gelder, was born on the northern half of the farm which had been divided and given to these two sons. Garret moved, with his father, Abraham, to Castleton, later called Seneca Castle, where all his ten children were born. Family tradition says his household goods were transported by ox cart, according to the Van Gelder Genealogy.

Garret's sister, Mary Ann Van Gelder, married John J. Schuneman of the Dominie Schuneman family. He was the famous "Dutch Dominie of the Catskills." The book of that title is still cherished by many. Dominie Schuneman's and his wife's gravestones which have remained on the property of the red brick home he built in the Jefferson Heights area of Catskill have been restored as part of the 250th anniversary of our local Dutch Reformed Church. The first small church building was located in what is now Leeds, not too far from where the second handsome edifice of stone still stands on Route 23 B. A part of this same original church, also served by Dominie Schuneman, is the current First Reformed Church of Coxsackie. Formed at the same time, it is also celebrating the 250th anniversary of its founding. Mary Ann and her husband, John J. Schuneman, purchased a large farm in Metamora, Michigan. Here her father, Abraham Van Gelder, and her mother, Catherine Van Voorhees, lived out their last days with them.

Like them, many others left this area along the

Hudson and other parts of the East for the less stony ground of central and western New York State. The Pelhams, who wrote the Civil War letters of the second section of this **Odyssey,** settled in Oswego. Because in those letters the men were mentioned as *going to the canal daily to work,* it was natural to assume they meant the Erie Canal. Inhabitants of Oswego will be glad to know that Oswego has been safely restored to the shores of Lake Ontario if it ever strayed, and the "canal" referred to was the Oswego Canal, one of the more important tributaries to the Erie Canal which it joined at Syracuse. It took a map and an excellent young people's book on the Erie Canal by American Heritage to set this matter straight and learn to what extent the Van Gelders were following the Erie Canal Route West via the railroad.

The welcome hospitality they received continued as the travelling trio visited more relatives in this area and found homelike accommodations everywhere — a good beginning for a trip that soon became more strenuous, sometimes exciting, and often downright uncomfortable.

Several more Exhibitions were held in or near these towns. Some were doubtlessly arranged by the relatives with the help of the brochures. When they moved on to Rochester, they were on their own. Rebecca writes back home:

Brockport, December 17, 1890
Dear Carrie, We are nicely situated here but have not heard a word from home in a week . . . Do write, at least a postcard twice a week. However, it may be difficult to keep track of us for awhile as we have no appointments and probably will not make any until after the holidays as every hall is full until then. We leave here to-morrow morning for Rochester and from there start for Niagara, then leave the latter part of the next day for Buffalo, and the following day for Cleveland.
Beekman took Harvey and Arthur to Geneva for a lecture, December 8th. We had a repeat at Seneca Castle, and also at Newark with one in between at Seneca, which was called "No. 9."
After seeing to the baggage at Rochester we found a laundry and went to see Beekman's sisters, Mrs. Sears and Mrs. Whitney. They are in ill health and there for treatment. We had dinner in their delightful boarding house. We missed only one of Beekman's family — a brother who was away. Papa called there and saw only his wife and thought her a little peculiar. He remarked to Beekman afterwards that Norton's wife was not very handsome. "Well," he said in his characteristic way, "She's just as good as she is handsome." At Seneca, Papa found a Mrs. Foster, formerly Miss Britt from Britt's Corners [now Story's Corners in the Palenville-Kiskatom area].
Rebecca closes her letter home, *When you go*

down to the house see if you find any traces of mice. She had left the Person Insect Powder and red pepper on the kitchen table. Also, she asked her daughter to see if there was any necessity to shoot the powder into the bureaus. The poison cheese for the mice had been left over the bedroom door on the transom.

Christmas Day back home at the Wardles was described by Carrie *with full particulars. . .*
Charles and Gerald have gone over to the church, so I will write you of our day. I am alone again. This is the ninth day that I have done the housework. I have got along very nicely, so well that I do not care if I get someone before the middle of January.
On Tuesday, I brushed up the rooms a bit, stewed the cranberries, and gave my kitchen floor the best cleaning it has had in weeks. Yesterday I baked a very nice jelly cake, got the suet and raisins ready for a pudding, peeled my vegetables, stuffed my turkey and cleaned out my bread drawer, (the first in a month I should judge).
The day has passed very pleasantly indeed. I forgot the pudding until it was too late to steam it, but it has been one of the pleasantest Christmases I have had and this has been due almost entirely to the fact that nothing was left to the last minute, so that I have been neither tired nor hurried.
An unexpected and somewhat troublesome present arrived Christmas morning and little Ralph found it most uncomfortable. A double tooth had cut through, but only on one side, so more trouble was expected from it. Ralph received from his Uncle Frank a sweet rubber doll, a white kitten, a large Noah's Ark containing over 80 animals, a silver teaspoon from Auntie Floy, a rubber ball from Emma, horse reins from Lizzie, a red cart, a picture book of pigs large and small, and a homemade picture book.

Gerald, not yet five years old, had three small handkerchiefs, costing five cents for three. an orange (still in my childhood and my son Bob's a "treat," now a daily morning happening, "oranges are no longer just for Christmas" would have been good TV copy), a box of candy from Santa. From Frank there was a gun that shot a small rubber ball, a nice big drum, a horn, and a set of very nice tenpins. Auntie Floy gave him two pretty collars, Emma a book, Lizzie a silver napkin ring with G.W. engraved on it, from Bennie [Curtis] a box of jack straws and the book his Grandmother had left for him. *"Could a child ask for more?"* asks Carrie.

The Curtis family lived next door in the red brick house built by Peter Van Gelder in Catskill. He was related to the Marquis de Talleyrand and was quite a character with old world manners that became effusive when, as so often, he had imbibed too much. Auntie Floy, a teacher, reserved, very English like her father, who often lived with us, was indignant, when

L. to R.: Gerald Knight Wardle in his dress from which he graduated at 5 years of age, and Ralph Harvey Wardle, whose dress I have.

he passed under her window at one of these times, tipped his hat, bowed low and said, *"Romeo and Juliet."* She sputtered, *"I'll Romeo and Juliet him."* The grown-ups had their gifts which Carrie also listed and then closed:

I hope you all enjoyed the day as much as we did though it has been so quiet — I should say so uneventful. Quiet it was not for with the drum, the horn and the piano going there has been noise enough. Before breakfast we had a **GREAT FAMILY MARCH.** *Gerald had his drum, Charlie the horn, I with the gun and Ralph bringing up the rear with his family of two dolls, a cat and a monkey in the red cart.*

　　　　　Carrie

When the travelling trio went to Brockport on Tuesday, they had found Cousin Rufus at the station. They left there Thursday morning for Niagara. After dinner they rode through the Park and about Goat Island and Luna Island. Rebecca's letter tells the tale:

The next morning we went down to the rapids, across the lower bridge both railroad and carriage, to the Canada side, up to Horseshoe Falls, back to the carriage bridge and Hotel. After dinner we went for a walk to the Three Sister Island, and Goat Island, etc. It was cold and the frost

effects were beautiful. Saturday noon, took the train for Cleveland, Ohio, via the Lake Shore route. It was after dark when we reached the city and much to my disgust I was left alone. Papa and Arthur went out to look after the baggage and look up a place to stay. They returned after an hour and found me sitting in that great depot alone. Soon after our train came in the man in charge locked nearly every door and put out nearly all the lights so I was left to my own reflections, which as time passed on grew not to be of the most lovely nature. I had waited three hours in Buffalo in the morning. When they returned, they had your very welcome letter forwarded from Brockport.

They had also found a place to stay — the Prospect House, an old house they said, but comfortable. It was a long way to it and we were tired and hungry. When we came into our room, I expressed myself freely, after taking a glance around; the dirt was altogether thick, the blanket on the bed something dreadful. We had our supper and took another room as it was too late to look elsewhere. We have made the best of it and will stay until papa says go.

The pattern throughout their trip included very frequent attendance at many church services, Sunday School, sometimes Epworth League, and almost always the evening service, as well as some of the prayer meetings and special services during the week. Sometimes Arthur would go to a different church. Sermons and texts were often quoted in letters and diary along with comments on their reactions. Many sermons were *good*, some *excellent*, but not all. Sunday Schools were largely attended, anywhere up to 1,000 being present. There was a great deal of good music, choirs, and orchestra. This was a time when many places had "opera houses" and used the large auditorium for many affairs. Even Catskill had its Opera House, which I remember being on the third floor of the large brick building on the corner of Main and Bridge, which is now two stories and occupied by Pulver and Stiefel, lawyers. Lectures were still very popular as during the period of the 1854-64 letters. The letter continues:

At the Jennings Ave. Church, where Arthur went in the morning, they had Sunday School which was not yet over — 345 children present, a full orchestra, plenty of fine singing and a most excellent sermon. Arthur was highly pleased and said, "I struck it just right all day." There were many fine people at dinner and the house seems to have a good reputation. I am not charmed. It is not my "style."

It was interesting to learn that the minister, John Wilson, was received into the church by my grandfather, the Rev. John Knight Wardle, M.D.; and the Rev. Ostrander of the Catskill Church was at one time his class leader. The Rev. Mr. Beardsley at Seneca Castle used to work at Rushmore's Mill near Orliffe Heath's father's place in Catskill. He said Mr. J.B. Foote was also Sunday School Superintendent then. The travelers went to the Euclid Ave. Methodist Christmas Exercises. *They were very good, but in no respect better than most of ours.*

The Inness 13th Regiment Band of New York gave an excellent program of Rossini, Verdi, Liszt, Donizetti, Massenet, etc. in the afternoon. There were four soloists. Great preparations were made according to the press for Christmas music at the Trinity Cathedral. Several Steiner and Mozart numbers were included. In the evening Arthur went to see "Shenandoah" during the performance of which he saw "Gen. Sherman" ride his famous black horse. *I think I would like to see that myself,* wrote Rebecca.

We expect to leave Thursday. I'm sure we could have quite a few appointments if it were a month ahead or we had come here a month ago. They advise us that on the way back we will be able to have Exhibitions in the area, so our time has not all been lost.

Arthur wrote back to his father from Akron, Ohio, that he had arranged for their program "Alaska" in the Trinity Lutheran Church, as follows:

The first $10 to us, the next $5 to them for heating as it is a very large church and they say it takes a ton of coal, and divide the remainder. I have good outlooks in other churches so if I can get "Europe" for one of them I think I may be able to get a sort of religious one in Grace Refd Church where they will be having extra meetings all next week. Please send me by return mail any directions you may have and list of hymns and other views which you have with you. I find regular rates here are $1.00 to $3.00 and we cannot get less than $1, even if we stay a week. Everything is very nice here. It seems almost a palace compared to the Prospect. I expect to stay here until Monday anyway and think you may as well come here also at that time.

Many hotels had very fancy letterheads. On one from Windsor Hotel, Akron, on December 31, Rebecca wrote:

Dear Carrie,
I hardly realize that Christmas is past and the New Year so close at hand. . . Papa and I took a long walk yesterday afternoon. Arthur went to Canton about 23 miles from here. . . made arrangements for Tuesday and Wednesday of the week after next. Next week being the Week of Prayer probably we will not be able to make any arrangements, just as with the Holidays. Papa and Arthur have gone to put up the curtain in the church which is large and handsome.
       Mother

From the first Charles and his father-in-law had cor-

responded about rents, renting ground for a garden, the tenant house, repairs, *3 left over chickens* which sold for $1.20, a double harness he could sell for $15, *Shall I take it?* and the sale of a horse. *Mr. Goff told Mr. Chichester your price was $35. I told him to get $50, if possible.*

Carrie wrote her mother that Maimie Elmendorf was getting along very well with Grandma's Sunday School class, though there were 36 present. Gerald, still four years old, had sung with the Infants and was very pleased. He was also one of four "Clappers" in the Christmas program. Rebecca wrote that Christmas Exercises continued even beyond New Year's. On the 28th, Rebecca went to the Broadway Methodist Church very early hoping to find Sunday School in session. Instead she found a Bohemian service and love feast. But in the afternoon at the Broadway Sunday School there were nearly a thousand children present — 440 in the infant departments.

As expected no halls were available through the holidays and the Week of Prayer after New Year's. But they kept busy. Rebecca was getting bills ready and sending them; getting tickets put up and sent where needed; looking after the washing, etc. She also partly made a skirt for Alice Ham which was directed to Carrie who was asked to press it and give it to Catharine Clark, *who sits near Alice at school.*

The Exhibitions were not the financial success they had hoped, but many expressed themselves as most pleased. One woman came to Mr. Van to say it was the finest thing of its kind she had ever seen. She had been to Chautauqua but his views were superior. High praise continued throughout the trip. They had received $46 so far from expenses and a share, but had given the best of satisfaction, and had had little expense. Charles sent a draft for $50 on January 3. He also sent information on selling his father-in-law's Law Library to James Franklin Taylor. Charles' advice was to

sell the law library cheap for three reasons — first you do not expect to use them; seond, new books are getting cheaper every year; and third the library is not complete. Several lawyers have spoken to me of the last as the most serious drawback.

He had paid $86 in taxes, and had $15 on hand, from rents, etc.

I am getting to be quite a plumber and have repacked faucets in all the houses and the tenants are happy.
Father [the Rev. J.K. Wardle, M.D.] has spent two Sundays here, preaching for the Presbyterians. None of your photos have appeared in Leslie's Weekly yet. I will send you the weekly paper with the account of the trouble at Leeds. They have had what a fellow calls "a hell of a time." Rev. Mr. George and Dr. Erway are both here in jail. Carrie wonders how a man would enter the ministry

knowing he was a kleptomaniac. It seems to me the statement in the Recorder puts him down either as a fool or a knave.

Charles also wrote his mother-in-law. On December 31, 1890, they had been unusually busy all winter and he had worked at the Tanners Bank every night until half past ten during that week. There were 16 inches of snow on the ground. It was very cold and the ice harvest was *jumping*. All icehouses wre being filled with ice about 12 inches thick.

By the way, old Fan is dead. Mr. Johnson had her out on his farm and turned her out in pasture with his horses and cattle as usual. He has an ox who bosses all the other animals around. One day when Fan and the other horses were eating together, the ox drove the other horses away, but Fan was spunky and would not move so he ox-horned her and tore her open and she died. Mr. Johnson says he will pay Mr. Van for her.

We are glad you are having such a pleasant time, Etc.
                        CAW

Arthur wrote his sister from Kent, Ohio, January 9. He and his father had gone ahead to make plans for future Exhibitions. *Thanks for the Christmas gift. Charles should have been with us when we visited the chimney and plate glass works at Ravenna. The window glass works were most interesting.* There follows a lengthy description of making plate glass. Also the workings of a flour mill. There were the car works of the Erie Railroad — 20 pairs of wheels on freight cars, shoebutton fasteners; an indicator for the caboose to show how far and how fast it went, etc.

Oh, we are seeing the country, I tell you. Catskill is too dead for me. You ought to see how these places are growing. All the time new manufacturing places are being put up. Please write soon and tell us all about home.
                        Arthur VG

Maimie Elmendorf, who was a friend of Carrie's, ran a private kindergarten and lived with us at the time. She wrote Mrs. Van about her Sunday School class, which she had taken over for her.

Your letter to the infant class made them very proud and they were delighted as only children can be. All of them thought they would have been delighted to visit the Sunday School with its 1000 children. During the session I found several opportunities to impress upon them Mrs. Van Gelder's text, "Thou God, seest me."

Yesterday while talking of Jeroboam and his sin in forgetting God, and worshipping idols, one of the small boys surprised me by sayinhg "Guess he didn't remember Mrs. Van Gelder's text! and forgot God was looking at him." The little ones all think so much of you ... The attendance has been about 50 average until yesterday when only twelve braved the storm. They have been very attentive since the first Sunday after you left. That

day George Wright and Willie Gallt were regular little "thorns in the flesh," so I put one in one corner and one in another, and after that they were just as good as could be.

This same William Gallt, who lived to be nearly 100 years old, often told me what a marvelous Sunday School teacher Grandma Van Gelder was.

The children also made three scrapbooks, red, blue and pink, each with twenty pages and forwarded them by express to Childs' Hospital in Albany. She had fourteen left in her weekday private kindergarten class. George Curtis, next door, and Tilly Englert were not coming any more, but she expected to get along well.

The trip remained interesting but built up to great excitement at New Orleans. From the Barnett Hotel in Canton, Ohio, they found the same trouble they had at Cleveland and Akron. Soft coal was used and a great deal of manufacturing done, so that before they reached a town they could see a great cloud of black smoke covering the place.

It requires a great deal of diligence to keep clean. . . We have enjoyed ourselves so much all the time so far. I went out every evening to the union prayer meetings, so I had a good chance to hear the different ministers as well as see their churches, but I can tell you one I did not like — the Universalist. He did nothing but poke fun at Yatman, the evangelist, who had been in Akron. After he "finished" Yatman, he took up Martin Luther and criticized his method of sanctification by faith.

In addition to these places, lectures were given in Ravenna, Kent, Wadsworth, Canton, Shreve, Belleville, Gambia, Howard, and Danville before going to Kentucky. *Gambia was lovely for situation.*

> January 20, 1891
> Kenyon House, Gambia, Ohio

Dear Carrie,
*Came here yesterday from Belleville. This is by far the nicest town we have visited. It is only a small place, no factories, but the Kenyon College, a military school, a ladies' Seminary and a theological Seminary. Our landlady, Mrs. Condit is very nice and we feel more at home than in some places. At Belleville, the proprietor at least tried to make us comfortable but the house was old and out of repair and the family, the old lady in particular, was something the same. . . made me think of a kind-hearted backwoods shouting Methodist. She joined the Methodists more than fifty years ago when, "they would not wear a curl or a feather, just one plain ribbon over the hat, and tied under the chin. I am going to send her the papers you sent us when I get through with them. No greater good could be done than putting **good** books and papers in such a family.*

Carrie wrote that Mr. Chapman, the revivalist, was coming for all the Catskill churches the next week. Apparently none too soon, or perhaps already too late. She reported Mr. Woodruff had gone to Canada leaving a large number of debts. And two ministers were under arrest for grave charges.

Aunt Ellen Van Gelder, a music teacher living in the Octagon House, was David Van Gelder's third wife. They had a son Howard, about Arthur's age. He became a successful electrical engineer. She wrote Rebecca:

Dear Sister,

Your interesting letter was eagerly read by both myself and Howard. He thinks a good deal of his Aunt Rebecca.

Yes we have had good meetings with Chapman and Smith — if possible even better than last year. The idea was expressed by some of the ministers that the work seemed to show itself more upon church members which in my humble opinion is quite as necessary, for I think if they were more faithful to their obligations and lived more earnest and devoted lives and the ministers were more concecrated and preached the truth as fervently and simply as Mr. Chapman we should nave no occasion for revival services.

The new members were received into the various churches March 1st. I could not count those taken into our church [the Dutch Reformed] but think 17 were baptized and as many received into membership. Among the number were Harry Goff, E. Conklin, Isabelle Brookes, Mr. Slingerland (of the ice house), Mrs. Joseph Weber, Mrs. Geo. Martin, one of the Plusch boys, John French [a cousin of Frederick Fiero] — perhaps Arthur will know him.

I knew him and learned that he had emptied half the wine in bottles of Fred's Grandma Fiero and filled them up with water. Anyway we had a few interesting bottles — one hand blown. Years later Florence, Fred's sister, went John French one better but too late for his redemption. I remember when a friend told us how Florence had gone down in her cellar and emptied out all the good old cherry wine — vintage 1890s probably. "I'm not going to have anybody drinking this stuff." What became of her antique bottle, probably only the garbage man knows.

I think also two of the Sax daughters that keep the restaurant near Doty's, I have heard nothing from the Baptists or Methodists, but J.B. Olney, Stephen Root (who has always been a disbeliever), Captain Palmer's daughter, William Palmatier were among members of the Presbyterian church. Dr. Van Slyke preached to the Endeavor Society and young people of the congregation — quite a departure for him. The last two evenings Chapman's meetings were held in the Nelida Theatre and when the vast audience sang together "There is a fountain filled with blood," it was very inspiring and brought to our minds what faintly the great chorus in heaven would be like — "The great mul-

Gerald Knight Wardle graduated from dresses to knee pants at five years of age.

litudes that no one can number."

W.E.M. Van Gelder   [Aunt Ellen]

Carrie told in her letter the big news that Gerald had graduated from dresses. He had worn his new suit with pantaloons for the first time that Sunday. He was much pleased and *looked wonderfully well in them.*

He is to wear his dresses until his birthday [his 5th on Feb. 1st] on week days. We bought a pretty gray checked suit for $4.50 and I shall make one or two pairs of pants to go with his gray blouse and black coat made last fall.

Mr. Addison was found dead in his barn a few days ago. We will send the Catskill papers soon. Also the magazine, "Christian at Work." Ralph is very babyish, wants to sit on my lap all the time. His teeth are painful and I think are making him want to be petted.

Carrie

Six days later, Carrie wrote that Ralph was getting very thin and pale, and far from well. She was watching him carefully, though she herself felt half sick and very tired.

The trio was now at Cincinnati. It was January 28 and Rebecca had been *copying some letters for Papa and Arthur to use.* It was hard for them to get press reviews since they left so soon after the Exhibitions, but she was going to try to have copies sent to Catskill.

*Have been getting some clothes ready for the laundry. I never wore such dirty clothes in my life only when house cleaning, hardly then. This soft coal dust is dreadful. It is on everything and into everything. At Danville, the cistern water and we had no other to wash in was **black**. I could not have washed my feet in it if I had been at home. I didn't clean my teeth for three days. How they managed to keep the table linen and the bed linen white was a mystery to me.*

Recd your letter. Sorry Ralph is not well. Wish I were there to tend him. We went to a prayer meeting last night much like ours in Catskill, except there were no young people. The one at Danville last Sunday was very much like one at Kiskatom, fifty years ago. . . A good share of the women kneel during prayer in this part of the country.

Rebecca continued saying they were talking of buying tickets to New Orleans with stop-over privileges. The stores in Cincinnati were many of them very fine and like those in New York. Mules were used instead of horses very often. At the Post Office they could not get letters addressed to her without a written order, nor could Arthur get letters for either of them. They would not even tell if there was a letter waiting, until someone came back with a written order. Arthur and Rebecca visited the Zoological Gardens up the inclined railway. After supper they all went to a lecture on the Bible and Art.

Lexington, Kentucky, was their next stop, but they were waiting to get some money from home. Harvey made some advantageous arrangements with the Queen and crescent Line for tickets to New Orleans.

The time table shows you our route from here. I do photographing for the Company for 2 one thousand mile books and half price for Mrs. Van. We paid $15 for the latter and got the others for photographing. The price of their books is $30 each and the lowest cut rate is $23 each. We also get transportation for 800 lbs. of baggage. This you see is a good thing as we get 150 miles extra travel on the line and can go on ahead and do some advance work and return to fill the appointments or take photos. . .

We have given 16 lectures in Ohio and after paying expenses and advertising and RR fares there is little left at any place and sometimes a loss. We have given in all 21 since we left home. I wish the above RR matter to be kept strictly as a family matter as we are the first ones that have tried and succeeded in this manner, and if it gets out others will run it right into the ground as everything else seems to be. I hope to do more in this line at some other time. If I succeed in satisfying this company I will be able through them to get in with the South-

ern Pacific RR as they are connected, so you see the necessity of keeping our own counsel. In Ohio I could do nothing with the other roads but have a partial promise for return tickets over the Nickel Plate from Chicago.

JHVG

He described Ohio as being fine rolling farming country, quite similar to Western New York. The valleys were deeper near Lake Erie and along the southern part of the state near the Ohio River. The central portion he found more level near Columbus with more black soil on top. Most of the other soil and the subsoil was of a light yellow color. They could have taken a steamer to New Orleans for $20 each, including food.

We can do nothing here in Lexington as all arrangements are made long ahead and lecturing is done to death here. They tell us the Southern field is poor lecturing field. It cannot be worse than Ohio. It takes ten days to go to New Orleans. If I do not hear from you I will telegraph as I am anxious to go on.

The telephone, though patented by Alexander Graham Bell in 1876-77, was never mentioned at this time. They relied on the telegraph as did folks in the Civil War. With its successful Morse code it was in wide use over much of the country. The first successful telegraphic cable crossing the Atlantic Ocean was laid in 1866. In 1900 when Uncle Frank Wardle crossed the Pacific (the last group of letters in this ODYSSEY) there was still no cable and they had no news from home from the time they sailed from San Francisco, stopping at Hawaii, until they reached Japan.

The Ohio River was crossed on a long high bridge when they started on February 2, 1891, for Lexington, Kentucky. They were now in the "south." Negro cabins soon appeared everywhere. The country did not appear very inviting. They missed the thrift and enterprise that were so prevalent in the state they had just left. As they neared the famous blue grass region near Lexington, there was a change for the better.

After dinner they walked about two miles to Ashland to the former home of Henry Clay. Shown through a few rooms kept just as in olden times they found it pleasant and interesting. Mr. McDonald, who owned the place, occupied the rest of the house. He was the owner of some famous horses. One was Dictator then 28 years old and seeming just in his prime. When the horse was 20 years old, Mr. McDonald paid $25,000 for him. On the farm there were 15 stallions and 40 brood mares and 18 to 21 yearling colts.

In a few days there is to be a great parade of all the famous horses with which the region abounds, one man alone having 800 to sell. It is said no place in the world produces so many valuable horses.

The next morning we left for Harriman, Tenn. *We crossed on the High Bridge over the Kentucky River, the track being 285 feet above water; the banks high and rocky. We crossed many ravines both deep and wide; crossed the Cumberland River. We also passed through 24 tunnels. It seemed for a long time it was mountains, tunnels, ravines and rivers. We passed 10 to 12 waterfalls some of which were so near we could have caught the water in our hands.*

At High Bridge, Harvey left the train to take photos, while Rebecca and Arthur went on. They came down to the valley of the Emery River at *railroad speed.* It proved to be a wonderful ride from High Bridge to Harriman which they reached after dark. They went right to the Key City Hotel. *My room,* reports Rebecca, *was cold and opened overhead into the 'Swearing Plumbers' room.* Next day, wandering through the mud, Arthur found rooms at Mrs. Chapman's, and Harvey showed up after dinner.

Harriman is a new and very enterprising place, and just a year old. The Byrd house, as it was called was the only one aside from negro shanties, until the year before. Now there are 3000 inhabitants, 300 houses in the main part of the city and 100 more at Walnut Hills, the suburb. The people come in faster than houses can be built so they put up 'shacks' as temporary residences.

They seem to be an exceptionally fine class of people and are taking the greatest care that their city charter shall contain only good. Much has been done in laying out streets that are wide and well-graded so far. There are several churches, though only one completed edifice, that being the Congregational, though the Methodist, the Methodist Church South, the Baptist, Episcopalian and Disciples all have regular Sunday services, Sunday schools, etc. All have building lots, the Church Extension Society came in to see about establishing Sunday schools and found several in good condition.

The Exhibition Building had specimens of wood, coal, and iron found in the vicinity and also many fine views of scenery and industries. Extensive steel works were being built. After holding Exhibitions on Monday and Tuesday they left for Chattanooga. Harvey suggested Charles send him more money. *Use the $50 note. I am sorry to use so much money but we are in the mill and must go through.*

News from home said they were all well, and though Ralph was not sick he was dull and very quiet. Charles reported the

arrest of Decker again last week, and after three days and two nights trial he was convicted at midnight of selling whiskey without a license. He forfeits his license and pays a big fine and may have to serve a term in jail. We think that settles him. The whole thing cost us $70. Do you feel like con-

tributing $5 towards it? The others have stood the expense on the other trials.

On a different note, *Harry Goff has been converted at the Chapman revival meetings and about 200 others.*

Chattanooga, the Diary tells us, had about 10,000 inhabitants at the time of the War; but when they arrived 25 years later, that had grown to 35,000. A large number of Northerners were in business there.

The Tennessee wends its crooked way half around the city and in times of water overflows the lowlands about. We crossed it and waited at the end of the bridge for a boat to go through the draw, and a queer looking thing it was, not in the least like our North River boats. [This must refer to the Hudson, so long called the North River.]

There were hundreds of logs floating downstream, caused by the breaking of some rafts or something of that sort. Lookout Mountain could scarcely be seen for the mist till they were very near the city. Terrible floods and rains hounded them.

Chattanooga, Feb. 11, 1891

. . . There are many colored people here — 'niggers' they generally call them. Arthur gathered some holly and I want to send it to you. It grows so high in the tall trees it is hard to get. There are two young men boarding here from the North. The son-in-law, Mr. Young is employed on one of the papers here. According to him with this afternoon's downpour we are to be "treated to one of the rare sights of Chattanooga — very high water in the Tennessee River." It is up to the high water mark now and is raining hard and the high water up in the mountains will not be here in less than 24 hours. Yesterday we saw water backed up nearly to the tops of the fences. At a short bend in the river near here the water cannot flow through as fast as it comes down so backs up in the city. In 1877 boats were used in some streets. The first floor of a hotel was flooded. The present prospect is that the water will be quite as high now.

The bed in our room is fairly good, but Arthur said his is like a board and he found two occupants that had paid no board bills. They made a raid on him so in self-defense he killed them. The table is good and the family pleasant. If only it did not rain so much!

Rebecca wrote to little Gerald about her trip to Missionary Ridge, on the electric cars. A Cyclorama represented the closing scenes of this Civil War battle.

The landscape views are worth the price of admission to those who love Nature. The "Battle Above the Clouds" did not amount to much compared to Missionary Ridge and Chattanooga. I had an idea of the peculiar deep blue haze that makes the landscape so lovely at times. I sat on Lookout Mountain waiting at sunset for a train to go to the head of the Incline to meet Arthur and Harvey where they had gone to take photos. The country can be seen far and wide with the Tennessee River winding about. It is a very crooked river with a short bend in it near the city which is called Mocassin Bend.

I guess you would have liked to have seen, and you would have laughed at what I saw when I got back from the trip. There were two little colored boys, each in a cart with a goat harnessed in front and drawing the cart. They rode along side by side for a while and then one of the goats saw a bit of cabbage leaf at one side of the road and started for it. Children laughed but the boy didn't care for the goat went on in a minute. There was a little hill. The goats went up. Then the boys turned them around and let them rest a bit. All at once they started up and ran as fast as they could to see who could get down the next street first.

The valentine you sent is very nice indeed. You must have worked right smart to put such a nice border around it.

From your loving Grandma

P.S. I was eating my breakfast when papa's letter telling about your new baby brother. . . I know he is a nice little fellow. Kiss him softly for me and tell

The End of the Goat Race described in letter to Gerald by Grandma. Alabama, 1891.

him his Grandma loves him.

The new little black-haired boy arrived about 9:30 on February 15, Charles wrote.

The only fault we can find with him is that he is a boy, our third. [Two and a half years later a little girl arrived. Me.] The baby is a quiet little fellow and sleeps well. We have Dr. Flemming and Mrs. Cole taking care of Carrie. I heard today that the Village Trustees intended to appoint me one of the Board of Water Commissioners. I would like to know if Father thinks I better accept.

Arthur's letter to his sister about this time is quite

a change of pace. Apparently being 8 years older Carrie thought he needed her advice.

Birmingham, Alabama

Dear Sister,

I received your letter. I was going to say your lecture but I thought I better not. I returned yesterday from Chattanooga where I had been doing advance work, and thought it needed an immediate reply.

I want to correct your wrong impressions. Now your letter is all very good advice **but as far as kissing is concerned** it does **not apply to me.** That is something I do not do and have never done, except once as I think you know, Lizzie Mets and Maimie Elmendorf, a lot older than I. . . I was just writing that to Maimie for effect and did not state I had done anything of the kind. As far as sending my love, etc. that is something I have never done, except to relatives. . . So there!

I dont know as it is any of your business who wrote that letter but if you are concerned about it I will tell you. However, I do not want my affairs to be told all over the town. Her name is Kate C. Condit Gambier and she is a nice girl, too. Any more of my affairs you would like to know? [Actually Kate was the daughter of their boarding house keeper in Gambia.]

I suppose mama and papa have written you all the news. There is a family next door in a "shack"(a small board shanty) who just came from New Mexico. They came the last 600 miles in a "To Kansas or Bust" wagon and crossed the Staked Plain of Texas. They say antelopes are thick there, sometimes 75-100 in a herd. Their skins are worth only 25 cents there. They killed over 30 rattlesnakes in the first 20 days they were there. I am going to write some fellows there if I can. He says that jack rabbits are so thick that they never shoot them and if they want to kill them they knock them over with a stone.

Yours with love,
Arthur

L. to R.: Gerald Knight Wardle, age 8, Winifred Wardle, age 5 months, Frances West Wardle, age 3.

The Van Gelders at Birmingham where they went on February 20 liked it better than Chattanooga though there was not the variety of mountains and valleys. Twenty years before there were few farmhouses, now there were 36,000 inhabitants. This amazing growth in population and industry which they found from Ohio through the South is surprising. It may not have been a "gold rush," but it was a "manufacturing rush" apparently. The next morning she wrote:

*Rain, rain, I doubt if I can get out. We feel now we are in the South and should be somewhat careful how we express our sentiments. We were talking with a gentleman near us at the table last evening about various churches. He spoke of the Methodist Church North and the Methodist Church South. I remarked it would be a happy arrangement if they could be united. He, in a very **courteous** but **decided** way told me he did not think so, adding that he failed to see any religion in a church so mixed up with politics. I did not tell him that there was as much political feeling south as north, if I **did think it.***

Papa learned last night that the church south here is very strong as well as wealthy, that they never have any entertainments in the church, and if we had one in the church the people would not attend so you can judge of brotherly love

Mother

Plans were to stay in Birmingham a week or more. There were Exhibitions arranged, including one in the parlor for a sick lady, the pastor's wife. Rebecca's final remark in this letter was,

There are a great many lovely places to visit in this great country, but I have yet to find one that I like better in which to live than our own New York State.

She believed people in her part of the country cultivated flowers and plants more than most. There had been a vast amount of capital from Eastern and middle states invested in the South and West. Exhibitions were held in the Presbyterian Church, in Woodlawn; the YMCA at Elyton; Bessimer, a colored Methodist church; and the Ladies Aid wanted another program. The Presbyterian minister thought he knew several places in New Orleans where they would be glad to have the programs.

Birmingham was started in 1870 by the sale of lots. In 1872 it was visited by cholera and received a setback. It did not begin to grow again until 1876. A man who was there ten years before in 1880 said there were only 3,000 inhabitants. The last census showed 35,000, and with the cluster of suburban villages connected with the city by dummy lines besides the Queen and Crescent RR and street cars there were probably 65,000. The next stop would be Tuscaloosa, an education center and said to be one of the finest towns in Alabama. After a short stay they would leave for Meriden, Mississippi, and expected to reach New Orleans by the end of the week.

His father-in-law also wrote Charles,

I have been so busy developing pictures and arranging for lectures and packing, etc., etc., that I can scarcely find time for letters or even to take memoranda we wish to preserve.

He apparently used developer laboratories he formed where he wanted to process his prints.

The updated news of Ralph was not encouraging. He would get a little better and then a little worse. Carrie wrote that he was more care than the little new baby.

Mrs. Cole was called away as Mrs. Holt had a daughter, so we have had our hands full. But with Charlie as night nurse and Nellie as day nurse we do very well. Nellie is invaluable, She is not always as neat in somethings as I would like, but she is so pleasant, so ready to adapt herself to any circumstances so good to the children that I could not have anyone better. I hope to keep her until the middle of May.

Francis is an unusually nice looking baby for so little a fellow. His hair is black like Ralphs and I think his eyes will be dark as Ralph's, but the shape of his head is like Charles.

I do not think you need be specially worried about Ralph. If you were here I do not think you could do more than we are doing except to take him out in the air . . . That I mean to do as soon as the walking is at all good. Every day I wish Arthur and Father were around to give me and the children a nice ride as of yore.

Charlie is going to teach Gerald to write soon. He is anxious to have the boys good writers. [This continued with all of his children, but we never were as good as he was.] Gerald prints all the capital letters and makes figures very nicely. He has been a very good boy lately and tries to be quiet but I fear he cannot learn though he has made improvement.

Carrie

Earlier Ralph was reported with stomach and bowel trouble again. Dr. Fanning had given him a tonic and they were feeding him eggs and broths etc. to build him up again. He was very tired of milk and would not touch it no matter how hungry he was, except a little in the night. Prepared barley, arrowroot, and a little rice he would take, but Mellen's Food and Imperial Granum from which they hoped so much, he did not like. Dr. Fanning's medicines had not helped him much, and they tried hypophosphite on their own. After a couple more days if there was no improvement, they planned to try Dr. Lamont's skill.

Nellie has been curling Ralph's hair, he certainly is a beautiful child and she makes a great fuss over him. You will find the family quite changed when

you get back — Gerald with pants, Ralph with curls and a brand new baby.

Nellie promised to stay until she went to her sister's but ever since she came Mrs. Jones has written letter after letter and offering her more money. She wants her to leave immediately. I think Mrs. Jones must be a very unprincipled and selfish person. She knows I am alone and with two such little children, one of them very sick and the baby. I would send for Mary for a month if they did not need her home just now.

Now do not be worried, because you could do but little and both Mrs. Stone and Aunt Ellen would help any time I needed them.

The final message was that Mr. Studley, a nursery man, had advised them in regard to the fruit for the place. They ordered plum, peach, quince, cherry trees, grapes, and blackberries, many of which I helped pick and can years later.

Arthur and his father took pictures of some mines, a trip Rebecca skipped. It rained all day and all night; so when they arrived from Bessimer and Arthur was to take a 2:15 A.M. train, he and his father slept with one eye open, until half past one. Arthur made ready for Meridan. At the depot he was told the train would be two hours late. He tried to sleep a little, without success. Then the train was four hours late. At six o'clock Arthur came back to the house through pouring rain. The train was not expected to leave until after nine. By this time the others decided to go with him since it was a through train. It cleared about the time they left Birmingham at 10 A.M. Just a few miles before reaching Tuscaloosa, they passed through a tract of woods where a cyclone had been at work. Through a narrow strip there was hardly a tree left. Some were torn up by the roots, some broken at the ground, and some had the tops twisted off. The country proved uninteresting. Only a few comfortable dwellings were to be seen. The towns were nearly all small with few nice houses. In spite of snow at Birmingham, blossoms had not seemed to be injured. Palms and palmettos with fan-shaped leaves began to be seen. They were only two to three feet high but full of purple blossoms. Wrote Rebecca:

I am getting tired of cities and towns and want to get out in the country and woods. Plans are uncertain. If we get no Exhibition we will go directly to New Orleans.

From my window in Meridan I can enjoy another fine building across the street. But I am intrigued by three yoke of oxen before a lumber wagon with hoops or poles bent over the top ready for canvas. There were six such wagons here last night with the canvas on.

This is a great cotton market. We saw quantities baled up on a large platform with nearly a dozen negroes working among the bales. In all the rain we have seen so much cattle without shelter. At

Harriman we saw cows picking at what they could find and what they did not find they did without. I wondered how they could give a bit of milk. Yesterday, I saw some so thin and miserable looking, it must have been all they could do to get about No wonder so many cattle die. Mules thrive under a great deal of neglect.

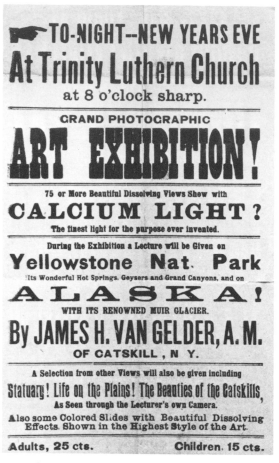

Dodger for Stereopticon Lecture Tour

For the past three days no trains had left Enterprise where a lecture was scheduled. Thousands of acres were under water in one place. On level and thinly wooded land they could see nothing but water on either side of the train. When they reached Enterprise, they found the school hall surrounded with water. Rebecca writes:

I was a short time with Mrs. Lee with whom we were to stay. Arthur soon came in saying we could cross the overflowing Warrier River and get a train on the Q & C road if we hurried.

We crossed the overflow in boats and the main part of the river on a bridge, part of which was broken. We got darkies, big and little to tote our things as we could get no dray to cart them. We went to the Q & C RR three quarters of a mile away. The station agent said it made him think of "In Darkest Africa."

The train instead of being ready at five would not start till eight. We tried to find a place to stay over-

night, but there was nothing available for Arthur. After we got on the train we concluded to go on to New Orleans. We reached there at 5 A.M. Wednesday, the eleventh of March. We waited at the station until 6 A.M. then went to 168 Camp Street where we were shown a lovely room over the parlor and told breakfast would be at eight.

The room had a good Brussels carpet, nicely papered walls, black walnut furniture, a stationary stand with running water and lace curtains. The bedstead was unlike anything they had ever seen — a "canopy top" lined wiht red satin — upholstered would be a better word. This was one of the times when they were *cosy as can be* with a fire in the grate. *Comfortable or not it all took a great deal of money,* mourned Rebecca.

In the afternoon Arthur went out canvassing and saw oranges in the yards, Palmetto trees 12 feet high, and roses up to the second story — all in blossoms, red, yellow, and pink. Some grew over the fence like the Virginia creeper they knew. Coming from the station they passed the French Market with many things for sale. There were large ocean steamers at the dock. The men went down to the river. It was very high. Seven in the morning there was a fire. Arthur went; but though the fire did not amount to much, he came home with the *finest bananas I have ever seen for 15 cents a dozen. We have seen but not yet tasted Chinese plums.* The same day Carrie wrote form Catskill:

From what you say I presume we will not see you before the middle of May. Or do you contemplate an Alaskan trip for the summer?

We had Dr. Lamont for Ralph yesterday. There is considerable sickness in town of the typhoid type and we thought with Ralph's symptoms it would be well to check with him. Besides I did not like to give Ralph the opium and mercury prescribed by Dr. Fanning. Dr. Elliot found no fever and left some prescriptions, one containing pepsin. Ralph has been a little brighter and more playful for a day or two, but it is pitiful to see his little form so wasted. He doesn't run about at all. . . lies in his cradle from morning till night unless we take him up and hold him.

Also that first day in New Orleans, Harvey wrote his son-in-law:

Dear Charles,
We arrived here at 5 AM after an all night trip. We still have some 1000 miles of tickets unused. We will return short distances and do some hunting especially on Lake Pontchertrain, which lies northeast of the City. When Arthur and I get down to business you can expect some large shipments of game. I am told there are wild cats, racoons, bear and alligators within the city limits. We have not seen anything so hostile yet.
The time has come to have our box shipped that I left in the kitchen of the Knickerbocker. I have

chemicals enough for the lanterns until we reach Galveston. Ship via steamer from New York to Galveston, care of Joseph Labadie. We'll make out a list for your guidance.
All are well. JHVG

Whatever the Van Gelders expected in New Orleans, it proved to be much more exciting. Mr. Beecher in his historical article on this tour in the **Quarterly Journal** of the Historical Society wrote:
These Catskillians, on Saturday, March 14th were to view the mob's rage over the Hennessey case and the hanging of one man on a lamp post and another on a tree's limb. Eleven were reported lynched that day. James Harvey Van Gelder was busy with his camera.

The mob scene surrounding the Parish Prison in New Orleans was photographed one hour after the outbreak, and **Leslie's Illustrated Weekly** newspaper printed it for the week ending April 4, 1891. **Leslie's Weekly** also made room for a contribution by Mr. John C. Wickliffe, one of the editors of the **New Orleans Delta** daily newspaper. It explains the reasons for the outbreak, that was heatedly discussed pro and con from coast to coast. Copies of the papers were sent home and one is in the Greene County Historical Society's Library. Further information was not needed or sent in the letters.

A JURY OF TWENTY THOUSAND
The lynching of the eleven men by the people of New Orleans on Saturday should be thoroughly understood by the people of the country before they pass judgment on it.
In the first place the affair was no riot. It was a peaceable, orderly assemblage of people gathered to right a fearful wrong. . . It was composed of respectable, reputable people and was led by business men, merchants, lawyers, doctors, and the leaders in business circles. It was not composed of young hot-blooded and excitable men. There were gray heads and gray beards in the committee, which marched in the lead and did the work. The vast assemblage of twenty thousand passed, both going to and coming from the prison, dozens of Italian shops and many Italian people; no injury was done to any Italian property, and no insult was offered an Italian person. The people marched out to the prison, executed the prisoners whom the evidence in the case had shown to be guilty, returned to the point of assemblage, and dispersed. This was not the act of a mob.
Signed, Yours truly,
John C. Wickliffe

Much of the article in **Leslie's Weekly** was repeated in **The French Quarter** by Herbert Asbury. One chapter in that book tells of the early beginnings of "Nouvelle Orleans" under the French Governor, the Marquis de Vaudreuill, 1743-53. The title of the chapter is "Criminals' Paradise." It tells of gaudy social functions, widespread government corruption, and the tolerance with which the lapses from the strictest moral code were regarded. While Spain dominated Louisiana, and during the years 1800-1803 when the province was "neither French flesh or Spanish fowl" vagabond adventurers from all parts of the world were encouraged to live in New Orleans.

Almost thirty-five years after La Salle descended the river and claimed it for France, there were only eleven men there who were not in the employ of the king himself. This included a garrison of one hundred twenty-four soldiers. The whole population was only three hundred. The belief that there was gold, silver, and pearls died slowly among the adventurous voyagers and couriers de bois who had arrived from Canada and Illinois.

The women who arrived were practically all deportees from prisons and brothels in Paris. The province was filled "by ransacking jails, hospitals, disorderly soldiers, black sheep of distinguished families, paupers, prostitutes and unsophisticated peasants who wandered into the streets of Paris and were kidnapped and shipped under guard." There were also political prisoners, river men, gamblers, pirates, and privateers.

These Sicilian Mafia criminals arrived in New Orleans soon after the beginning of the great wave of immigration from southern Europe before the Civil War and within a few years were operating in well organized bands in various parts of the city. One group, the Stooagherra Society, was organized as a branch of the Mafia by four men driven from Palermo by the Sicilian authorities. They arrived in New Orleans early in 1869. New Orleans was the Mafia headquarters, but branches were established in New York, San Francisco, Chicago, and other large cities. Over the years the Vigilantes and other reform groups made occasional attempts to control the vice that was rampant. The Mafia, the police believed, in 1885 had about 300 members. Tony Matranga was the president of the supreme council of twenty. Extortion letters were prepared, murders planned, and assassins assigned. The clever Matrangas decided to invade a new field then monopolized by the Provensaro brothers who unloaded ships laden with fruit from South and Central America. They employed several hundred Italians and had contracts with the shipping companies. Laborers received forty cents an hour and sixty cents at night. This was reasonably high for that period. The Provensaros were very rich and politically influential, but there was no known connection with the Sicilian group. In fact, they paid tribute regularly and hired the men sent to them by the Matrangas.

By the middle 1880s, the Matrangas coveted the profits made by unloading fruit ships and notified the Provensaros that thereafter they would take over. The new group made enormous profits by reducing wages to ten and fifteen cents an hour and forced Italians under threat of death to work for these miserable wages.

Chief of Police Hennessey was convinced that murders in the Italian colony would not cease until the Mafia power was broken. He began to collect evi-

Lynching of the Mafia murderers, New Orleans. *Photographed by J.H. Van Gelder.*

dence and wrote to the head of the Rome police for names and photographs of several members of the Esposito band who were supposed to be in New Orleans and active with the Matrangas. An anonymous letter warned him in July that the Mafia would kill him unless he ceased his activities.

Instead Hennessey said publicly that he would present evidence at the trial of the Provensaros — a result of a vendetta with them and the Mafia in which Matranga had been wounded. Two days before he was to appear on the witness stand, October 15, 1890, Hennessey was waylaid on his way home and shot. Before he died he said his assailants had been Italians, though he had not recognized individuals. A typical Mafia double-barrelled shotgun was found in the shed from which the shots were fired opposite the Hennessey home. Various others had seen the assassins running away.

On the day of the funeral of the Chief of Police, thousands lined the streets. There was talk of lynching. Many Italians published notices that they had no connection with the Mafia. Of twenty-one Italians arrested, nineteen were indicted by the Grand Jury late in November. The trial of nine of them including a 14-year-old boy who had signalled Hennessey's arrival began on February 16, 1891. Eminent counsel headed by a former District Attorney defended the Mafia. An outstanding member of the defense was Dominick C. O'Malley, a private detective whose career in New Orleans had been interrupted by a ten-month term in the Workhouse for such things as carrying concealed weapons, intimidating witnesses, jury fixing. Seventy-one jurors of the regular panel and 1,150 talismen were summoned before they could obtain a jury.

Wickliffe wrote in **Leslie's Weekly:**
Convinced as the people were of the guilt of the accused, they were staggered by the strength of the case made out by the State. Eyewitnesses to the killing came out and identified many of the men at the trial. Circumstantial evidence was most conclusive. Politz, a defendant, broke down and confessed he was present at the meeting when the death of Hennessey was decreed.

When the case went to the jury on March 12, 1891, they brought in a verdict the next day. Despite all the evidence as valid today as then, the verdict was they could not agree on some and acquitted the others. Almost simultaneously came proof that the jury had been tampered with by Mafia gold.

The acquitted men were still in Parish Prison under indictment of conspiracy. But they toasted each other and their lawyers in wine sent in by friends. State's witnesses left the city or barricaded their homes.

Down by the docks Sicilians tore down an American flag, trampled it, and raised it upside down under the Italian flag.

But while all these celebrations were in full swing,

a meeting was being held as a result of which this notice appeared in the morning newspaper of March 14, 1891.

MASS MEETING!
All good citizens are invited to attend a mass meeting on SATURDAY, March 14, at 10 o'clock A.M. at Clay Statue to take steps to remedy the failure of justice in the Hennessey case. Come prepared for action.

This was signed by 61 of the most prominent citizens of New Orleans, among them William Parkinson. Grandpa Van Gelder arrived with his camera at Clay Statue and found crowds already filling Canal Street and up Royal and St. Charles Avenue.

The signers of the call appeared, marching three abreast and headed by William S. Parkinson and John C. Wickliffe. With Walter Dengre, these three ascended the steps of the pedestal of Clay's statue. Each spoke three minutes about the history of the case and what they intended to do. They received from the crowd the sign of approval they requested as well as a roar of applause.

Wickliffe announced he would be second lieutenant of the execution party, James Huston first lieutenant and Parkinson, Captain. The signers formed ranks and marched to a gun store and armed themselves. Once inside the prison surrounded by the crowds, they proceeded with great deliberation. Each member of the party had a list of eleven Italians believed to be guilty beyond the shadow of a doubt, and he was instructed not to harm any of the others whom he might encounter.

In less than an hour Parkinson clambered to a windowsill and announced to the mob that the lynchers had finished their job. He marched his men out of the front door of the prison, was raised to the shoulders of some men and led the cheering crowd back to the Clay Statue. He urged the crowd to disperse.

I ask you as an endorsement of what has been done, and in pursuance of the promise we made, to return quietly to your homes. The lesson we have given will have its effect. If it does not we will repeat it.

No investigation of the lynching was ever made. The Mafia was never again strong in New Orleans. The Van Gelders, like the city fathers, were again involved in their own affairs. Rebecca wrote home that Arthur and his father had been alligator hunting.

They were tired enough when they got home and hungry but they had the alligator. What to do with it was the question yesterday and it took all day, so we were beset with delays and disappointments. But now it is arranged to tan the hide and have it sent with the head and claws to Catskill in about two months when done. Arthur has been trying to stuff a bird he shot. He killed a snake also, a mocasin, we think, from his description. He had no idea what a deadly foe he conquered. He was describing it to a gentleman today who told him what it was.

Grandpa wrote on a slip of paper tucked in a letter, *We had our alligator steak today. It tasted somewhat like sturgeon, rather sweet and somewhat tough.* This is the alligator whose hide and great jaws of teeth were kept under Grandma's sofa in the parlor when I was young, and which little Wardles crawled around with to scare littler Wardles.

Mr. and Mrs. W.T. Jennings, president of the Tanners Bank where Charles worked, sent them a postcard that they were staying at the St. Charles Hotel and were leaving Monday for Florida, so the Van Gelders visited them. The U.S. Barracks and trip along the levees to the National Cemetery brought home again our Civil War losses. Buried there were 23,000 Union men. One wonders if among the graves is that of Eugene Pelham, the 16-year-old son of the Pelhams of Oswego, New York, (110th Regiment).

A Jackson monument recalled the General's involvement there in the War of 1812. Beautifully kept "old time" plantation homes were along the way when a large steamer passed the swells washed over the top of the levee, glistening in the sun. Rebecca felt *a little strange thinking what might happen if that wonderful body of water should break through. The levees are carefully guarded night and day during the flood season so that in case a break occurs it may be repaired at once, but in spite of all the guarding the water gets the better of the situation sometimes, and causes loss of property.*

New Orleans, the Van Gelders remarked in one letter, was the most interesting of all the places they had visited. And this without any mention of the unmentionable carryings-on, so widely known. The book, **The French Quarter** quoted before, had a whole chapter on "Storeyville."

New Orleans had a reputation as "the promised land of Harlotry." The "ladies of the night" flocked there from all over the United States along with their "fancy men" and other male parasites who fattened on their fallen sisters, according to this book.

It was almost a century and three quarters since Bienville and his working party of soldiers and convicts came, before authorities and the people generally awoke to the fact that unless suppressive and regulatory measures were carried out their city could be one vast brothel.

It was after 1890 that the voice against rampant uncontrolled vice began to make itself heard. It was March, 1891, that the Van Gelders witnessed the lynching of the Mafia. It was also 1891 that police proposed medical examinations of "All women and girls notoriously abandoned to lewdness." Respectable ladies objected; it was an "insult to womanhood." Did all this escape the Van Gelders or just

escape their letters. Probably some of both.

Not until the end of the century was prostitution confined to one area, called Storeyville, and it soon became the most celebrated red light district in the United States.

It lasted until 1917 when the redlight district was closed and prostitutes moved into various business and residential sections. The Federation of Women's Clubs appointed a committee to help prostitutes, but they did not need it. The operation of the New Orleans experiment at Storeyville over a period of 20 years proved that segregation was the best method devised to control vice. But Storeyville declined. Sociologists advanced many profound reasons for the phenomenon but the principle influence was probably public sentiment and a radical change in the viewpoint from which premarital relations were regarded. There is considerable truth in the classic remark of Countess Willie V. Piazza: "The country club girls are ruining my business"

End of quote! No comment!

The Diary reports:

Friday, the 27th, Arthur left for Franklin. Harvey and I went to a cotton press and on board a schooner just in from Central America and loaded with bananas.

Harvey and I left for Franklin Monday morning, taking a line of road up on the east side of the river for nearly 30 miles on account of the broken levee which caused the waters to flood the Southern Pacific track, over which trains had run however until that morning.

The water was so deep the morning Arthur went that it nearly put out the engine fires, and the road was so uneven the train was in danger of going over. We had crossed on a ferry, and took the Southern Pacific on the new road built from that point to another beyond the flooded district.

The night before Rebecca felt homesick, but a cheery letter from Arthur made her feel like going further West. She said he seemed to find friends everywhere he went, and pondered, *Greek and Latin are good, but this trip will be of value to him, I am sure.*

They expected him to skip Franklin, but he changed plans and arranged for them to spend a week there.

Arthur had his reasons. He had arisen at 6:30, and his father went with him to the train. In the French Quarter they got so much breakfast for 25 cents that he had to leave some for lunch. (Did they have "doggie bags" way back then?) Leaving his father he sailed 12 miles up the river to the place where he could take the Southern Pacific. The tracks below that point were flooded from a great break in the levee. He wrote his sister Carrie from Franklin:

As we approached the banks of the river, the great plank was let down and we boarded the train. As I was looking with all my eyes over the extensive swamps, where plenty of snakes and turtles lay on stumps, and an occasional marsh hen or an alligator would hasten away from the approaching train, a fine looking man sat down next to me. I asked him if there were any interesting things for photographing at Franklin or New Iberia.

I intended to go to Lafayette as planned, but after talking with him a while I found that he was Superintendent of the Episcopal Sunday School and owner of a sugar refinery. He lives in Poughkeepsie, NY, in the summer and here in the winter. It was evident he was a very influential man here. Being urged by him to stop, when the train arrived here we got off and he directed me to the boss of this hotel, the Parkinson House, no bar, and said he would call around soon. He came in about an hour, went to see another man and sent a friend of his. This man invited me to church. There I met several prominent citizens and enjoyed the service very much.

A fine horse and carriage arrived the next morning with Mr. Ferris of Poughkeepsie. After arranging for a lecture, he directed his clerk to show Arthur around the bayou. Then Mr. Ferris took him around the place and introduced him to all the prominent men. A farmer from Rochester, New York, who had 15,000 acres, invited them to dinner. Arthur wrote:

That's the kind of people to get in with. I wish you could have been along when he showed us his yard, such beautiful roses, so many mockingbirds and blackbirds singing, such fine hunting dogs and such delicious fruit.

Franklin was a genuine Southern town with a leaven of Northern blood and business capital according to James Harvey's description of *this Acadian land, and center of the sugar producing country.* It was 101 miles west of New Orleans. Mr. Parkinson, the hotel proprietor, was the brother or half brother of the Parkinson who led the New Orleans avengers on March 14. In the morning they went for a drive to Irish Bend, probably seven miles north. It was a beautiful day to get photos.

Attendance was small at the two exhibitions given in Franklin, either because of cool weather or because a lecture on the Mafia just previous to his was with a very poor oil lantern. He and Arthur went on for a lecture at Centerville and expected to meet Rebecca the next day on the train for New Iberia where an exhibition was booked.

A horse and buckboard belonging to Mr. Parkinson took them to several interesting places. The Oak Lawn plantation was owned by a man who also lived at and owned the St. Charles Hotel in New Orleans. One room in the house, which was looked after by a housekeeper all the time, had been a guest chamber for Henry Clay. It remained with the same furniture he had used. They saw the hands plowing and hoeing out on the plantation and the levees built along one side to keep out the overflow from the Great Lake, which was sometimes made high by back water from the Mississippi. Down at the Shadyside Plantation Mr. and Mrs. Branett invited them to dinner, took their pictures in the flower garden, and directed them to the Sugar House. This contained machinery for every part of sugar making from crushing the cane to packing the different grades of sugar in barrels for the market. Cane could be brought in from the field in the morning and the next day be ready for market. The very end of the last year's crop was 75 barrels in the form of *black syrup.* It was waiting the coming of the boat down from the Teche which was near the refinery.

Northerners in business in the South were noteworthy in numbers. The Arlington Plantation owned by Mr. Baker, formerly of Rochester, New York, raised rice and cotton. He was particularly proud of his cattle which contrasted with the very inferior native stock. At Franklin they had good milk and plenty of it, a welcome change from a long period of only condensed milk.

New Iberia had the next lecture in the opera house for the benefit of the Public Library. Salt mines were on their agenda the next day. The elevator went down 175 feet. After a repeat Exhibition the next day they left for Houston. The country was very level. They regetted they had decided to skip St. Charles which turned out to be thriving and beautiful.

They crossed the Sabine River, dividing Louisiana from Texas, while it was still light, arriving at the Tremont House in Houston after 9 o'clock. Papa wrote to Carrie:

In Texas at last. Since Barnum Bailey is no more we will try to give them the "greatest show on earth." We will attempt to make Texans believe they will never forgive themselves if they fail to see it.

Your Mama seems to enjoy herself most of the time. She still gives curtain lectures in private. Says she will never go with me again unless I keep brushed up more, dress better and toes out and head up all the time, etc., etc. Well, as I was not born that way, I suppose we will have to leave her home to look after the Grand Babies and we will go on and have a good time seeing the country. Would like to go to the Land of the Van Gelder ancestors very much. I imagine Louisiana is something like Holland. The one has levees, the other has dykes. Both are flat countries.

Have taken some good negatives of this Teche country — large plantations and mostly devoted to sugar, although rice is also grown here. The greater part of the old plantations have passed out of the old planters' hands and many of them are now owned by Northerners. It costs from $100,000 to $150,000 to put up a first class sugar house and refinery with the best modern machinery. They are run night and day and Sundays for about three months. They lie still the rest of the year except for the poorer grades and savings from waste.

> Yours,
> *J.H. Van Gelder*

Rebecca did not let Harvey's reference to her *curtain lectures* pass unnoticed.

*If you had seen him coming through the streets of New Iberia you would not have wondered at it. He had been to the depot to get some things from the old trunk that he wanted. The things were not wrapped or folded. Among them was a pair of shoes and a pair of pants with the suspenders dangling down. I will leave it to your imagination, the appearance he made and my confusion as he came in the hotel **AND HE THE LECTURER OF THE EVENING AT THE** Opera House, the second finest in the State of Louisiana.*

She also reported that after much pursuasion he had a new suit and wore it Sunday for the first. She did not consider it very handsome but it *did nicely for the present.*

A short stay at Houston and the Van Gelders were on their way to Galveston off the coast of Texas. One thing they found for the first time on the prairies they crossed were wild flowers. An envelope still contains many they sent home. At last I learned that all the boxes of shells that were in the attic and had Grandma's handwriting on them were picked up on Galveston's beaches and shipped to Catskill. Rebecca writes:

The ride over the bay was delightful. The city of Galveston in the distance with a light mist surrounding it, tinged with neither pink nor gold, but a cohor in between. The two made a more charming picture than anything I had seen in a long time. It was different from the landscapes that had pleased us so many times. [Rebecca's ability to paint increased her awareness of color.]

Mr. Labadie and two of his boys met us at the train. We were very warmly welcomed and spent nearly two weeks with the family which consisted of Mr. and Mrs. Labadie, Miss Emily, four sons and two daughters at home, the youngest a dear little baby near Ralph's age.

Sunday morning Arthur went to Mass with Louis, while Mrs. Labadie, Harvey and I went to the Episcopal Church just across the way. It is 40 years old and has a fine interior. The special attraction was a solo by a lady from St. Louis. She had come to the city to attend the Sangerfest to be held in the city during the week.

We all got letters. Papa got one from the Queen and Crescent acknowledging the receipt of the photos with which they were well pleased. He sent about 62, I think. Frank Leslie sent $5 for the prints of the Parish Prison and Clay Monument.

Arthur and Lewis had a day's experience in herding cattle and considered themselves therefore *expert cowboys.* An acquaintance of the family, a *cattle king* up in Hitchcock, a new town on the mainland, wanted to separate 500 steers from the rest of the herd. They were in the saddle from 9 A.M. to 4:30 and rode 40 miles. They were two highly delighted and tired boys having done their duty in rounding up and separating cattle, killing rattlesnakes, prairie runners.

The week-long Sangerfest may have interferred with their ability to make arrangements for lectures, but did not spoil their enjoyment of the concerts. They saw the torch light procession for President Benjamin Harrison and went to the Beach Hotel and shook hands with him. Arthur and Lewis saw him again at the Presbyterian church. The Labadies went with them out to the Cotton Mill, Bagging and Twine Factory, and also the Water Works. They were all quite new with superior machinery.

Rebecca wrote to Carrie:

I have just been cleaning Arthur's coat and vest that he has worn most of the time since we left home. They are getting worse for wear, but I am giving them a thorough cleaning occasionally and they do very well again for a while. The pants I am going to wash today. They have been in coal mines, the salt mines, hunting in swamps, torn on fences, exhibiting in halls and opera houses, to nearly all manner of church services, besides travelling about 2000 miles. He has worn his cutaway some. His light suit is a great comfort now. It is warm here.

I bought a fine straw hat trimmed with velvet, lace and a spray of leaves for $3.50. I bought a fan for 25¢. I want a sun umbrella and a pair of silk gloves. I looked for thin gauge drawers but could not find any. I think I shall have to trouble Charles to go to Doty's or elsewhere and get me two pair.

The friendly pleasant visit at Galveston with the Labadies began to end when Arthur started ahead for Houston and nearby communities to set up exhibitions. The Labadies had been boarders at the Van Gelder Cherry Hill House in Catskill. Their home town of Galveston suffered from yellow fever, from hurricanes like the terrible one I remember hearing talked about in 1900, and from such pirates as LaFitte. After the great hurricane a seawall was built. Two causeways connected with the mainland. Arthur started out early, but gales of wind and rain made the crossing dangerous. He took a later train. Usually the causeways were not used in high winds lest the trains be blown into the water. His parents met him a few days later in Houston, and they resumed the pattern of work and sight-seeing. In answer to a telegram, Carrie wired back that Ralph was getting every care possible. *Do not miss your chance to visit your brother in Kansas.*

As they were entering San Antonio on May 5 the city seemed to be set down in the middle of a mesquite forest. They took an electric car in the afternoon along the public highway two miles to the San Jose Mission, the second of the old missions. Rebecca recounts:

The front wall must have been very beautiful in its day. Part of the wall on one side had fallen down and so had much of the arched roof. There was a Mexican family living in one end of the old granary. Thursday we went out to the "Post" which is on ground high enough to overlook the country for long distances in every direction. On the way back Arthur and his father set up the cameras for the exhibition at the Y.M.C.A. We stopped at the Alamo. In the old Cathedral there had been several worshipers, one, an old Mexican woman kneeling very devoutly with a little boy beside her, who was concentrating on less devout matters.

We left for Stafford Junction the next afternoon reaching there after 9 P.M. and had to leave again by 4 A.M. The sun was up when we reached the hotel. I lay down on the sofa in the parlor and was asleep in about a minute.

Arthur and Harvey went out prospecting and found a rather queer looking place to stay, but it was quite comfortable. The house was built by putting up poles close together, plastering it outside and in. The inner wall was then whitewashed and decorated by dipping a sponge in indigo and patting the walls at regular and irregular spaces. The ceiling overhead was made of sheeting fastened down with narrow strips of wood and all calsomined. The furnishings included a marble-topped black walnut bureau, a nice black walnut bed, and a pair of good woolen blankets.

Harvey gathered a whole page of notes on San Antonio before they left. This Texas City was the first prominent settlement near the head of the San Antonio River and was granted a charter by the King of Spain about 1733. It was incorporated with other towns, January, 1837, by the Republic of Texas. The Republic of Texas remained independent until annexed by the United States in 1845, an action which triggered the Mexican War.

Santa Anna, the Mexican general, politician, and president of Mexico, 1833-36, with 6,000 men came into the country in 1825. His advance troops arrived the same day that Lt. Col. William Barret Travis retired to the Alamo with 150 men. Another 32 men arrived from Gonzales. When summoned to surrender, the Texans replied with a cannon shot. The Alamo fell Sunday morning, March 6, 1836. All 182 men perished, including Jim Bowie and Davy Crockett.

Grandpa's notes continued:

The first meeting of the San Antonio Literary Society was held in 1800.

Wild turkeys were so plentiful they were a drug on the market at 15 and 20 cents a piece.

Sunset was the first Railroad and reached the city in 1877; connected with the Southern Pacific in 1883.

In 1857 mail arrived from San Antonio at San Diego, California, in 25½ days, *the fastest time on record.* The city was lighted for the first in 1855. The first electric train was running September, 1890. The San Jose Mission was the second dedicated to St. Joseph and founded in 1720. The granary with its strong and curious flying buttresses and arched stone roof is still there and in it a family still makes its home.

At this time Rebecca made the last entry in her Diary except for a schedule for the rest of the trip.

Arthur was too ill to go Monday from San Antonio, so Harvey took the stage to Stafford Junction and on to Devil's River. We came a day later and found instructions at Stafford Junction to stop at Painted Cove.

News of the trip did not end, however, for the letters continue to trace their goings and comings. From El Paso, May 20, Rebecca wrote that they were ready to go forward even though there were still things of interest there. She told of her first lesson in photographic printing. Harvey managed to develop most of his own pictures en route. Once a druggist whose dark room he apparently borrowed tried to help and succeeded in ruining some. The heavy, dirty work of filling the cylinders continued periodically during the whole trip. They got dusty as well as tired and hungry from a visit to a Smelting Works, which was full of interest to them. Arthur came back with specimens of ore containing lead, silver and gold.

I went with them over into Mexico Saturday and saw the city of El Paso del Nort, which looks strange enough to a Northerner. There are so many low one story houses with flat roofs.

Water rent is extra here. Where we take our meals they have a meter on the faucet and pay by the gallon. The water bill there runs about $3.70 a month. I am certain of one thing, we will be glad when we can let the water run all we want without worrying about the money value of every quart.

The climate they found very healthful, but the country round about was very desolate looking, though it could be very fruitful with irrigation. Those who could afford to have water could have grass. Some varieties of trees grew well with water. The China tree was seen most often. It had quite a delicate blossom resembling lilacs in odor. Alfalfa was interesting enough to send a sample home in a letter.

On a postcard from Mexico, Grandpa had written simply: *We are in a foreign land.*

From El Paso at the extreme western tip of Texas, and bordering Mexico, they went north through New Mexico, stopping at Las Vegas and Santa Fe. The Gallinas River divided them from the eastern part of

Las Vegas. It was more like a Northern settlement than the adobe buildings in the other part. As happened often their boarding house was run by a Northern woman, this time from Buffalo, New York.

Monday in coming from El Paso, we found the cars warm coming over the "staked plains" as they call them here. I call it the desert for it is the most barren and desolate looking region imaginable, but as I have said in my letters before, very fruitful if irrigated.

We found a great change after sundown as we were coming north and getting into higher altitudes. About midnight it was cold. I put my wrap on and after a little man came through the train and built a fire in the car. At 4 A.M. we reached the junction where we changed cars for Santa Fe which is 18 miles from the main line.

Mother

At Santa Fe they stopped at the Alamo Hotel kept by a Mrs. Gough also from New York State. It was a queer looking place. The great majority of the houses and stores were adobe, in most cases only one story. The oldest house in the place was 200 years old and had a second story, not very high. There were two *old Cathedrals.* It was very cool since Las Vegas was 6,500 feet above sea level. Santa Fe was still higher, with snow-capped peaks in all different directions, one over 14,000 feet. While the men were busy, Rebecca and a woman she met on the train visited a cathedral and an Indian school called the Romona Home.

After dinner and a nap, we walked about town and visited the "Old Curiosity Shop" in which we saw a great deal of trash and some curious old things among which was an old trunk made of the hide of a buffalo. It had been a grand affair in its day and used by Government officers in the transfer of valuable papers years ago. On the corner of the roof over the entrance was an old Mexican oxcart with its cumbersome wooden wheels cut out of solid wood and which I should think would require a good horse to drive without any load.

Just before tea time we went to Vespers in the Cathedral. There were a large number there, the greater part Mexican. A very few others were well dressed. It was a strange looking audience — more Mexican women than men. They do not wear hats at all — just shawls over their heads. There were some seats but many worshippers either kneeled or sat on the floor. Most of them seemed very devout. A little inside the gate, stood a large cross. Some kneeled before it and kissed it, but these were nearly all elderly Mexican men. A very few young men knelt before it.

The next day they visited the Historical rooms and saw an old pair of bellows made from buffalo hide which had been in use among Indians for four generations. Other trunks of buffalo hide were of different workmanship, and showed some skill in making the locks and keys. They were very large and heavy. They saw some stone gods but when they tried to designate them as "Aztec," the spelling was more garbled than phonetic, almost illegible and graced with a question mark after it. On view were Indian paintings, pottery, specimens of different ores found in the territory.

The Historical rooms were in one end of a long row of one-story adobe buildings in no respect different from many others. Just across the street was a nicely shaded plaza near the center of which was a monument to a man killed in our Civil War or in one of the wars with the Indians. The Post Office was in the other end; the Government Palace in the center. *I've no doubt it was beautiful within, but it was not beautiful without.* Arthur and his mother went for a walk in the ravines and low mountain peaks.

I easily forgave them for such casual mention of "staked plains" as they travelled north from El Paso to Santa Fe. Their ignorance was no more abysmal than mine which however had been challenged by Arthur's descriptions of them written to Carrie from Birmingham, Alabama. He had met a couple there who had crossed the "staked plains" from west to east, 600 miles in a "To Kansas or Bust" wagon, killing rattlesnakes, coyotes, and rabbits galore. A little resesarch at the library, and I came home with a fascinating book, **Mavarik Town,** (by John L. McCarty) the story of old Tascosa. Since earliest times it had been an easy crossing of the Canada River for beast and later for man. Tascosa was at its peak during the 70s and 80s, ten years before the Van Gelders first heard the words, "staked plains" of Texas.

The "staked plains" or El Llano Escatado, in the panhandle of Texas turned out to be a microcosm of the early Wild West, filled with such prestigious names as Coronado, Billy the Kid, and Carson. It was also an area with a more winter free route to California during the Gold Rush.

Tascosa was at first a camping ground for Indians and explorers, then the Comanchero trading point. A group of Mexican pastoral settlements followed. In its heyday it was a trading center for the open range and the legal capital of ten counties of the cattle empire. Known as the stamping ground for the most notorious of the "bad men" of the West, cattle thieves, and cowboys sought it out for pleasure and mischief. Both Anglo-American and Mexican "Little Men" got together to fight off the "Big Men," who in general represented foreign investors and who tried to control the country. It was the sheep men of the open range against the cattle men who fenced in land and water. Barbed wire fences were first introduced in Tascosa, so trail herds had to go elsewhere. In less than a quarter of a century the town had risen and fallen.

The hoped for railroad passed them by and people

began to move to Amarillo, homestead claims, or return to their old homes. The valiant newspaper editor kept printing his paper to a negligible constituency until 1891. The "man with the hoe" finally replaced the fenced in cattle empires. For many years he has not been seen on the road in an old jalopy, and power farming has taken over.

Tascosa got one more bit of publicity later when a Boys Ranch opened there and became famous through a major movie (Boys' Town) filmed by Metro-Goldwyn-Mayer. Easterners find it hard to realize how young the West still is and how its pioneering history was "just yesterday."

There was a Hot Springs about five miles out from Santa Fe on a branch line. The Van Gelders had not decided what they would do as there might be an Exhibition that night, but they knew they would soon head for Pueblo, Denver, and other sights in Colorado before reaching Smith Pine in Spearville, Kansas.

Arthur mailed an added note on the train. They had decided to go on to Pueblo or perhaps further, arriving in Denver the next morning.

Denver, Colorado
June 2, 1891

Dear Carrie,
Arthur has just come from the Post Office again without a letter. We came through Pueblo last Saturday and left a postcard for the postmaster to send any mail for us that reached his office before June 5th, to Denver, but nothing has come yet. It is a week, yesterday, since we have had the last word from you. We left word at El Paso to have any mail sent to Spearville but I see we are not going to get there as soon as we first thought.
Colorado is a large state and full of wonderful sights so I feel sure we will not get to Smith's before the middle of the month anyway, perhaps later. Today we are going to see the city. I have been too tired to sightsee before. We had to be up early to take the train at 9:15 from La Junta where we stayed Friday night, paying $3 for the privilege of occupying two rooms from 9 o'clock in the evening to 3:50 in the morning.

In Denver, Sunday, they attended *the finest church we have yet seen* and heard Dean Peck of Denver University. In the afternoon Rebecca went to Sunday School and *was delighted.* Arthur joined her at a Young People's Society of Christian Endeavor meeting in the same church. They heard Chancellor McDowell in a most excellent sermon. The organ was one of the best in America.

The men made arrangements for an Exhibition in Georgetown and Silver Plume, while Rebecca washed and mended and rested. A lecture was already booked for Colorado Springs, and perhaps for Denver. Their plans were never so unpredictable as during this period; and it caused great distress about little Ralph, whose life hung in the balance.

They urged sending letters to several places. As it happened, letters and telegrams all went to the wrong places at the wrong time. In one letter Harvey wrote he was afraid they would have *to send Rebecca home. She is so worried about Ralph.*

Silver City, Col., June 3

Dear Carrie,
I sent a letter yesterday from Denver to which place we return tomorrow. Friday we have an Exhibition at Colorado Springs. We came up and up this morning through the wonderful Clear Creek Canyon to Georgetown. There Arthur got on the train and we came over the "loop" and around the curves and up and up the mountain sides to this Silver City, 9,050 feet above sea level. The mountain peaks above us are snow covered. Gray's Peak is only a few miles away. The sides of the mountains on either side of the creek are almost straight up and down and I can see the entrance to very many mines. Some cabins are way, way up. Papa and Arthur have gone to get views and go to mines if they have time.
All well and happy as we can be considering that we so want news from home.
With love,
Mother

They wrote again from Denver on June 5 and called at the Post Office. There was a letter of May 25 that said Ralph's problems seemed a little better. But a postscript by Charles reported him not so well the next morning. He was *wasting away fast — nothing but skin and bones.* Carrie added,
I cannot lose hope. It seems harder than ever to give him up after all the weary waiting the last month when we thought he was going to get well. Of course his recovery isn't hopeless, but if you want to see him you had better stop only a day or two at Smith's, and then hurry home.
Charles wrote two days later:
Ralph may last 4 to 6 weeks if he really has to die. We have not resorted to stimulants at all. So dont deprive yourself of visiting with Uncle Smith. Remember us all to him.
Harvey wrote from the Denver Station where he was waiting for some special rate tickets to come through. The baggage man would not check their stuff without the tickets. He hoped Ralph was better but added:
Mrs. VG takes a very gloomy view and tinks that probably you have had to part with Ralph.
I wish we could have been with you to aid and sympathize, but you know you have our sympathy at any rate.
Yesterday we walked from Georgetown to Green Lake 10,000 feet high and 2½ miles from Georgetown. The mountain peaks were still 2000 to 3000 feet above the little lake. We made snowballs and ate some snow on the way there.

Georgetown was fifty miles west of Denver and in mountains 8,476 feet above the sea. They had visited Silver Plume (9,176 feet high), 4 miles by rail and 2 by wagon road. The lecture made expenses there and back from Denver.

Colorado Springs
June 7, Sunday

Dear Charles,
Mrs. Van has gone to church and Arthur went to YPSCE. We arrived Monday about 5 PM with an Exhibition that evening. Tuesday we are to illustrate a lecture for the Methodist pastor on Pompei for which I get $10. Also one on Thursday the 11th, leaving the next morning for Pueblo. We will not stay there long unless we go into the mountains from there.
We expect at all events to go to Dodge City by the 17th or 18th and a day or so later to Spearville, Ford County, Kansas. I write this so you will know where to write or telegraph us. Always put General Delivery on our letters. If not, in large cities it leads to delay. Also write a postcard every place you expect us to be. Mrs. Van gets almost beside herself if she does not hear every few days. She is so bound up in Ralph that I fear we will have to let her go home if he is still alive. She is completely unstrung hearing he is worse.

The day before they had gone by electric car to near the foot of Cheyenne Canyon about four miles away. Then they climbed up the canyon to Helen Hunt Jackson's grave, probably 1,200 feet above. *It's a strange and romantic place to be buried.* At Georgetown and Silver Plume and on the road to Green Lake, the men went into two silver mines which *are not surpassed except at Leadville and perhaps a few other places in Colorado.*

At Colorado Springs they found a temperance town with very wide streets and electric cars that ran in every direction. They had waterworks and electric lights in every room of their boarding house. Pike's Peak was close by.

In an effort to bridge the miles in spite of post office delays, Charles wrote on June 5 that he had telegraphed to Pueblo on May 31, when little Ralph died, and also sent letters as advised. None reached them for over a week. His letter:

Our darling fell asleep without hardly any pain. He was not well Saturday and seemed to have a cold. We called the doctor about 1 o'clock and at 3 A.M. our darling laid his head back and gave an almost imperceptible gasp and was gone. Gone to be among the angels and free from all suffering and care.
Carrie has born the grief bravely, but this morning she is feeling the loneliness of Ralph's absence. I am sorry we did not have time to let you know but we did not know he was leaving us until within five

minutes of three, Sunday morning. The autopsy which we thought best to have showed consumption of the bowels but he died of paralysis of the heart. I send this to Denver in hopes it will catch you there.

But it was a postcard from Charles with the sad news which finally reached them in Colorado Springs and Rebecca replied immediately on the 9th.

I cannot tell you how full of sorrow my heart is. I cant help thinking if I had done differently it would have been better, but having done what seemed best at the time, it is unwise in most cases to regret. Papa is talking of going to the great mining town of Leadville high in the Rockies, but I shall not go with him. I shall go to Smith's. I am so anxious to hear from you.

They visited the Garden of the Gods, Manitou, Williams Canyon, Ute's Pass and Cheyenne Canyon, all in Colorado Springs.

Catskill, NY June 7, 1891

Dear Mother,
It is a week since Ralph went away from us. I think you must have heard before this. We have received letters from you since we telegraphed, and I am glad you did not know before this.
Floy has been a big comfort. Lizzie has been here. Frank was held up by illness but Bertha who has been in Philadelphia on her editor's business for the Kindergarten Magazine is expected soon.
Still sympathy is of little use after all. The hurt is still there however our friends may love and sympathize with us. I enclose a lock of Ralph's beautiful golden hair.
        Carrie

In answer later to a question about Gerald's reaction to his brother's death, Carrie wrote her mother that he often spoke of Ralph; and when he saw his clothes, he wanted to kiss them; but he did not seem to grieve.

Do not regret not being here. We did everything possible and he was so quiet and Francis is such a good baby that we could care for them nicely.

The travelling trio had kept the Pine family in suspense in Dodge City and Spearville, Kansas, where Rebecca's brother, Smith Pine lived. Earlier, Lulu, Smith's oldest daughter by his first wife, had written Aunt Rebecca:

Pa has been very busy on the farm lately. He expects to go to Dodge City to get some trees today. Carrie's baby must be only a few days younger than our new little brother born Feb. 6th. Laura and Willie think him very nice and call him "sweet boy and Bay Bro." They play outdoors every pleasant day. Each gets his stick for a horse and go trotting off.

Lulu told of visiting Mary Imel's school over in the

Imel district where her father had taught so long ago. Lulu's school closed in March. She had only taught part of the term as she caught whooping cough and then pneumonia. The School Board let her father substitute for her. He taught from Thanksgiving until the first of March. She added that Percy Shaffer, whose family, like so many there, had come originally from the Kiskatom-Lawrenceville area of Greene County, was going to work with her brother Walter in the drug store in Dodge City. Walter's and Lulu's mother had burned to death more than eight years earlier. Eva Shinn, the second wife who became mother of a large family, added a note of welcome for *a long visit.*

It was June when the Van Gelders finally caught up with the Pine relatives and friends. En route they had found Eddie Shaffer and his wife and children at LaJunta. He had harnessed up his team and driven them out to see his home three miles in the country. They took a train and arrived in Dodge City at 11 P.M. where they found Walter Pine and Arthur who had preceded them.

We are at the Arlington Hotel with Arthur. Walter

Garden of the Gods. *Photographed by J.H. Van Gelder.*

boards with Dr. McCartney who owns the drugstore. His practice is so large he has no time for the store and Walter is in complete charge. It's a good position but very confining.
In the evening we visited the Shinn's, Eva's brother. This morning Walter got a fine team and carriage and we went for a drive to the "fort." It is now used as a Soldiers' Home.
It is beautiful here now because of the abundance of rain. We got back about 2 P.M. and asked Walter to have dinner with us. As we came out of the dining room whom should we meet but Smith. He was in town on business and heard we were here. He will meet us tomorrow at Spearville Station.

The Stereopticon Lecture Tour was winding down, but there was still one lecture arranged for the next week. They planned to spend two weeks at Smith's in Spearville, and then a day or two with M.F. Lawrence and at MacPherson's.

Irrigated farms in the area were worth $40 to $50 an acre, but they learned that many fine farms had been mortgaged as high as they could go and then abandoned when the mortgage ran out. Harvey called it *a land of boom and depression, magnificent with water and of little value without rain or irrigation.* Nevertheless he was soon seriously considering bidding on a property to be sold at the foreclosure of a $300 mortgage, June 23. It had cost Smith $1,000 in exchange property, but Smith thought it could be bought for half the mortgage and costs or even less. Harvey was ready to risk $200, but did not think he would be tempted to go higher. He felt the house in the rear of the property was worth $200, even though there were many empty houses around. With the current rains and a couple of more wet seasons or the big ditch that would probably develop soon, he believed the place would boom again. They already had some interest down in Fowler which they planned to visit but felt prospects were very poor. Rebecca's remark was, *I dont suppose my $1000 investment is worth very much.* Rebecca's father had given each of his grown children a farm. Rebecca's was the now famous Catskill Game Farm. A farmer ran it for them. Grandpa built a pond and ran a pipe down to the farmer's kitchen, but he let it get clogged up with mud and stay that way. However, the pond is still part of the Game Farm. The Wardle children spent many happy days visiting there. I often drove with Grandpa for the day and occasionally the family stayed over in the south end of the farmhouse, which Grandma retained so she could go out there and paint the mountains, still a favorite pasttime of hers. She had studied art at the Charlotteville Seminary.

Walter Pine, who eventually became a doctor and started a hospital, came up from Dodge City to visit them at Spearville. He *liked driving fine horses better than mixing pills.* His half sister, Ruth Pine Disney, trained as a nurse at his hospital. (She is my age and has a son Robert also. He was in charge of all the installations for listening to outer space during the Geo-Physical Year. Of the many remote installations, the only places he did not go to personally were the North and South poles.)

Ruth's brother, Howard, is a retired attorney. He lives in Santa Barbara, California, and is involved in researching the Pine genealogy.

Rebecca wrote home:

The little baby here is good as can be. The children are nice and bright and especially fond of their father. Their mother is a very pleasant lady and Lulu, Smith's oldest is a very sweet.

The country round about looks much better than it did when I was here before; the prairies are all green and beautiful. More of the land is cultivated; the crops look good.

Her vivid description of that earlier visit via Chicago in 1883, tells of a night sleeping under a wagon on the prairie. Her brother Smith, who had lost his wife in a terrible fire, had decided to teach school at Duck Creek about 20 miles from his home. So Rebecca got there just in time to help move, settle, keep house for him and his two motherless children, and make a simple one-room house on the prairie a cozy home for the winter. This letter belongs here even if written eight years earlier.

A fast train from Albany reached Chicago in 22 hours and two hours later, Uncle David Scofield met me at the station at Elgin. A five minute drive and we were in his pleasant, hospitable home, just in time to attend a grand missionary meeting. The speakers were two ladies from India, whom Uncle David entertained at his home. Eighty years old, he is enthusiastic about missions and has a library full of papers and magazines on the subject. He is working hard to establish a school for training and education of young women for medical service in India.

More than 20 years later I was to be impressed always with Grandma's own bedroom whose spacious walls were covered with pictures of Methodist missionaries. She seemed to know them all by name and what they did. Her tables and bookcase were crammed with missionary magazines and literature. For years and years she was president of the Missionary Society of the Catskill Methodist Church. It often met in her parlor in the Cherry Hill House.

The Chicago visit in 1883 was crowded with concerts, a fine temperance meeting, *essays written and read with great credit by local women,* a drive around the extensive and beautiful grounds of the State Insane Asylum, a visit to the Elgin Watch Factory, where 1,900 workers made 1,200 watches daily. There was a Chicago Museum and Lincoln Park to visit.

Shortly before leaving for Kansas, she wrote home of a

walk along the shore of Lake Michigan, nearly a mile, I guess, to visit Potter Palmer and the new house he is building. The lake was just lovely.

Potter Palmer came from our own little Potter's Hollow at the northern end of our Catskill Mountains. He was the owner of the famous Chicago hotel, the Palmer House.

Today Aunt Lizzie and I are painting a little but get on rather slowly because we go out a great deal. There are no end of places to go here.

You do not mention how the new lecture room on the church is getting on. How about the organ?

Years later, Grandma gave me a painting of Lake Michigan. I fancy it had its beginning at this time. Her easel was always up in her room.

Seeing the 500 new houses being built and all these other happenings she attended must have accentuated the contrast, when a few days later she would experience a very primitive existence in the prairie state her brother had chosen as his home. When Rebecca saw her brother, his ten year-old daughter, Lulu, and fourteen-year-old son Walter, in their prairie home, she felt the object of her long journey had been attained.

I despair of making you home folks see how a prairie looks with its little houses dotted here and there. They have two to four rooms, and occasionally a cellar, but never a garret. Stove pipes go straight through the roof, protected by tin. Cactus is very handsome, particularly the prickly pear cactus. Cattle feed on buffalo grass and are sleek and fat.

Smith had already started to teach at Duck Creek. Since there was no school at Spearville, he decided to take the motherless children with him. He hired a one-room house one mile from the schoolhouse. His brother-in-law, Glennie Lawrence, helped Rebecca and the children gather together what household goods would be needed to take to Duck Creek.

Imagine us with Glennie having the household goods in the lumber wagon and leading a cow, a slow cow, behind the wagon. Walter, Lulu and I followed in the buggie. (All wagons are "buggies" here except lumber wagons.) We started to find Duck Creek, having a good road part of the way and then only a faint trail. Delayed by rain and then some needed repairs at Spearville, it got dark early with the clouded skies.

Glennie said we did not need to go so slowly as he with the cow. My reply was, "Since the road is new to all of us and landmarks few, I think we will stay together."

Rebecca enjoyed going through the Prairie Dog Town, only a short distance from Spearville, which was a station on the railroad by then. There were about 20 prairie dogs, 3 owls, and happily no rattlesnakes. Late in the afternoon they crossed the old Santa Fe Trail used by travellers and freighters until the railroad came through. They came to a very bad draw, as the dry bed of a creek is called. It took a long time to get across and up the bank. It was getting very dark; and they were still seven miles from Duck Creek, with only the faintest trail. Walter now went first with the lantern, Glennie with the load and the cow, and Lulu and Rebecca in the buggie. Rebecca thought Walter should ride, and she gave him the reins. Rebecca sat way at the end of the seat and held the lantern as low as possible to see the trail. Duck Creek did not appear. Rebecca called out:

"Glennie, have you any idea where we are?"

"Not in the least," he replied. *"We need to get further West, but we cant find the trail. We better stop where we are. We might go in the wrong direction. If it rains we are as well off under the wagon as in it."*

We picketed our horses and cow and since we had a rather late lunch and had passed a watermelon patch, we decided to prepare immediately for the night.

Taking our strawbed and putting it under the wagon, and fastening an old quilt up as a wind breaker at the side, bringing the buggy up along side, putting underneath it a camping blanket and featherbed, getting more blankets, pillows etc., putting sugar and salt and other things likely to perish in the rain under the wagon, we regarded our work as finished, and retired to our apartments. I took off my hat and tied it to the reach, put an extra shawl over my shoulders and another over my head and laid down to sleep. A strong east wind was blowing a mist in my face. All I could do was draw the shawls and blankets closer and go to sleep.

After a while I was aroused by the sound of something treading around and making a sort of snuffing and snorting sound. I raised my head cautiously and there was one of our horses near my pillow.

After calling several times I succeeded in awaking Glennie, and in a few moments the camp was again quiet. There was a bag of oats near my head.

Rebecca fell asleep again only to be awakened several times by the barking of the dogs in the distance. Finally at dawn they awakened and began preparations for *our forward march. Our toilets were made still not having a drop of water.* They had no idea where the sun was and counted on Walter's pocket compass to head them aright. They found Mr. Richardson's where Smith was boarding and had a nice breakfast of biscuits, wild duck, wild plums, and coffee. Mrs. Richardson inquired if they had been afraid. Did they not hear the wolves? They had been right in the region of prairie wolves and wild cats. *I've no doubt you heard them and not dogs,* she told Rebecca.

The school was one room, but *the finest in the county, and paid the best, $45 a month.* Smith would teach for three months and maybe longer. George Some-

body was going to care for Smith's cattle back home.

The one-room house he rented had no cellar, but it was plastered. Unfortunately, so was the floor and Lulu and her aunt scooped that up. The school was one mile away. They had brought extra stove pipe to go through the roof, but a chimney had been put in which *placed us immediately with the aristocracy.* Even plastered walls were not common. They used the rope that had been tied around the old trunk and hung curtains as partitions for the night. In sight of the house were 1,000 sheep tended by two little girls 10 and 12 years old. Rebecca soon decided that with a little more settling, Smith would be very cozy for the winter.

On a trip to Dodge City they saw a train of freighters coming up from Indian Territory. The area had been set aside for five civilized tribes after the Louisiana Purchase and became Oklahoma. There were twenty wagons fastened together two by two. The first had a high box and cover *like the emigrant wagons.* They were drawn by five span of mules each. The driver of each pair of wagons sat on a mule nearest the wagon.

A lumber wagon took them to church in Dodge City, *and a nice one, too,* said Grandma, *It had a spring seat which I got.* There were about forty in church. The minister pursuaded them to stay to afternoon Sunday School, so they were divided up two by two and "Brother Pine and his sister will go with me," said the minister. The room they all used was parlor, sitting-room, study, library, and bedroom. There was one more sleeping room and a kitchen. The walls were papered not plastered, and it cost $13 a month.

When it became time for Rebecca to start toward home and look after her own family, Lulu begged, *Dont go, Auntie. Carrie is there and we have nobody.* Rebecca made a visit at MacPherson's 100 miles further east in Kansas. Her last letter remarked,

People on the frontier make the best of everything, more than Easterners. Children learn to ride early and bright young girls care for herds of cattle.

These old memories of 1883 Rebecca now left behind as they began to head home. Most of the news of the current Kansas visit was not in the letters home but saved to share when they reached there. Rebecca writes from Lyons, Kansas, on July 3, 1891. A pleasant visit with Mr. and Mrs. Houston, (Mary Shaffer Britt) who joined the Van Gelders in a visit to F. Lawrence, included a thirteen-mile drive over the prairie, delightful both in the early morning and on the return after five o'clock. They saw Mrs. Herman Weber's son there. These family names persist to this day in Greene County, New York, from which so many migrated west. They had seen Larnard which seemed an even more pleasant place. There was plentiful fruit — cherries, plums, peaches, apricots, and some apples, as well as nearly every kind of vegetable, doing well with all the rain.

After dinner at noon, Papa and Arthur went out and returned with a fine team of horses and two-seated carriage. We went first to the salt mines near here, then out about the prairie past a great field of corn and wheat. Harvesting, two weeks' late, is just beginning. We go to McPherson this morning and will stay there until Tuesday. Then to Topeka and Kansas City. After we leave McGifferts, I shall be ready to go home, but Papa wants to stop quite a few places, so I suppose it will be the last of the month anyway before we get home.

      Mother

Information is more than a bit sketchy from Kansas City on. Rebecca wrote a long letter to her Sunday School class which Maimie Elemendorf would read to them. There is a mere postcard stamped in Chicago, but no mention of any visits to her Uncle David Scofield. If still alive, he would have been 88 years old.

Chautauqua, with or without all three "u"s, and situated on its beautiful lake south of Buffalo, afforded time for a letter home.

Chatauqua
July 20, 1891

Dear Carrie,
Papa and Arthur have gone out to get some photos if the light is good enough. I am packed and ready to start. We reached here Saturday evening and went to a Bible Study of the book of Ruth at 9 A.M. this morning. Sunday services were at eleven with a good organ, good choir and a piano. Papa and Arthur went to another Bible class at 2 P.M. by Lewis Miller of Akron, Ohio, President of the Chautauqua Association.
The Primary class was so crowded I went to a vesper service instead. It was not quite as good as I expected. At the close the leader made a prayer so long I got tired and so did all the rest, I judge from appearances. I thought of Mr. Matthews who prayed, "Lord, help us to pray short." In the evening we all went again to song service which was very fine, and we had an address which Papa said was the best of all by Mr. Montgomery of Buffalo.

This final letter of this group found in my attic closed with the news of arriving in Niagara that night. There they hoped for letters that would help them plan when they would arrive home. There is no intimation that they stopped for another short visit with any Van Gelder relatives around Seneca Lake, New York, their first visiting area on the way south and west.

PART VI
BETWEEN TRIPS

Between trips when the seven-month Stereopticon Lecture Tour ended the summer of 1891 in Catskill, this entrepreneur on the maternal side of the family already had plans. Grandpa hoped to do more with his lectures *and new slides.* He was very involved in community affairs. Arthur had missed most of his junior year. When he graduated from Catskill High School in 1892, he entered the School of Mines of Columbia University. His parents also decided to go to New York City. In addition to some lectures, Grandpa researched the Van Gelder genealogy from its beginnings in New Amsterdam. Arthur Pine Van Gelder compiled all the information in 1945 after he retired to co-author a **History of the High Explosive Industry.**

That first year in college, Arthur appeared as manager on a flyer advertising the illustrated lectures and helped his father set up equipment. There are records of some lectures held in schools. The most flattering report came from the New York Genealogical and Biographical Society Meeting.

Earliest known ancestors went back to Hendrick Van Gelder, (1706ca-1753), who came to Greene County after the Revolution. The earliest of three researched lines date back to 1630, and there is unconfirmed evidence of some connection with some of them.

The Pynes (later Pine) and Van Gelders were not known to each other for some years, but both had their farms in Manhattan and Westchester areas fought over by the Revolutionary armies. Both arrived in different parts of Greene County (then part of Albany County) about 1791.

The 1890s were busy years. The Chicago World's Fair in 1893 drew members of the family. I delayed my mother's visit there by arriving naked and unnamed on August 7, 1893. I eventually saw some of the Exhibition buildings which had not been razed, when my father sold Locomobiles and later Fords throughout the West and South. The family moved to Oak Park, near Chicago, where the last Wardle baby, Charles Athow Wardle, Jr., was born. This was the eighth child, but little Ralph had died. The cradle had been kept rocking by Constance in 1895. She studied

T RAVELS,

S CENERY

AND

H ISTORY

⁕ Graphically Described ⁕

AND

⁕ Artistically Illustrated ⁕

BY JAMES H. VAN GELDER, M.A., OF NEW YORK.

JAMES H. VAN GELDER, M.A.

What is said about his Illustrated Lectures by the pastors of churches and by the newspapers in various American cities.

A course of Illustrated Lectures of the highest order may be arranged at reasonable rates.

Also competent stereopticon operators furnished.

For Terms, Dates, &c.,

Address the Manager,

MR. AUTHUR P. VAN GELDER,

School of Mines,

Columbia College,

New York.

Flyer for Arthur Pine Van Gelder's Lecture Bureau in New York City.

John Pine, Jr., my great-great-grandfather. He moved to the Wilderness near South Cairo when both armies of the Revolution raided his father's farm in Westchester County. He was an early supporter of the church and all public enterprises. He married Esther Sutherland.

Constance Wardle. Debut as Aïda at Brooklyn Academy of Music.

Charles Athow Wardle, Jr.

Carrie Van Gelder Wardle, Oak Park, Illinois

Constance, Philip, and Alma, all under three years.

Charles A. Wardle when an agent for the Locomobile and later for Ford cars. Early 1900s.

voice in Italy and debuted as Aïda in the Brooklyn Academy of Music. A planned debut in Italy was cancelled when she was called home by mother's death in 1923.

The cradle was next rocked by Philip Van Gelder Wardle whom after his two years of chemistry in Cornell, the government kept glued to Uncle Arthur's high explosive plant in World War I and who liked to confess he played hookey from school to play baseball with some biggies in town. There was a tiny baby Alma who was carried on a pillow. The three were photographed the day before Constance was 3 years old. Alma died at 16 after a sad illness which lasted from Christmas Day until Good Friday. Rheumatic fever was not readily diagnosed in those early pre-penicillin days.

The earliest memory I have is of Dr. Elliott sitting beside the bed where I was suffering from terrible leg pains. The next recollection is of an almost impossible climb up steep little Walnut Street. I was so tired I can feel it yet. Yet it was never diagnosed, even later when I could attend school in third and fifth grades only half days. Years later when my husband died in 1950 now common tests had not reached Catskill as a routine matter. Only a few weeks after his death, the volunteer health association of which I was executive director was promoting a doctors' teaching clinic. Help that could only be given in earlier days by family and neighbors is today given by professionals and volunteers with excellent results. Volunteerism, not customary in other countries, saves U.S.A. millions of dollars. Other countries leave all that to government as a study tour to Europe in 1953 proved to me.

The next early memory was of the blowing up of the Maine, the famous battleship of the Spanish-American War. When McKinley was assassinated, I have a vivid recollection of my five-year-old self going alone to Grandma's front parlor and squeezing out in secret some genuine tears, and there was no TV to help build up the emotions. There was Grandpa Wardle's funeral to recall in 1899.

The Rev. John Knight Wardle, M.D., had retired but still preached in the area. When he took dinner with us on such occasions, he often went up to the balcony off the attic of this Odyssey with a glass of milk and to my surprise a cigar in his hand. Mother too went up there during thunderstorms and watched the storm sweep over the Hudson Valley and encompass Church's Castle now known as the famed Olana. It was built like a Persian Castle in mosaic by Thomas Cole's only pupil, Frederick Church, a famous artist of the Hudson River School of Art. The view from Olana is superb, giving the whole sweep of the Catskill Mountains and several miles of the Hudson River.

Grandpa Wardle was considered stern in manner, but his letters to the children of his first marriage show him to be warm, loving, and wise. One letter expressed sorrowful regret when *none of my older children came home for Thanksgiving*. The second marriage was not happy for him or his children.

The most interesting of the letters from this branch of the family was one from 1880 written by Frank after a long trip around South America. He had two sisters, Elizabeth and Florence. Elizabeth, the eldest, had been keeping house for him, possibly during the years he was a minister. The letter was written to Florence, the Auntie Floy, a teacher, who often lived

Florence (Auntie Floy) Wardle

Church's Castle, now called Olana, Persian type with mosaic. Built by Frederic Church, Hudson River artist. Copied by Frank W. Wardle from J.H. Van Gelder glass plates.

with us. Frank was very fond of her and extremely generous, putting her through Cortland Normal School in 1882, and a special course at Cornell, besides a travel tour to San Francisco to a teachers' convention.

Our voyage was a long one from the 30th of November to the 29th of December . . . The voyage has shown me many entirely new phases of life as it exists in the tropics! Flowers are blooming and fruits are ripening. People clothed in the lightest of white linen suits . . . I spent 2 days in the quaint old Spanish city of Panama where for 300 years moss has been growing on the tile housetops . . . Our party bought some 200 pineapples — some costing only 3¢ each — oranges 50¢ for 125 — great bunches of bananas — over 100 for 25¢

At San Jose (Mexico) the sailors caught a large tiger shark 17 ft. long . . . Near Acapulco we saw several grand volcanoes in active irruption . . .

A letter to sister Lizzie in 1881 describes San Francisco as California Mexican in style.

Sunday is a great gala day. Every saloon, gambling house, billiard hall is open. Even Americans hardly know when Sunday comes . . . My first day in town became acquainted with a gentleman . . . During our talk (it was Saturday) he said "Tomorrow Mr. Wardle I'll drive you out about 15 miles and give you some fine quail shooting." When I

told him that I usually observed Sunday in a different manner from that he seemed astonished and said "Why everyone goes shooting or driving Sunday, even the minister."

In a letter to sister Lizzie in March, 1881, he wrote: *In regard to your seeking employment in one of the government departments I very much prefer that you will not do so. There is no necessity for it and I do not wish you exposed in the many ways I know government employees are. . . All I want you to do my dear girl is to be just as happy and useful as you can — improving the time in faithful self culture — fitting yourself thoroughly for whatever sphere in life God in his providence may in the future call you to . . .*

He also listed books to read — marked in red in the letter.

A letter of recommendation written in 1887 from a principal and superintendent of schools in Middletown, New York, tells us much about Florence.

Miss Wardle was a superior scholar and completed the course in our teachers' training class with marked success . . . [She] has since taught with success for about five years . . . would be a decided acquisition to any one of our higher seminaries.

She did hold such a job.

On December 23, 1887, Uncle Frank was in Brooklyn. He said in a letter to sister Florence that as a Christmas present he would send her tickets to Cali-

To California and Return $200!

HO! FOR CALIFORNIA.

A SPECIAL EXCURSION will leave New York City from New York to San Francisco on July 5, stopping over Sunday in Chicago. The round trip ticket, one half the regular fare, is

$91.75.

The plan of the trip in going is as follows:—
One week between Chicago and Salt Lake City.
Spend the second Sunday in Salt Lake City.
Stop one day at Manitou, giving an opportunity to ascend Pike's Peak, and take in the beauties of the Garden of the Gods.
Pass over the Denver and Rio Grande R. R. by daylight, stopping over night at a convenient place between Pueblo and Salt Lake City.
The D. & R. G. R. R. is famous for its magnificent scenery; it passes over the backbone of the Rocky Mountains, and gives one such a view of mountain scenery as cannot be obtained anywhere else in Europe or N. America. This is the unanimous verdict of all who are thoroughly familiar with the scenery of both continents.

COST OF TRIP FROM NEW YORK AND RETURN.

Ticket (round trip,)	$91.75
Association Membership,	2.00
Meals going and coming,	15.00
Extra cost between Denver and Salt Lake City,	10.00
Sleeper going and returning,	21.00
Other expenses,	5.25
	$200.00

☞ THE EXPENSES OF THE ROUND TRIP WILL NOT EXCEED $200.

The expense of meals on the way, can be reduced by providing lunches.
Other expenses will depend upon the places

MARSHALL PASS.

Flyer describing trip taken by Florence Wardle to a teachers conference.

fornia to a

grand rally of all leading pedagogues in San Francisco, July 17-20. . . provided that among the 500 ladies and gentlemen who are going you find you have a friend, which I presume is a forgone conclusion as all the leading luminaries in the educational world with their wives and sisters are going and it will be the greatest educational gathering ever held in the U.S. [Round trip half regular fare $91.75]

As you will have no expenses connected with the trip let me suggest you squander some of your hard earned dollars on some thoroughly nice and first class traveling suits — for 6 weeks association with the same people you will need 3 or 4 at least to vary the monotony. . .

A letter to Floy, January 25, 1897, tells of a new venture:

My little business opens up favorably and already I have secured the contract to advertise the largest new office building in N.Y. "The Bowery Green" cost $3,000,000, 3,000 tenants.

I wish you could see my nice little office, solid oak furnishings and floor — pale nile green walls — rugs and my fine old desk from Venice — one of the prettiest little offices in this town. I have a 50-year-old maid as my stenographer and typewriter — smart as chain lightning. I chose her in preference to a "Venus De Milo" who applied at the same time. . .

We have tiny after-dinner coffee spoons made of old Norwegian coins, and a server and sugar spoon all with twist handles from Uncle Frank's London trip.

It is difficult for me to figure just how soon the oldest and the youngest brothers were both seeking treasures in the West. Uncle Frank wrote from the Gold Mining Camp in 1898-1899. Charles added the sale of Locomobiles to his Phoenix Life Insurance agencies in the Hudson Valley area. On the stationery Frank is listed as secretary and assistant treasurer.

Then letters began to come to Carrie and to each of his children weekly from Texas and California. In the spring and summer of 1901 he was setting up automobile dealerships and wrote Gerald:

As you are the man of the family while papa is away you shall have the first letter.

Early experiences with a fast-growing business selling horseless carriages were both encouraging and disappointing. Letters that Uncle Frank included in the Genealogy tell of Charles' venture:

Entered employ of Ford Motor Co. of Detroit. [First sold Locomobile in Catskill] salary of $2,500. Then went on tour setting up agencies. He did too well by them and sold out entire output one year ahead and as a reward on December 31, 1903, Ford told him they had no further need of a sales manager and so dismissed him. A shabby treatment with Ford Co. 8 months.

In letter to brother Frank, Charlie states

We have sold 1600 machines which have paid a net profit of $45,000 on only a capital of $100,000. Of $72,000 I have sold prior to May 1st, this Co. has only delivered about $4,000. They have fallen down completely in deliveries and orders are being cancelled for non-delivery.

Carrie had written from Oak Park, Illinois, as early as January, 1900. She was as always writing poems, articles, or diaries but reports rejections. I have an article that was published in the **Ladies Home Journal** about Sunday afternoon activities for children, an art she had practiced happily on her children. There are poems published in the **Kintergarten Magazine** even before her friend Bertha Johnston was editor. Boxes remain of her diaries, poems for us children, and articles on a variety of topics.

Letters from Frank and the others were written to his brother John who worked in Brooklyn. He left home at 14 years and had many difficult years. Frank paid a year's tuition for Alfred at a theological seminary. Though he did not continue in the tradition of being in the ministry, Alfred held very fine positions in the YMCA, and was state secretary of the New Hampshire YMCA in Concord.

It is his grandson, Alfred H. Wardle, who has done some interesting research on the Wardle side in England. Disappointed that the Wardle name he bore was traced back only to his great-great-grandfather, he has found Wardle or Wuerdle towns as far back as the 1300s, but without confirmation of its being part of our line. A visit to England netted him two more generations, and he is not finished.

His father was Warren Wardle, who summered on Cape Cod where my other first cousins live — children of Alfred — Elizabeth Wardle Nickerson, Ethelwyn Wardle Notoro, and John Knight Wardle, Jr. I have a fascinating letter and letterhead from Africa where John found traces of an old Wardle and his chemist or drug stores.

Though earlier relations with Grandpa Wardle's second family were difficult, it seems we younger Wardles have happy memories of Aunt Emma and Aunt Ethelwyn, who had excellent educations to be teachers. Uncle Harry and Uncle Arthur Wardle owned the Wardle Drug Store in Hudson, New York, for many years and Arthur was Dean of the Albany College of Pharmacy and a member of the Hudson School Board. Uncle Will was less well known but was successful in business.

Back in Catskill and New York City Charles was again in the insurance business. He also took more interest in the Water Works as Grandpa Van Gelder aged. In 1910 he wrote to Carrie:

I had planned to come home this week, but on account of a water works matter will postpone it till after election day. We have a satisfactory report from engineers and it is now up to Mr. Ferguson more recently interested and myself to find a market for the power.

This was about the end of active promotion of Lake Kiskatom Water Works Electric Power, when finally voted down.

Letterheads Tell Tales, Too

CHARLES A. WARDLE,
General Agent
HUDSON RIVER COUNTIES.
Office 330 Main St...
CATSKILL, N.Y.
Telphone 99-2.

THE *"Locomobile"* COMPANY
OF AMERICA.

Main office of Company
II Broadway, New York.
Works: Bridgeport, Conn.

CATSKILL, N.Y._____190__

THE CROWN PERFUMERY COMPANY

Telegraphic Address—BRIGHTNESS, LONDON. LONDON PARIS, NEW YORK

Show Rooms & Offices,
112 & 113, FORE STREET,
LONDON, E.C. 140 FIFTH AVENUE Sep 9 1895

ESTABLISHED 1872

TRADE MARK.

1ST PRIZE MEDALS AT ALL EXHIBITIONS. RETAIL, 177, NEW BOND STREET, W.

NEW YORK OFFICE,
160 FIFTH AVENUE

HIGHEST HONORS
CHICAGO EXHIBITION.

Dear Charlie

Since your letter of 24th ult about the young man wishing to Study Pharmacy here I have been making some inquiry about among the Druggists with the result that in the present depressed condition of business I can find no one who has any position to offer him —

Our special Drug Salesman has just returned from Canada & will now go out among all the Retail Druggists and I will also ask him to inquire and do all in his power to find something

Hope you and Carrie and the family are all very well and especially that Carrie has fully recovered. We are still at Lauchmont & shall remain until I know definitely what the future has in store for me. As yet Thomson says nothing and has not intimated when he will come over but about the last of this month probably.

With much love — Yours as ever,

F. A. Wardle.

Ford Motor Company

AUTOMOBILE MANUFACTURERS.

JOHN S. GRAY, PRESIDENT.
HENRY FORD, VICE PREST. & GENL. MGR.
ALEX. Y. MALCOMSON, TREASURER.
JAMES COUZENS, SECRETARY & BUSINESS MGR.

WORKS & OFFICE,
688-692 MACK AVENUE.

Detroit, Michigan, Nov. 13, 1903.

Mr. C. A. Wardle,

    C i t y .

Dear Sir;

    In consultation with the directors to-day, a resolution was passed to the effect that, as our product is practically sold for the coming year, that our plans will have to be modified in regard to yourself, and the resolution was to the effect that we should pay you from now to the first of January and allow you to take the time to look after your own interests; at the same time assuring you of our best wishes and good will.

    Any assistance that we can lend you or recommendation that we can give you will be most cheerfully granted and we assure you that the decision taken is simply because of the rapid sale and provision for our output that has been made during the past few weeks.

    Wishing you every success and assuring you of our best wishes, I remain for the Board of Directors,

        Yours sincerely,

        John S. Gray

        President.

FRANCIS R. WARDLE

GENERAL

Advertising

Ten Years Experience
in Successful Introduction
and Advertising.

Connection with the leading
Advertisement Writers
Designers and Experts.

Plans and Estimates
Furnished without Charge.

CATALOGUE MAKING, A SPECIALTY

156 FIFTH AVENUE

PRESBYTERIAN BUILDING, 20TH ST
ROOM 403 NEW YORK.

Feb 8/97

Dear Hoy,

The work of getting my new business started and a week of illness both for Isabel and myself, explain my non writing.

I send under separate cover copies of the N.Y. Evg Post and the "Soul in Distress" in which you will see my first & 1000 contract for advertising the "Bowling Green" Office Building —

And now good bye my dear, with love to you ever.

Yours affectionately
    F. R. W.

PART VII
GOLD MINING IN OREGON AND TRAVELS IN THE FAR EAST

A man mined for gold in the rugged mile high mountains of Oregon, and two years later found himself in China in the middle of the ferocious Boxer Rebellion. Francis Robert Wardle and his wife Isabel wrote letters back home telling of their dramatic adventures.

Uncle Frank was the most venturesome of the Wardle brothers. He was the oldest son of John Knight Wardle who had arrived in the United States from England in 1846 with his father, Hugh Wardle, a druggist. The young son John was 18 years old and put himself through medical school. He established a good practice in New York City, but soon gave up medicine for the ministry. This was a move he could hardly escape with his own Wesleyan convictions and his mother's ancestry. His mother, Ann Eliza West, was a daughter of Robert Athow West, A.M., and was from a long line of Methodist ministers and missionaries some of whom were co-workers with John Wesley. The Rev. John Knight Wardle, M.D., my grandfather, came to Greene County as pastor of the Catskill Methodist Episcopal Church in 1879-81. My father, Charles Athow Wardle, was only 14 years of age. His mother had died when he was three. He broke away from the step-mother and step-brothers and sisters and worked in a drygoods store. Catskill was his home most of the remainder of his life. Thus the letters with many fascinating experiences got into my attic.

Uncle Frank's first trip as secretary of the Jupiter Gold Mining Company was described in a letter to his brother Charles dated June 18, 1898.

I have just returned from Kirby, Josephine County from a six days' trip on horseback, fifty miles south of here to and among the Siskiyou Mountains separating Oregon from California, where I went to examine two properties we own there — one a gold-bearing on Althouse Creek (400 acres yielding $10,000 to the acre) and the other 1000 acres of copper ledge, etc. I found both properties solid and of genuine merit and unquestionably of enormous value, but needing capital for fuller development.

The Althouse Gold-bearing placer is 4200 feet up in the Siskiyou Mountains, in the middle of a splendid forest of giant pines and surrounded by the finest mountain peaks and deep valleys imaginable. I really saw nothing finer in Switzerland or Norway.

Some of the trail was ticklish, especially rounding sharp mountain corners — just room enough for a pony to place his feet — a stumble would have sent us down a 3000 foot precipice. Our guide

Rev. John Knight Wardle, M.D., my grandfather.

Ann Eliza West Wardle, my grandmother

and packer expected to see me, a tenderfoot, get rattled at some point so when I rode quietly without remark he said to Col. Straight, "Well, he's game." Coming back Thursday he put me through a further test of nerves by galloping his

Francis Robert Wardle

horse along a 3500 foot precipice in a really terrific place. My horse insisted on following at the same speed. I would not willingly have done this foolish thing but I had no choice and so for nearly a mile said nothing. When it was over I was bathed in a cold sweat. The guide let himself loose with more heartiness than he had before shown, "There are only five men in this country who would have dared do that." I did not tell him my feat was entirely involuntary. Do not mention it to Isabel. I think it tried my self-control rather more than anything else that has ever happened in my journeyings.

I panned gold out of the gravel — some old placer ground that was from prehistoric times. I saw about $5000 the former owner had taken out this Spring — also bought some water rights ... I have thoroughly tested all over the claims. All we need is proper capital.

I shall soon return to Evanston and try to raise the money we need. When this reaches you I shall be near my 46th birthday, a pretty old man to be wandering around the wild mountains of Oregon as a gold seeker. But I never was much of a stay-at-home.

A full page ad had been printed earlier in the Dobbs Ferry **Register,** November 4, 1897, before he went West. He enclosed a copy of it to his brother with the instructions:

Take out ads in both papers in Middletown. I want either a whole page or nothing. You can offer whatever amount of stock is necessary up to 50

shares to each paper. We have a big deal here, but as yet dont know if it will amount to anything.

During this first scouting trip to Oregon, he had left his wife, Isabel, in Evanston, Illinois , with her brother, Judge Church. Frank wrote:

Evanston is a charming place on Lake Michigan, and Isabel is fond of her brother's interesting family of nearly grown young people — and they have a large circle of friends.

From New York to Portland, 3000 miles, for only $40, instead of $80, he gloated when he reached Grant's Pass, the end of the railroad travel, June 8, 1898. Thence it was 30 miles by stage to Kerby, their Assay Office and headquarters of their operation.

A tremendous adventure was in store for Aunt Isabel when these two tenderfeet set out over the many miles to camp. She had not been on a horse since she was a child. Colorful descriptions of this trip to camp, their rustic home, and the Christmas supper to which all the men in camp were invited were written to Florence, her sister-in-law.

I was very glad to get your good letter of home news, every little particular is more eagerly read when one is shut in a far away wilderness like this. The strange sense of loneliness and isolation, way up in these mountain peaks, each one shut in by all the others — so there is no view — just a little glimpse across a deep gulch over a thousand feet below us to another peak — the one directly opposite — so cold and bleak always because the sun never shines on it all Winter long; while we on our side, have a flood of sunshine all day when it is clear — and there are many such days.

Isabel Church Wardle, Uncle Frank's wife.

Jupiter
Printers Error

THE

~~Juniper~~ **Jupiter Gold Mining Co.**

Dobb's Ferry, N.Y.
November 4, 1897

(OF THE STATE OF OREGON).

CAPITAL STOCK, - $1,000,000

In Shares of TEN DOLLARS Each.

For sale at par, issued full paid and non-assessable, with a

BONUS OF 25 PER CENT. IN STOCK
EVERY THREE MONTHS.

For the first year while the works are in process of construction.

OFFICERS.

HENRY HARMON NEILL, President.   JOHN ROLLIN CHURCH, Treasurer.

GEORGE DAVID LINN, Vice President.   FRANCIS R. WARDLE, Secretary

Treasurer's Office Dobbs Ferry Register, Dobbs Ferry, N. Y. 56 Beaver St., Room 96, New York.   **Secretary's Office** 156 Fifth Avenue, Room 403, New York

---

We came on December 14. The day began with a drizzling rain, which stopped shortly and up here had been snow. We left the valley at 8 A.M., just daylight, drove four miles then got on our trusty horses. Remember I have never been on horseback since I was a child. Immediately the climb began, up, up, crawling along steep sides of mountains — then down again to cross a tiny bridge of logs, over the stream and on up again. Are you dizzy? Then look not to one side for you will see your trail is only a narrow path beaten out by horses feet, and like the mountain slopes down many thousands of feet sometimes, a misstep — and you are lost, for there is nothing to catch and hold you. But these beasts are surefooted. It is wonderful to watch them pick their way! At last comes a climb straight up a sheer 1000 feet. The horses stop to rest every few minutes — then on again — until a log cabin comes in sight all snow covered. Surrounded by huge Sugar Pines and Firs and Larches, all with a mantle of snow. A bare little place we come to, for of furniture we have bought just five plain chairs, and three cots! The carpenter made us a table for the main room, another for the kitchen — everything awaited the Mistress' contriving out of packing boxes.

Behold then a bare room, fireless even — as we had arrived some two or three hours sooner than Uncle Frank had thought we would, so that preparations that he had ordered had not been begun. But soon we had a great fire on our big hearth — another in an airtight stove, and we were warm in a jiffy.

The first thing I did was to throw a piece of red felt over the table for a cover (my boxes were all opened) and our spirits rose at once. Always carry a red felt table cover into the wilderness!!! Then in a short time the camp cook gave us a good dinner, and we went to work in earnest, made up our beds, unpacked most needful things and as early as we could went to bed. We slept warm and well. Uncle Frank with great wisdom and forethought, had had heavy light grey building paper put over the logs in all the rooms, and a ceiling made of unbleached muslin, so we do not have to heat the peak of the roof, and the rooms are much warmer and cozier and lighter. Day by day saw comforts grow. On three sides of the main room (20 feet square) I had shelves put up, one set draped with cretonne for a cupboard, another some pieces of red felt cut into fringe and tacked along the edges, each shelf covered with enameled cloth — this holds pictures of all of you with more in wire frames on each side — my clock and one or two tiny things I brought along in my trunk . . . another shelf — books and work, etc. . . . Some other shelves are devoted to business papers entirely.

There are two bedrooms ten feet square — one has two windows. Each has a curtain over the opening into the main room, which is both dining-room and sitting-room. The kitchen proved not quite as dry and warm as we expected, so I did not dare put our maid out there at night, so she has one room. As yet I have made no bureaus but hope to do so out of packing boxes. A shelf and a curtain in the corner make a closet, and I have a little stove that warms my room in the morning very quickly.

Under the double window I have a divan made more roughly than anything you ever saw — the boards are what are called "shakes" made chiefly for shingles and are split right out of some of the magnificent trees — some boards eight feet long, being almost as straight and true as if they came out of a saw mill. On this a mattress covered with pine cone pattern cretonne and a ruffle of the same at the bottom.

Then I made two big pillows out of excelsior and cotton wool and covered them and the bed pillows which I borrow during the day, with turkey red, green and orange cotton goods. Five cent scrim curtains drape each window. A lot of posters Mary sent me are tacked all over the walls, with a few photographs I had. I also made groups of pictures from the papers and magazines, and so the room looks warm and bright and gay.

It is already said to be the best furnished cottage in the county and from what I have seen, I can easily believe it to be true. . . And yet it all took only a little taste and contrivance to bring it about.

As to our household arrangements, I have a most excellent young girl for a Companion, as they are called here, and my good Jessie is entirely unobjectionable and a very good cook — as neat as wax — and very systematic — so I am more than fortunate, if she remains contented. I do all I can

Shares for the Jupiter Gold Mining Co.

to keep her so. I am teaching her typing and she has the use of my sewing machine — eats with us, of course. There are no social distinctions in this country.

Details continue for six pages of single-typed legal size onion skin. Frank had wanted to go alone, but Isabel felt she could bring some graces of home if only her strength was equal to the undertaking.

It is not easy for a woman of my age to begin such a hard life, but with my peculiar difficulties it is especially hard. But I am happy and contented — and dirty as a pig! Our fireplace which sometimes is a joy, at others is but a grief and trial. I am sure I am almost ham colored already and this morning the floor was gray with the ashes thrown through the night. . . Every five minutes I must fill the capacious maw with wood. . . . We keep no fires over night.

How would you like to pack every drop of water used down a steep hill from a ditch and sometimes in this dry season to pack it 500 yards further up? In time we hope to overcome this with a pipe to the house, but that means getting piping and other supplies in from the Pass — 50 miles. Sometimes, as yesterday and today, all is frozen up and we are filling every vessel and pitcher with snow that slowly melts and leaves us so little melted water!

Already today in the undrifted areas there is three feet of snow. For this we are thankful — the more snow, the more gold, and the more that melting snow fills the ditches and washes the gold down the sluice boxes where it is caught in a "riffle" and at certain times is gathered up. This may partly explain to you why the miners do not help themselves — if you cannot understand the inate honesty of these hardy men. They may be and are trusted implicitly. They also have little opportunity the way the system works, but dishonesty rarely exists, here at least.

A high point was the Christmas supper. Everyone came. The camp cook outdid himself. No one missed Santa Claus.

We had all the miners — eight of them, including ten woodchoppers come and take supper with us. I do not believe one of them had ever seen so well-furnished a house!! The camp cook, a very good one, came down bringing extra dishes and table. Putting the two together we had a very good spread of ham, cold chicken, tea biscuit, fresh bread, fried potatoes, tomatoes, squash, and pickles. And then apple and squash pies, stewed peaches, baked apples and two kinds of cake, with a good cup of New York English breakfasttea!!! They all seemed to enjoy the novel condition and if their table manners are not quite up to our standards — they are good honest men, — picturesque in their flannel shirts and blanket coats — some like Joseph's coat of many colors.

This is where Aunt Isabel leaves us on that first Christmas, 1898, at the Jupiter Gold Mines. Under five feet of snow on January 10, 1899, Uncle Frank wrote:

Dear Wardles:

All you'uns back there in Civilization!!

This is the fifteenth day of our latest continuous snow storm. It began two days after Christmas (which was a charming, bright day with the thermometer at 53°) It was ushered in by great winds and a fall of temperature to 18, then the snow began falling — steadily — night and day, day after day, until now we have five feet of it on the levels where it is not drifted and from ten to thirty feet in the drifts. This latter depth is on the crest of Weston Peak almost a thousand feet above us as we are looking out of our front window.

I don't suppose you can hardly realize the isolation from the world. Most of our letters are from ten days to a fortnight old when they reach us, and so are the newspapers. It takes six days from Grant's Pass by Railroad for our Eastern mail — then one stage brings it to Brownstown, 18 miles. This is our nearest Post Office, and there the mail sleeps quietly in a pigeon hole until our packer, old man Sissul, feels inclined to walk up the trail another 11 miles farther — usually once a week, though sometimes after heavy snows we hear nothing for two weeks and more. Absolutely shut in.

We are sheltered by our rough log cabin and warm with two stoves and a big fire place going. There is something like Ten Thousand pounds of provisions in Camp and unlimited firewood — for the cutting. We are not unhappy — quite the contrary for these great snow storms mean "The Miners' Delight." After this snow quits then there will begin to blow the soft warm "Chinnok," a wind coming from the warm Japanese Current that flows along this coast. It will melt the snow, almost like a fire, and then our ditches will fill up with the precious water we have so long been waiting for. Then from the ditches, reservoirs and Hydraulic piping the water will pour down into our "Giant" and "Ground Sluice" and there will flow down through our flumes and riffles a thick, mushlike stream of yellow mud and carrying with it the precious grains of Gold for which we have worked so hard.

Our foreman who has had large experience says there will be some weeks when we shall secure as much gold in one week as many men earn in a year.

All this the Snow Storm means to us — so we are happy, the harder it snows and blows — the more money for this company. All this relates to the "Placer Mining" portion of our business. The

Quartz Mining part is entirely different and involves an expensive Quartz Mill and costly machinery, so we have a Lease pending with a Chicago Syndicate, who will erect such a mill at their own expense and will simply pay us a fixed Royalty on the Output. The Placer mining portion we retain in our own hands and shall operate that part ourselves.

Without going into any more business details — I will only say that we have been fortunate enough to secure and now to own a valuable mining property that has gold in it and so our future is assured. It is personally a great satisfaction to me to know that my confidence in this property — from the very first — has proven well placed and confirmed by the Mining Engineers who have examined it.

Our Log Cabin — 30 x 20, with Kitchen Annex 20 x 10 — was finished Dec 12th — and on Dec 14th I brought Isabel and Miss Masten, the maid of all work — up over the 15 miles of rough mountain trail — all on horseback. Her letter sent to one of her family — will give you many of the details of the trip and our rough mountain home. I wish you could see us here — far up in the wildest and finest mountains of this Coast. It is a strange new life, very different from what we have been living, and yet having a peculiar charm of its own (when it does not storm too long or hard). Ordinarily, I would say the climate is much better than the winter climate of the East — warmer — dryer — and much more agreeable.

On the Average 20 days in every winter month are brilliantly clear and sunshiney and with the thermometer at about 40 degrees — so that we go about without any extra wraps — though we have to wear warm wool underwear all the time. The air has a peculiar quality of tonic dryness and lightness that we did not find when down in the lower Oregon valleys. Our altitude is 5200 feet, almost the topmost crest of the Siskiyou Mountains. We do not find this height oppresses us in any way, except that we can not indulge in very violent exertion, without becoming somewhat short-winded.

As yet Isabel's headaches are not benefitted by the change but I hope they will be before the Spring has passed. Early Spring and Summer in these high mountains are ideally lovely and delightful — a perfect mass of flowers everywhere and a climate like mingled Cream and Champagne — at least so I found it in early June this year, on the occasion of my first visit out here. We write our letters whenever we have time and then set them aside until someone is "going out" — this sometimes means a week or even two weeks waiting before we can mail the letters. We look upon all these things however as a part of the general struggle and sacrifice that we determined to make in order to seize this great opportunity for achieving at a bound what others often struggle a lifetime for, and so we do not complain, but take it all philosophically as a part of the price we must pay.

But it **is** a great change! There is no doubt of that — from Murray Hill, New York to a log cabin in the Siskiyou Mountains, Oregon, and for people nearing "50" it rather showed some courage and power of accommodation, don't you think so?

Our Mining Superintendent — Colonel Straight — was taken seriously ill early this fall, and I have been alone in charge here. At the first we had about fifteen men employed but have now got down to our regular and permanent force of less than half that number. These men are engaged for the winter at about $45.00 a month and board and are kept busy mining the soft "placer" ground, which when washed with water yields an average of 84 cents in gold per cubic yard. This has been the average yield of 18,000 cubic yards so far moved and washed during the seasons 1896-7-8 and this ground steadily gets richer as we go farther up the Gulch.

I have had much new work to grasp and understand but find in mining as in everything else that I have attempted that plain common sense and steady application solve all the new problems that come up.

When I first went into this mining business I had not the slightest idea that it would result in my spending a winter in these mountains — as a Mining Superintendent — but as circumstances arose which made this necessary I did not hesitate to step in and do my level best, and it looks as if all were coming out in good shape and prosperously in spite of "the tenderfoot manager." I can not possibly say at this early day how long it may be necessary for us to stay here — certainly until June next, but I hope by that time to have the Quartz Milling portion of our business safely in the hands of the Lessees — the Chicago Syndicate, and our Placer Mining operations under the permanent charge of a competent paid Superintendent — if I can find one — so that at last my dear wife and I can travel about and see something of this great big world of which we have seen so little. I would like while we are on this Coast, if it proves possible, to take advantage of our nearness, to visit Alaska next summer and possibly in the fall or winter to take the trip to Japan — stopping over at Hawaii on the way. Even with a limited income these things are possible for one already here — as the time and cost of the trip across the continent is saved. However it is quite too soon to forecast as yet. For some months, we are perched up 5200 feet on French Peak — digging in yellow mud for yellow gold — and until we "have made our pile," we must stay here and push the enterprise to a successful finish.

Please send this around to Charlie and Carrie — to Florence and to Lizzie, and let us hear from all of you. If father would be interested, I would be pleased to have him also see the letter.

In regard to the book or magazine so kindly suggested by Lizzie and Floy, while we are sincerely obliged for the thought, it really would not be necessary, as we take all the magazines already, and as for books they would be quickly ruined here with the smoke and ashes from our wood fire, as we have found to our cost, so pray don't think of sending anything. With love from us both to you all.

News of the death of his father on March 4, 1899, came in a letter written by his sister Florence. His reply on April 16, 1899, includes the only news of the gold camp for the previous three months.

I received your letter speaking of father's last days and the circumstances surrounding his death and funeral — and want to thank you very sincerely for sending me so full and faithful an account. While Charlie has been very good in sending me some particulars, he relied upon you to give me the more detailed account — and so until your letter, and the papers you sent reached me, I was ignorant of many details — which you supplied.

Yes, father was a strong and good man, and has left his mark upon many lives and churches. Your letter gives me a painfully vivid realization of how much he suffered during the closing days.

Were the family at Hudson kind and attentive to him — and sympathetic and why were only Charlie and yourself with him when he died?

We are so far away here and all news reaches us so long after the facts have occurred, that almost all the things we hear of as happening back east, seem like a far-a-way tale, not closely or vitally connected with our present life, but father's death has not been so — and I find myself thinking about it very frequently and reviewing the past.

The weather for the past fortnight has been generally warm and pleasant, and when so, it is lovely beyond words to describe — dry, tonic, and peculiarly soft and invigorating. At last we are getting a good supply of water in our ditches and are mining quite steadily and making an immense hole in the hillside — 200 feet wide by 50 feet deep — representing many thousands of tons of placer ground washed out. What amount of gold we shall get from it remains to be seen and can not be determined until we make our general "clean-up" some time in May — but we have occasionally "panned out" a part of our race way and on one occasion we got $485, on another $228 and on the last about $65. There may be several thousand dollars in the long flumes and sluice boxes, but we can not tell before the clean-up. Several parties with money are trying to buy this property from us outright and if we can get a fair price we will sell it and then my money troubles will be over, though at present I am as hard up as ever in my life. If we sell our mine for a good sum, I shall spend the summer up in the Puget Sound region and possibly take the short Alaska trip — traveling about and showing Belle this wonderful country.

And now dear sister, good bye. Write me when you can. Your letters are always welcome. I am working hard and usually very tired, that is why I don't write more to you-uns. With love, as ever, Yours affectionately.

Among the recollections which he included in the Wardle Genealogy compiled later, he says:

Reviewing my father's life and character, he was a man of absolute honesty and integrity... He was devoted to his church work and was an intelligent and forcible preacher and wielded wide influence . . . He was also a great church organizer and cleared off several heavy church debts aggregating $80,000 besides building new churches and parsonages. . . .

Now that my father has passed away from us forever I look back upon our life from a longer perspective and with a fairer viewpoint and feel for his memory a deep and lasting respect based upon the sterling qualities he possessed. He was a man of fine strong mind, a very wide reader. His memory was phenomenal. I do not think his children ever felt for him the warm affection that parents often command, but they can never fail to respect his memory as a great and good man, and a strong man even if not demonstrative in his affections . . . From inheritance he was rather stern and somewhat severe and very positive in manner, especially with his children whom he ruled strictly according to old ideas . . . As each child grew up to mature years this became sometimes difficult to enforce and there was occasional friction now regretted by us all.

Faint memories of the funeral of this grandfather whom I scarcely knew remain in my mind. I was five when we sent to the services across the unbridged Hudson River. I only remember that when we were returning to Athens afterwards, the river was full of great slabs of ice banging against the boat. The ferry was obliged to turn back to Hudson. We stayed overnight in a hotel.

It is Christmastime 1899. They are back in San Francisco. No letter is available to tell what had actually happened concerning the gold-mining venture, nothing since April, 1899. On December 18, 1899, Frank wrote from 614 Sutton Street, San Francisco. They were living in a third story back room in a cheap boarding house. Isabel had been sick nearly half the time and *that does not make it very hilarious for her.*

We had one bright gleam of comfort — even if short when last week Prof. Joralomon and his wife invited us down to spend Sunday at Belmont. They are teaching in a Boys' School of 140 students, but they have a lovely place and are very comfortable. . . .

They took us to Palo Alto to see Stanford University. A splendid monument. Isabel has some cousins here — the Sandbergs and Raymonds with whom we ate Thanksgiving dinner, very pleasurably — 14 at a round table. Beyond this we have not been about much on account of steady cold rains — that is, Belle has not. As for myself, I start out at 9 A.M. and chase opportunities until 5 or 6 P.M. every day of my life. Am trying to find some salaried position for myself and purchasers for our mine, neither yet successfully, but I get up each new day and plod steadily through each day's work by itself trying neither to lose hope nor fear but just fight steadily on as long as I have any fight left.

Once upon a time this sort of thing — alone in a strange country with but few dollars ahead — would have daunted my steadiness of nerve but now I just keep steadily at it.

Six months later the silence is broken with a letter from Isabel on June 10, 1900, just a few days before they made their momentous trip to war-torn China. They were still in San Francisco. She had been out of the hospital only two days, after eight weeks there and several operations.

I am crawling around a little each day — hungry for a sight of Dearest, who has been away from me since the 30th of May in Portland on business. He has probably written Charles the astounding news that we sail for Japan on the 22nd! The doctors approve the voyage . . . but I don't know if I am awake or only dreaming. You shall hear from us from the "Flowery Kingdom."

On board the S.S. China, Uncle Frank's first letter home reflected only the calm Pacific with no expressed concern for a very uncertain future in war-torn China. They had sailed June 22, 1900.

Smooth seas and sunny skies for seven days have been our lot, since we left San Francisco. Honolulu will afford us a chance to send back our first steamer letter.

About 75 of our fellow passengers are returning Hawaiians who make the evenings pleasant with their soft island music and strumming of guitars. The S.S. China is quite full — 125 first class cabin passengers and a horde of returning Chinamen in the steerage who gamble continuously and smoke opium.

We have a returning China missionary, Rev. Sheffield, whose daughter is now in Peking — if

indeed she is still alive there. We shall know nothing of the Boxer Rebellion and what is transpiring in China from the date of our departure until we reach Yokohoma, July 11. You back in the States have daily cables, but we know nothing.

Isabel is surprised at the deep indigo blue of the Pacific, the bluing in a wash tub could be no bluer. . . She is proving a good sailor excepting one day in bed with one of her bad headaches. She has done exceeding well. The 19 days' sea voyage will prove of great benefit to her as the doctors predicted. We have not fully awakened to the astonishing fact that we are actually sailing for Japan and China.

Yokohoma was reached nineteen days after leaving San Francisco; and Frank wrote from the United Club, No. 5 Bund Street, telling of more pleasant days at sea, after *stopping for a day at Honolulu, over which the American flag now waves gloriously. These Sandwich Islands are a series of volcanic peaks rising abruptly out of the sea.* Isabel's later letter had told more of their day there, arriving before breakfast and driving about

*this loveliest of spots, made glorious with tropical blooms and fruit and palms. Whole trees are masses of scarlet or orange . . . We drove seven miles to the Pali precipice, up, up a good steep road. Pali divides this strange island and who could ever forget the splendid panorama for a 100 miles if he has stood in the narrow pass and looked down and over the valley beyond to the ocean — so blue from pale turquoise to deepest indigo! Our **Pali**-sades sink to insignificance. After tiffin at the hotel — you never had luncheon after you step on board the steamer — we drove again to Waikiki where the splendid surf rolls in and it is here that you see the famous surf board riding through the great breakers. Among the women are many beautiful faces. Their favorite dress is a Mother Hubbard, stiffly starched and spotlessly clean. There are good schools. We passed poor Queen Lil's home, where she lives in lonely state. Everyone returning to the steamer had one or more pretty leis around his or her hat or neck. They are made by stringing together as many carnations, chiefly, — as you wish each stripped of its calyx and pushed close together . . . We left 78 of our 110 passengers and therefore had a quieter time the rest of the voyage.*

Seagulls swooshed through the great upside down washbowl of the Pacific to whiten themselves in the *indigo bluing* rinse, so labelled by Uncle Frank. Uncle Frank tells us:

Two days later we passed Midway Island the new U.S. possession for a cable station. This morning, July 11, at daylight Japan came into view — green mountains and glasslike water covered with queer-looking junks and queerer looking Japs [In

1985, the typewriter seems to hesitate to write the short form of "Jap" with its current derogatory connotation, proving we do progress from unmeant and unrealized snobbishness to more awareness of the dignity of all human life.]

We are domiciled for a week at the Oriental Hotel and no less than five men have put me up for this club. Having heard no news since leaving San Francisco I am shocked today on landing to learn how serious and probably fatal have been the past three weeks developments in China . . . To-day's probability of Dr. Sheffield's daughter's massacre is far worse and tonight he is prostrated.

Yokohoma is a strange place. I cannot attempt to describe it. Surroundings are too strange and unfamiliar. I have been about all day in a jinrikshaw most of the time. It is just a big baby carriage with sturdy little two-legged steeds trotting steadily along all day; his legs looking like inverted Indian clubs so enormously developed are the calves. If you are going up hill, an extra coolie will push you and feel amply repaid if you give him 5 sen (2½ cents, U. S.)

I do not see how I can get over to North China Ports but must try if it is safe and possible. I place Isabel at Nikko, Japan's loveliest summer resort and summer home of the Japanese Imperial Family. Then I will go to Tokyo and Tientsin. If not, then to Shanghai though 5000 refugees from that point are en route here. All hell seems to have broken loose in China.

And so it had. Even with the experience of many who had lived in China for twenty years or more, it was still hard to get all the pieces together or understand the happenings and cross currents. Uncle Frank wrote:

You know quite as much as we do here and rather more as the Japanese government exercises a strict censorship at present. 30,000 Japanese soldiers are en route to China and 40,000 Russian Cossacks ditto from Manchuria. Meanwhile, everything is in suspense and fear. Our three large cargoes of lumber en route to Tientsin, Taku and Port Arthur are worth $300,000. If anything goes wrong it may prove very serious for us. And at best it will be almost impossible for us to do new business until these disturbances settle down.

To get a perspective on the "inscrutable Chinese," influenced beyond our imagination by thousands of years of civilization, events leading up to the Boxer Rebellion need to be related. The Empress Dowager, Tz'u Hsi, was the dominant figure in court after 1852, lording it over the Emporers who were usually minors. The European powers wanted freer access to Chinese markets and more equal political relationships. The Opium War back in the years 1839-42 was caused by edicts of the Imperial Chinese government prohibiting opium trade. Great Britian won the war easily over the weakening Ch'ing dynasty. The treaty of Nanking followed. It opened five ports to British residence and ceded Hong Kong as a naval and commercial base to Great Britain, established regular tariffs and allowed intercourse with British and Chinese officials on an equal basis. Diplomatic intercourse such as existed in the Western world was unknown to the Chinese. Questions regarding foreign residents and trade were decided by Imperial decree unilaterally. The United States and other nations followed up with similar treaties.

The Sino-Japanese War, 1894-5, ended diplomatic struggles, and in 1897-98 there was a scramble for concessions by the Western powers. It was U.S. initiative that advanced the "open door policy" in China and ended the attempts of other powers for spheres of influence and the movement to partition China.

In 1898, the famous reformer K'ang Yu-wei won support of the young Emporer for the sweeping changes of "the hundred days" which the Empress Dowager crushed with the support of the conservative elements. The Anti-Foreign Outburst of the Boxer Rebellion was a popular reaction to the threat presented by European powers in the years 1895-1900.

The Boxers were a secret society, sometimes called "The Society of Harmonious Fists." They attempted to destroy all Christian converts and drive all foreigners out of China, including the missionaries. A few High Chinese officials supported the Boxers, and the Empress and her conservative coterie gave them a measure of support even from the beginning.

The Boxers of the early days were simple peasants. The movement was born in Shangtung. They hated missionaries more than any other group of foreigners. Probably most peasants thought all foreigners were missionaries because they rarely met any other "barbarians" since diplomats and merchants seldom travelled in the countryside. The movement spread to other provinces. Emily Hahn in her book, **China Only Yesterday** says:

All over the Legation Quarters, foreigners were beginning to seriously question the situation, but nobody but the missionaries worried too much. Certainly not the diplomats.

Thousands were beginning to join the Boxer Movement. A few warships were sent to the China coast by American, British, Italian and German command.

Great damage and destruction began to be reported, yet an Englishman wrote, "Of course Peking is safe, that goes without saying, but merely because there are a few foolish women and children and some non-descripts and a good many missionaries, we will order a few guards."

A clipping from the **Portland Oregonian** is dated August 3, 1900, and is headed "North China Situation." The editor's introduction says:

Writing from Nagasaki, Francis R. Wardle sends

a most interesting letter regarding the situation in North China. A great deal of history has been made since this letter was written, but it presents the views of an impartial observer, who has had exceptional opportunities for looking over the situation.

"From the inception of the present disturbances in China, there has been a strange failure on the part of Western governments and peoples to recognize the significance and gravity of the movement now in progress, and this is not altogether to be wondered at when many old residents in China were similarly minded and were caught unawares, right in the very midst of the storm center.

"The Boxer revolution is only one symptom of a profound and widespread anti-foreign reaction among the Chinese people. . . Here and there warning voices were raised and precautionary measures urged, but as one refugee expressed it,

"We had lived so long in China that we had come to believe the Chinese would never do anything but talk — certainly not fight. It was the old story of Wolf, Wolf! And yet for more than a year companies have been assembling at daybreak and drilling themselves in the practice of arms, and among the Chinese themselves the prediction has long been current that in a short time every foreigner would either have fled or been slain . . . .

"Since coming to the Far East I have heard it sometimes stated that the missionaries have caused all this trouble. But this is not the case, or rather it is not the whole case. The movement in China is broader than this — a reaction against everything new in favor of the old — and many influences have brought it on; the operations of foreign syndicates, the violations of ancestral graves and traditions by railroad construction, and the coercion of the Chinese by foreign governments, all these are factors quite as much or more than Chinese objection to missionary propaganda. Political intrigue has been a subtle but powerful cause in spreading and increasing ferment, and probably if the inner history of the movement ever is written that old arch-hypocrite, Li Hung Chang, will probably be found like the witches in 'Macbeth' — stirring up the devil's brew.

"It is the common impression here that ever since the visit of Li to St. Petersburg he has been scheming how — having sold out the country to the Russians — he could 'deliver the goods.' It is an open secret that this whole movement has exploded prematurely. It was planned to come off in September . . . The unexpected uprisings of the Manchurians and their fierce attack upon the Cossacks guarding the railroad to Port Arthur has, for the present at least rendered any such purpose abortive. The Russians have their resources taxed to the utmost to maintain themselves in Manchuria and protect their railroad. This seems to be the latest turn of the wheel in that strange game the allies are playing.

"Another factor not to be ignored or underrated is Japan. Everyone who has seen the wonderful organization and high efficiency of the full army division Japan has now put in the field speaks of it in the highest terms. Col. Mead, just from Tien Tsin, told the writer that the Japanese not only outnumbered the Russians and all the European forces combined, but they had higher military efficiency.

"The Japanese brought everything complete to Taku and while other nationalities were waiting for lighters and facilities for disembarkation, the Japanese brought their own lighters, artillery, and commissaries along with them and quickly disembarked and reformed and went forward to the relief of Tien Tsin . . . though the honor of saving the beleaguered Europeans from massacre really rests primarily with the fierce Cossacks composing the Russian force.

"No one back home can possibly realize the horrors of that fierce Tien Tsin attack of July 14 and 15 . . . Described to me by a United States officer present at the time . . . he said, 'Almost every European house in Quarter was torn and riddled by the Chinese bombardment . . . The Chinese fire was well directed having been trained by German artillerists. Over a million Chinese were crowded into the native quarters. One could not walk ten steps anywhere in the city without coming upon dozens of bodies torn by shells and rapidly decomposing. Pigs, chickens, men, women and children strewn in one horrible sorry mess . . . And when pestilence threatened, thousands upon thousands were thrown into the river and carried down toward the sea. . .' The details become too gruesome to add to. 'No one doubts' he concludes, 'the capture and sack of the imperial city when the allied forces reach the capital, and should it be found the Europeans have been massacred, terrible will be the vengeance wrecked upon the offenders."

By August 6, from Nikko where Frank had settled her for two months while he was away, Isabel wrote of her stay in Yokohoma and then in Nikko:

I wish I could put windows in this letter to let you see what I am seeing for I can never tell you of them. Such a gay scene, the pretty little women in their bright kimonos and gayer obi or sash, wonderfully arranged hair. Mothers and girls are dressed alike and almost all with lesser people strapped on their backs, leaving the hands free in most sensible fashion. One would think the rolling, bobbing little heads must sometimes loll off, but all seem safe, and I have yet to see a maimed or crippled person. The streets are full of these gay little people all day — they scuff-scuff or clatter by on straw sandals or clogs — without grace or ease of movement. A huge oil paper umbrella and a piece of straw matting is their rain outfit. The coolies wear a sort of straw thatch. The little shops, the fronts all open to the street are full of the liveliest things which are all so very cheap, but alas! Uncle Sam won't let us have them unless we pay for the privilege, so we must close our eyes to the exquisite teacup at 25 and 50 cents each, for which we should pay at home 4 or 5 dollars! It almost passes belief. In the markets and cook shops are strange things one does not know if they are made to eat or play with!

We had letters to many people and were handsomely entertained many times, always at tiffin. I have a cousin here in Yokohoma, a wealthy man. They have one of the loveliest houses full of specimens of Japanese art. They gave us a very handsome tiffin served by their two "boys" clad in cool grey kimonos, their feet in white digital stockings and straw soles so that their movements were noiseless, their ministrations as silent. A good cook received 10 yen a month (5 dollars), other servants less, and all feed themselves without fear of their stealing as they do not eat our food. I think the Japanese are better cooks, the Chinese better servants, they have more head — more reliable — and all house servants are honest. The coachmen look very cool and picturesque in their white kimono — sash of green or whatever color his master chooses — a white inverted straw washbowl for hat and his master's initial or crest on his back. I had a lovely ride with such a one with my cousin's wife.

All things have an end and business concluded in Yokohoma, dearest brought me up here to Nikko, Japan's loveliest mountain resort. We stopped over night at Tokio — the Capitol — over 1,000,000 inhabitants much older than Yokohoma but far less interesting and bright than Yokohoma. Of course it is here that the Imperial Palaces are, but without lots of red tape, visitors can see only the old moat surrounding the equally old walls, protecting the buildings within. Then we had five hours ride in funny little English cars — through miles and miles of rice fields all so patiently cultivated in the most primitive ways, every inch of ground not actually hilly is cultivated, so that Japan looks like a well cared for farm laid out in tiny plots. Everything is diminutive like the people. How neat and tidy are the tiny thatched roof cottages with their ridge polls planted with something green. At one station, I bought a Japanese lunch — put up in the daintiest wooden box, a new unsplit pair of chop sticks included in the price — 10 cents (20 sen). It consisted of rice — more rice

and rice — each separate parcel supposed to be different — but all equally tasteless and nasty! After vainly attempting to master the art of chop sticks — we were alone in our section — I threw the whole thing out the window, ashamed of adding this bit of untidiness to the speckless neatness of the fields through which we were passing. Of all the foliage, the bamboo pleases me most, each stalk looking like a huge ostrich feather — a patchful of them is the most graceful thing imaginable.

Dearest brought me here to Nikko on the 20th, leaving the next morning. I am very sad over the separation, but it was the price I agreed to pay for coming, so I will not complain. He sailed from Nagasaki for Port Arthur, to be gone two weeks. After that I know not. Disturbances in China alter his plans of course, but I have no need to be anxious for his safety as he cannot go to dangerous places. They are under military closure.

This is a charming spot in the heart of the mountains, not far enough up to be very cool in the daytime although the nights are delicious, and also it rains just as easy as nothing. Exertion is a burden. There is a place called Chinjuije eight miles further on where one must ride in a chair on the shoulders of four men, and feel like a sacred idol in a procession! There it is cooler and less moist but for a time I shall remain here.

Here within ten minutes walk are the most beautiful of all the temples in Japan, the only ones I have seen. It is fatiguing work, and having seen these we have seen the best and all are about the same; only here is the finest coloring and carving and lacquer work and gilding. Ridge poles and cornices are a blaze of gold, real gold that has stood the rains and storms of centuries, gleaming in the forest groves just as brilliantly as ever. In the finest temple, Ieyasu's, there are columns of gold and lacquer that cost $10,000 each.

Panels of wood with figures of birds or beasts so carved that the graining of the wood makes the feathers or fur. The ceilings of rich lacquer beams framing painted panels are marvels of art. To enter here one must remove his shoes; then he may step on the porch of pure unbroken lacquer of brilliant polish, and stepping over a superbly wrought sill of bronze, enter the severely plain but beautiful temple. I mean plain as to shrines and images for in the Shinto temples there is none, but it would be hard to find space for a pinhead that is not a marvel of workmanship. There are dozens of these temples with their wonderful gates — and various houses for storing temple foods — all are the same type — and all most gorgeous inside and out with color and gilding and carving. One may, day after day, wander at will about the beautiful grounds.

Now is the season when the white clad pilgrims go by in thousands to climb the sacred mountain Nantaisan soaring nine thousand feet above the sea, tapering regularly as a pyramid and forested to the top. Here is a shrine — shrines all the way to the top — here the pilgrims paste a paper prayer — go their way — to be as wicked for the rest of the year as they choose!

The Imperial family have recently arrived at their summer home here, everyone turning out to see their approach — the ladies alas in picturesque European dress, the men in semi-European dress — chiefly hats of the '49, high hats of huge size well pulled down over the ears and the nap all brushed the wrong way!

In the Temple grounds, people rent the houses of the priests for the summer. I have taken tea with an acquaintance in one with its pretty slide panels and straw mats and where the booming of the great bell struck on the outside with a huge wooden beam tells the hour. The sound floats over the river to our hotel pleasantly. I am tired. I am not a guide book but have tried to give you a few impressions of my own. I will send your Carrie an illustrated postal of the lovely temple gates but faintly colored. They should be deep and strong reds and blues and gold.

In contrast, the gaily dressed young and old were few and far between when I visited some of the same places in 1967. Our group travelled from Tokyo to Nikko by Tobu's Deluxe Limited Express train — 81 miles in 105 minutes instead of five hours. Then by bus up the thrilling hairpin Iroho-zaka Driveway along the Daiya River seen deep in a gorge. They had recently built a second road as there was one-way traffic. One road had 19 hairpin turns; the other 21. I can't imagine riding a jinricksha high on the shoulders of coolies up that mountain to the famous Lake Chuzenji surrounded by gorgeous high mountains.

The Toshogu Shrine combines Shintoism, the native Japanese religion, and Buddhism as easily as the Japanese do today. Our guide for Japan told me, "I am a Shintoist and Buddhist and influenced by Confucius." The magnificient blend of artificial splendor and natural beauty includes the avenues of 13,000 Cryptomeria trees planted in 1625 and reminding us of our own famous redwoods in height. Many more than 100 stone and bronze lanterns are seen. Somewhere at some temple I remember there were 1,000 stone lanterns.

The famed "Three Monkeys" over the door of the stable for the Sacred Horses, one of the 22 buildings, is part of the shrine. Every child knows these monkeys with their "Hear no evil, See no evil, and Speak no evil" expressed by covering the ears, or the eyes, or the mouth. The three little monkeys I remember may have been brought by Aunt Isabel from there.

I bought a Japanese scroll, guaranteed to be old and painted by a famous artist, at a shop half way up where we lunched. A member of our travel group who was an expert in Chinese and Japanese art helped me pick it out. He had been very prominent in the evacuation of the Japanese from China after the war. Many times we took off our shoes at temples, teahouses, and homes we visited. Most of us sat, unnative fashion, awkward and uncomfortable, but were served by real Geisha girls in beautiful kimonos that often cost over a thousand dollars. They cooked for us where we sat. The food was as usual delicious. I only disliked cooked or raw chrysanthemum leaves. The Geisha girls played ancient instruments but the thick coating of white on their faces was never cracked by a smile or expressioin of any kind. They were strictly chaperoned and had to be back at the dormitory by 9 or 10 o'clock. The true Geisha girl is a trained professional entertainer, skilled in dancing and repartee, and for us tourists, at least, in cooking at the table. She may or may not be a courtesan.

A charming letter to my brother Francis, 9 years old, says:

Your very nice letter written on the typewriter has just been received here in Nikko. What a big boy you are getting to be! I almost fear you may be raising a mustache and carrying a cane before I see you again.

You ask what Japanese boys do — well, in the first place they do not wear trousers and jackets as you do, but just such a long gown as the girls do — made usually of dark blue and white cotton with a narrow sash around the waist. On their feet they wear wooden clogs tied on or else one toe slipped through a thong — and on these high wooden clogs they run as fast as you can, but they make such a funny noise, especially when a lot of people are passing. Often the boys do not wear clothes, but these are the very little ones.

The boys play with queer toys, are fond of catching one of the many big bugs, or dragon flies, and while they are still alive they tie a thread about the body and then swing it about, not too hard, for all Japanese children are very gentle. The flies make a great buzzing. There is a very strange bug here that the natives call oni-mushi-devil bug. It is nearly two inches long, about one inch broad, is hard like a beetle and has on its head a sort of sharp notch then in front is a long thing about an inch long that has another notch on it. This long thing is jointed and the bug catches another bug or worm on this horn and then throws it back against the notch in its head pinching it to death. The bug is also called the stag beetle because this horn in front is so like a stag's. . . Boys put strings on these bugs too, and harness them to some little thing and let them drag it.

But we only see boys of the poor people and they have to work very early even if it is only to carry *on their backs the baby sister or brother. Then they carry a little dirt in a sort of rope basket and put it on the road to mend it, or they pick weeds from the little rice fields. Everything and everybody is so small. The men are hardly larger than Gerald [five years older] and the women only as big as fourteen-year-old girls. But they are all so pleasant and smiling and polite, even the peasants all bow to each other half way down to the ground, placing their hands on their knees as they do so. All the girls and boys bow to me in the street and call out "Ohayo" pronounce it Ohi-o, and for good-bye they say Sayenaro, Sa-yon-**ah**-ro. I described before the jinrickshas. It is just a common wicker armchair with bright red cushions in it, then long bamboo poles fastened on either side and four coolies carry you on their shoulders. They take little short steps and the motion feels like a gentle trotting horse. If they step quickly like a run it "joggles" a good deal as little Lord Fauntleroy said of his new pony.*

The ride up to Chuzenji was beautiful, a good deal like the clove road in your mountains, and cliffs were higher and the gorge wider with the maddest torrent of a river you ever saw, and lots of waterfalls. The fall leaves had our same October coloring. The hotel had only paper walls between the rooms, the windows are screens that slide back and forth. So are the doors with no lock. We had to sleep on cotton pads with the same, smaller for pillows. But they have learned how to cook for foreigners so we did not have to eat their tasteless food. I took a row on the lake in a "sampan" and a man and a boy rowed with a queer wobbly kind of oar which they use over the stern of the boat. They did not put up the queer square sail.

Next week I am going to another beautiful mountain hotel called Miyanoshita. Many think it more beautiful, but I do not see how it can be, yet they say mountains are more numerous and higher. I think I shall stay there a week and then come back to Yokohoma for a few days to go through the wonderful shops. Then I'll take a steamer and go through the Inland Sea which is very like the Thousand Islands in the St. Lawrence River, down to Nagasaki and stay there until I can go to Shanghai, China, where Uncle Frank will be by that time. We shall stay there perhaps two or three months before we sail for San Francisco again.

Uncle Frank is in Chefoo. Get your map and see where that is in North China. He is not in any danger and writes me that he is very well, but that it is a most uncomfortable place in every way — dirty, bad people, tricky and difficult to deal with and a very hot climate — no comfortable inns anywhere. He is so busy he has not had time to write even to me but has sent me two telegrams to say he is well and safe, but all the same I shall be very

glad when he gets back to Shanghai.

Tien Tsin is the entreport and gateway to Peking, situated about 30 miles up the Pei Ho River and 80 miles below the capital, Uncle Frank explained in another article, "Dark Days in China," in the morning **Oregonian**, October 15, 1900. Tien Tsin had important commerce. The European section was substantially and handsomely built of brick and stone, with broad macadamized roads, a park, library, large Astor House Hotel. This was called Gordon Hall and used as a hospital, and Gordon's Hell when it was also bombarded. There were handsome foreign consulates and stores, like a well-to-do European town. Beyond lay the native city, a far-reaching vista of strange, "fantastical" Chinese structures and of one-storied mud-brick buildings.

It is now a solitary waste of burned dismantled dwellings, amid which famished wonks (half wild dogs) were hungrily tearing the bodies of Chinese killed during the bombardment, the great fire and still greater slaughter following the capture.

Tien Tsin was first attacked in June and Chinese servants who had been in the employ of Europeans for 20 years and were cognizant of the attempted attack, gave no warning. Had the defense failed they would have been the first to loot and murder every European. The Chinese

Shansi Massacres

OREGONIAN, PORTLAND, NOVEMBER 4, 1900.

SERIES OF MASSACRES

TERRIBLE FATE THAT BEFELL AMERICANS IN CHINA.

Under the Guise of Friendship, Chinese Officials Sent Them Into Death-Traps.

1900

TIEN TSIN, China, Sept. 17.—I referred in a former letter to the terrible massacre of missionaries just reported from the Shanse Province at Fen Chou Fu, Tai Yuan Fu, Shou Yang Hsien, Tai Ku Hsien, Hsiaoi Hsien, Yang Ning Chou and other places.

The following is the official report as taken down by C. D. Tenney, Chinese Secretary to the Provisional Government at Tien Tsin:

Journey of the Messenger.

The report was brought in two days ago by Fu Chi Hao, a native helper of the missionaries in Fen Chou Fu. He brought with him a piece of blue cloth, upon which the missionaries had hastily written in pencil that the man was trustworthy, reliable and was well-informed about the situation. This messenger came by way of Taku, Shau Yang and Huai Fu.

At the last named place he heard that the missionaries at Huai Fu had at first escaped into the mountains but that the Boxers had caught them and delivered

rily stunned, she quickly recovered sufficiently to partially raise herself from the ground and begged that her life be spared. The soldiers, disregarding her cries, threw her into the flames of the now rapidly burning house and she was consumed.

It is very hard even to write such terrible and harrowing details, but unless the truth is told our people at home will never realize what fiends from the nethermost hell a portion of these Chinese soldiery and officials are, and will be inclined to utter protest when the iron hand of retributive justice shall attempt to control the savage instincts of these people.

It would be a righteous thing if every official concerned should first be executed and then his body be burned and the ashes scattered to the winds, thus destroying his line of ancestral worship, a punishment far worse than death to these people.

Following this attack on Mr. Stokes' house and the death of Miss Coombs all the foreigners were gathered in Mr. Farthing's house, their own being burned, and they were she'te ed there until summoned by the Governor to his yamen. As nearly as the list can now be made it is as follows: Mr. and Mrs. Stokes, Mr. and Mrs. Hsi C I M. Mr. and Mrs. Baynon and two children, English; Mr. and Mrs. Farthing, servant and children; Mr. and Mrs. Wei, of Ping Yang Fu, C. I. M.; Dr. and Mrs. Lo, C. I. M. All these persons were killed in the massacre at the Hsun Fu's yamen at Shou Yang Hsien, previously referred to.

The Massacre at Tai Ku Hsien.

At this place, on the 7th of the sixth moon (July 3), 300 or 400 Boxers wearing red badges, attacked the mission *had built cages in which they proposed to exhibit their prisoners before executing them by progressive slicing.*

After the capture of the Taku forts the Chinese Imperial troops made common cause with the Boxers and for days kept up a cruel artillery and rifle fire upon the European Quarter, with modern Krupp guns and Manchurian rifles.

Much more is said of the bravery of the missionaries, women and children, fighting and caring for the wounded, and of the kinds of soldiers the various nationalities proved themselves to be. The powers poured in troops, and Tien Tsin's Main Street was a vivid and motley parade showing most strangely and fantastically the "pomp and circumstance" of war. Thousands of swarthy Sikh cavalry, natives of India, in flaming red turbans, splendid big men with coal black beards and fiery eyes marched.

Behind them march the neat little Japanese infantry in their natty black and yellow uniforms, looking by comparison like boys on dress parade from some military school, but fine fighters never-the-less. Then with a characteristic free, swinging step, come a company of Americans, in rough serviceable blue flannel shirts, khaki clad fellows built for work and war and thoroughly respected for their famous get-there qualities. A moment's pause in the procession filing by and then comes a long train of gray Syrian mules in the English Commissariat service, guided by Indian coolies, barelegged and dusty; then a squad of Russian officers dash by at full gallop, in white uniforms with a finish of gold and crimson stripes, followed by the slower tramp, tramp of some Austrian infantry, with great fluttering bunches of cock's feathers of dark green half hiding their helmets. After this you may see a body of England's Jack Tars and marines in blue, with brawny bare arms, and with a rolling gate of the sea, hauling along one of the big naval guns.

A witty mother with many theories of child training remarked "The first child is a great disillusioner." So a visit to China reverses many preconceived notions, especially when one not only sees the Chinese as they are but gathers ripened judgment of level-headed men who have lived here 20 years. Within this great empire are untold possibilities of power, of wealth of development and of good, and if the curse of the utterly corrupt and unscrupulous officialism can be removed, new China can be given her chance. The first exodus of the Pekin refugees, now happily relieved by the allies, is coming down to Tien Tsin, and in my next article I hope to give you the story of their experiences.

The article "Russians in Manchuria" says the size of this country, the Gibraltar of this area on the Gulf of Pechili, is half the size of Europe, one of the finest countries in the world. There is no better land nor more splendid resources anywhere in the world.

The port or harbor is only a small narrow basin. Into it day after day, I saw coming and going a great fleet of warships and transports, with troops and supplies of immense amounts. Russia is at last formally and most fiercely at war with China.

With the first gray dawn, thousands of dark-skinned half-naked coolies pass grumblingly and quarreling to the daily unloading or loading in the harbor. They take the place of both carts and horses all through the Far East and in every sense are the "beasts of burden." Over them stand rough Cossack foremen with knout in hand and which they do no hesitate to apply liberally.

An illustration of Russia's purpose permanently to occupy Manchuria, and also of the lavish expenditure in the accomplishments of her purposes, is the creation of a brand new city, ready made to order is a case in point. The new city is Dalny meaning distant. The work has been in progress for two years under the very able Engineer Woldemar Sakharoff. He presented me with a colored map of Dalny that is to be. He told me that he has spent considerable time in America studying our methods of Western town building.

An official report of the terrible massacres of missionaries by Chinese Secretary to the Provisional Government at Tien Tsin, C.D. Tenney, is quoted by Uncle Frank and dated September 17, 1900.

A report was brought in by Fu Chi Hao, a native helper of the missionaries in Fen Chou Fu. He brought with him a piece of blue cloth on which the missionaries had hastily written in pencil that the man was trustworthy, reliable and well informed about the situation. At one place the missionaries had escaped to the mountains only to be caught by the Boxers and turned over to officials. He names nine in another city killed August 15. The district manager gave the party the most solemn promises that they would be conducted safely to Tien Tsin. They were taken 20 miles and foully murdered by the magistrate's orders.

The native messenger was with the missionary party and says when they had gone 20 li one of the Chinese soldiers with whom he had struck up a friendship warned him that the government troops were waiting just ahead to kill them and urged him to escape. The magistrate had said the missionaries were good people and wanted to protect them, but he was distrusted and replaced. The messenger witnessed the massacre.

Others were put in chains with iron collars about their necks and sent to Tai Yuan Fu with no food. A governor ordered a list of foreigners under pretense of sending them under safe escort to Tien Tsin. On July 9, he collected 33 of them in his yamen, closed the gates and called in the Boxers to slaughter them. The 33 heads were exposed on the city walls. Over 40 native Christians were also killed and the next day 10 Catholic Priests. At one mission some escaped but a woman who stayed behind a moment to help a native was thrown into the burning building.

It is very hard even to write such terrible and harrowing details, but unless the truth is told our people at home will never realize what fiends from the nethermost hell a portion of these Chinese soldiery and officials are and will be inclined to utter protest when the iron hand of retributive justice shall attempt to control the savage instincts of these people.

Among documents captured from fleeing Imperial Government officials, and now on exhibition in the Tien Tsin Custom house are government offers to the Boxers of 100 taels, about $139 Mexican, for each foreigner's head. This should finally settle the question of official complicity with the Boxer movement.

In spite of many other instances related of cruel massacres, there are also a few Chinese who tried to help them. At Nang Ning Choo two Swedes and their child escaped down the Yellow River on an official boat. The Magistrate robbed them of all their goods, but afterwards gave them a little silver and sent them on a boat. At Chen Tai a Brigadier General friendly to the foreigners kept the Boxers out of the city, but it was doubtful if he could continue, in which case he would lose his head and all foreigners would be massacred. This ends the story of the messenger, believed on checking to be substantially correct.

A general feeling of deep disappointment and an anxiety at the lack of full appreciation of what is required by both England and the United States was expressed by Uncle Frank as he completed his accounts of the general war situation. He noted that the Chinese openly boasted to the Russians that neither country would enforce a strong vigorous policy on this Far Eastern question. Russia and Japan seemed to be the only two nations thoroughly in earnest here and with a definite program. If it should prove true, he continued, as now rumored, that Russia has agreed to give Japan a free hand in Corea in exchange for Japan's similar concession to Russia in North China, then the English and Americans may as well quit and go home, unless they are prepared to support their will by something more than words.

The only real memory I have of the Boxer Rebellion is when my mother told me with great satisfaction of the fact that the United States had turned back their share of the indemnities China later paid. It was to be used for Chinese students to study here.

Awaiting Uncle Frank at Shanghai following his trips to Tien Tsin and Port Arthur, Aunt Isabel wrote to Auntie Floy, Father's sister, who taught in Catskill High School as well as in Cortland Normal and often lived with us. The date is October 23, 1900. She describes the weather.

It is like our own October but there is no coloring like our maples because there is no foliage to speak of. A drearier, uglier country can not be imagined, flat as our prairies, mud flats so that graves cannot be dug anywhere but irregular mounds are scattered all over the country, or a rough plaster grave made, or quite as often the very thick coffin of wood set on the ground anyway. The coffins are made of wood four or five inches thick. The troops up North found the new ones very useful as ice chests!!!

Shanghai impresses one, at first sight very favorably, the fine substantial three and four story English buildings along the Bund are very European looking. The houses are large, high ceilinged and difficult to heat with only soft coal fires in grates. We are wondering if we can keep warm this winter. Closets in the East are unknown. Everyone is supposed to keep all belongings in a small wardrobe. Needless to say we can't do it and trunks still bother us with incessant folding and refolding of garments.

There is no sewage in Shanghai. The toilet is universally a commode in one's bedroom, a corner screened off for this and the bathtub which is a huge, coarse earthen vase, about four feet long, oval in shape. A coolie brings two or more buckets of water in the morning and must dip out the same after use.

We have two pleasant rooms in a boarding house, private table. Chou (food) is poor, but there seems to be nothing better so we must be content. The Hotel is worse and terribly expensive. Japan is far ahead of Shanghai on the matter of hotels and comforts, and its picturesque beauty. I am vastly disappointed in the place in every way. The shops are very poor and to my amazement there are no places where we can find fine porcelain or curios from other Chinese cities — Ningpo and Canton. There are two or three silverware shops but the work is crude and coarse — so different from the fine Japanese work. It is a distinct surprise to find the Chinese are not the clever artisans we have always thought them. There is one fine silk shop here, silks of all kinds, but alas so dear as to be quite prohibitive for "us folks."

There are no pretty drives here, really nothing to do, dreary enough for those who needing to make it their home, enter the narrow social life of the town. We do not care for that and have not tried to make acquaintances. I met one or two pleasant people in Nikko — one dear little Irish lady with a fine baby — a "broth of a boy" whom I like very much. She has had us to tiffin in her tiny little house and has taken me to drive. There are one or two business acquaintances kept up as a matter of policy rather than attraction.

Reading matter like everything foreign is simply awful in price — paper covered books cost from 15 cts. to 1.50 gold! Everything far dearer than at home except tailoring. One can have a dress made for 3.50 Mexican — that would be 1.75 gold!! But English cloths are very high, flannels and hosiery very high. All these we expected to get here, supposing they would be so cheap and good. America is a pretty good place to be born in — to live in and to die in. I hope I attain the latter felicity some day!

Now perhaps the foregoing has in a measure prepared you for some disappointment in regards to your desire for a real Japanese silk dress. I can only tell you first that no one buys black silks either in Japan or China. The color is never good. One young lady in Kioto who had ignorantly bought a fine black taffeta, could only wear it nights — it was almost green. Usually they dye them to order at purchaser's risk. Also I tried for myself in all the Japanese cities to get for myself a "pretty" silk but could find absolutely nothing that I would wear, except the lovely rich Kioto brocades — at 4.80 (2.40 gold), and one must buy a whole piece as they are found only at the wholesale houses. Then I thought I would find something here, but find I do not want them or such as I like are too expensive. I will try to get you some samples if I can, and I think perhaps you will not want them as much as you now think. Remember the duty is 60 cents on every dollar.

I have been very industrious trying to find some trifles to send to you all for Dearest, pleasant work if we could only find them. Dearest has given me a list of over 35 people to whom he wishes or feels he must send some trifling remembrances. If you find a bit of embroidery it will be **old** and therefore rather faded but valued the more on this account by collectors. Modern embroidery is not interesting or pretty. If I could afford it I would buy any quantity of old embroidery and they are fascinatingly beautiful, almost the only thing I find to enthuse about. Ivory and wood are dear.

Several lovely old embroideries were among the Chinese "trifles" sent the Wardle family. One, I remember being told, was worn by mandarins, and the peasants had to knock their heads three times on the ground as the mandarins passed. Beautifully embroidered women's shoes were hardly four inches long and not more than an inch wide at the instep. These were worn by Chinese ladies with bound feet. I still have them.

She had spent *ten days of enchantment in Yokohoma again,* after leaving Nikko on the fifth of September. She met many people from there at Nikko so that she had a delightful time, weather cooler, and regretted when she left on the fifteenth for Kobe. There she was taken into the home of an old friend of her brother's who had visited Japan many years ago. Mr. Olmsted was also a business acquaintance of Frank's. I spent a very pleasant week with them in their modest home. She explained that Mrs. Olmsted was a daughter of old Dr. Otis of New York, who had died a little earlier.

I think her mother lives in Catskill at her old homestead and yet I cannot recall her maiden name. Mrs. Olmsted is going to spend the Winter with her daughter Edithe in southern California and Mrs. Olmsted goes there to meet her, the first visit back to the States in 10 years. They know all the Days in Catskill.

In Kobe she found nothing of interest.

During that week I went by rail to Kioto, two hours away, the most interesting city in all Japan from a purely native standpoint and its lovely situation lying in a plain surrounded by lovely hills beautiful in every phase of light. From the number and size of Temples — here are the largest — if not the most exquisite in all details. Nikko forever holds that supremacy. I could see but one temple thoroughly. Others I drove around and saw in the distance and ever and always one may hear the sweet tones of the great bells. In Kioto, I saw the wonderful cloisonne and Damascene metal ware made, not in great factories but in a tiny upper room over a tiny shop. There you will see patient pupils toiling under the master's eye. Lovely porcelains — Satsuma ware and the wonderful brocades. This too is the home of the matchless embroideries — that also need the purse of Fortunatus. I wanted more time. There is so much to see. I had a warm welcome back at Kobe and went

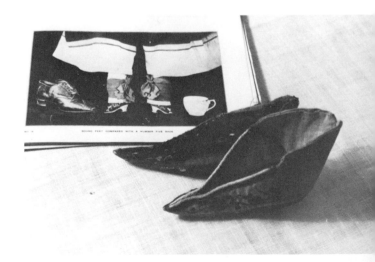

Embroidered Chinese lady's shoes brought from China in 1902 by Uncle Frank Wardle. Note contrast in size with modern shoe.
Photograph by Winifred J. Clark.

one hot afternoon for tea with the British Vice Consul whom we met coming over. He showed us a wonderful collection of butterflies, his hobby. Then on the 20th, Mr. Olmsted put me on board the old China where the officers greeted me kindly and were attentive during my two days sail to Shanghai.

When I visited Kyoto, (as we spell it), in 1967 a big point was made of the fact that it was the real home of true Geisha girls. Interesting too was an afternoon I spent alone in the Emporer's Palace Gardens with the old, old moats and palace buildings. Kyoto was the capital before Tokio, though Nara near Kyoto where the deer bow to you, is the oldest capital. Thousands of lightning bugs used to be trapped and let loose all at once on the hillsides. Poems were written and read, and culture was at its height.

In the spacious grounds two young Japanese students came shyly up to me and asked to walk with me. Like all students they wanted to practice their English. I took their pictures under the ginka trees that were making a yellow carpet on the palace grounds.

Aunt Isabel wrote on September 25, 1900:

I was interrupted here and yesterday noon Dearest arrived and proposed a trip to the native quarter within the old, old walls, probably the most memorable sight we shall ever see. He is writing an article about it so I will leave most of it to him. There are no foreigners within this section. One cannot imagine one willing to be there, such dirt and filth everywhere!!! The old Willow Pattern Teahouse, 500 years old, I am sure has never known soap in any part, dark with age and soot and smoke. It is very strange and interesting and with our guide and friend we sat upstairs and drank some of the best tea. A large portion of tea leaves is put in a cup — hot water poured on — and at once poured into another cup to drink — then fill it again until one has had enough.

To finish our investigations we visited an opium joint outside the native city. There was nothing repulsive about the scene at all save of course the picture of people giving themselves up to any vice. The smokers lay on curious pine couches, two on each with the lamp or cup of tea between them, chatting pleasantly, very quiet and placid. In No. 1, first class 50 cents Mexican is charged for the use of the couch and opium and so forth. No. 2 pays 30 cents. There were several well dressed women there. One was in no way disconcerted by my close inspection of the method. It is a sad subject, but one thing may be said, it was at least a decorous vice, no noise or brawling as by drinkers, and the Chinese rarely drink. In this regard they are better than the Japs who are great drinkers, chiefly Sake. I have rambled on, seem to keep going like Tennyson's brook — forever.

What would we not give for a good American meal. English food is so heavy, so much meat, nothing dainty, as we conceive it.

Disturbances on the South continue. Should there be any outbreak all business would be suspended. It is hard to be patient and understand the supineness of the Powers in dealing with the question. That old vixen, the Empress, ought to be tied up forever, but they let her go on replacing peaceable governors with others unfavorable to foreigners. They may have a whole kettleful of fat in the fire if they do not look out.

"Shanghai, The Native Quarter" is the heading for the **Oregonian** article written by Frank and dated October 26, 1900. The European part of the city reminded him of *a small provincial copy of Paris, its Bund not being unlike certain features of the Champs Elysees and the Boulevards, and when one travels down into the French Quarter the reminders and resemblances multiply a hundredfold.* The European population comprised ten thousand English, French, German, American, Portugese and other nationalities. He estimated some thirty thousand Chinese — shopkeepers, artisans, servants, and others who also resided in what was still called "The Settlement." It is modern with electric lights, paved streets and walks with stalwart Sikh policemen in flaming red turbans. The streets are lively with a motley procession of carriages, jinrikshas, Chinese chairs, and wheel barrows and *the ubiquitous, perambulating beast of burden, the coolie with his bamboo carrying stick, shouting, pushing, shouting and dodging, a veritable pandemonium of squirming, perspiring humanity.*

Many foreigners never saw or knew the native part of the city. It was surrounded by a high wall, which is pierced according to Chinese custom by north, south, east, and west gates, made of heavy wood covered with sheet iron. Officials close and bar these gates every night at ten o'clock. They approached by the west gate and were assailed by *such a variety of stenches that one was reminded of the old city of Cologne, where it is said seventy smells meet you at every corner.* I wish Uncle Frank had told us where Cologne got its name! He had secured an experienced guide from the Astor House, and in company with Mr. H.H. Delane of Portland and others made the tour of filthy streets, not more than six or seven feet wide shut in and semi-darkened by strange and fantastic overhanging balconies, banners, signs, and lanterns.

The street served as both roadway and public sewer, as well as a playground for some thousands of ragged and dirty little Chinese children. There are no mental standards with which to make comparison. It is sui generis. It is judged there are at least a million Chinese packed in, but there is no census in the sense of our term. All the members of a trade or handicraft are grouped in one street or quarter, much the same as in some old European cities. The shopper passes along from shop to shop easily comparing workmanship and prices. When you stand at one open front shop, the adjoining owners and their constituents all join in freely and tell you all they know and more about the owner and his wares. The Chinese know nothing of what we consider privacy and when the little shop fronts are taken out or down in the morning the whole city is literally turned inside out.

One of the most interesting visits we made was to the quaint "Willow Pattern" Tea House, which has been rendered familiar to the whole world by appearing as the popular pattern of most of old-fashioned blue china dishes of our childhood. Who does not know the crazy stairway that winds in such impossible and inebriated fashion all over the plates, in superb disdain for Newton's law of Gravitation, which by the bye was not even discovered until long after the Ming dynasty. But when we saw it there was no resemblance to our childhood fancy, but a shabby, ramshackle sort of place in the middle of a stagnant pond of green slime. Never again can I in fancy follow the pair of Chinese lovers up and down that impossible staircase or lean pensively over the rustic bridge gazing dreamily at that clear and sparkling water! I shall remember only the squalor of the real thing, as it is. Parenthetically, it might be that if some of our armchair diplomats in Washington saw John Chinaman as he is at home, they might modify their fine theories in consequence.

In place of glass, unknown in China before the advent of the foreigner, the quaint windows are glazed with thousands of little pieces of translucent shell and mother-of-pearl, producing a delightfully soft toned effect of light and color.

The article's description of Chinese tea drinking is not like the ceremonial tea our tour group was served twice in Japan. Uncle Frank says the Chinese consider our occidental way crude and barbarous as they do our *tearing our food with knives and forks.* When they were seated, an old man in attendance brought a large bronze kettle of boiling water, after he had placed little cups of very thin China — each nearly half filled with dry tea leaves and red tea blossoms — on the small square table in front of them. As soon as the boiling water was poured, the cup was quickly covered with another slightly smaller, thus preventing the escape of the aroma. Then still another set of cups was brought, making three sets in use, and into these each guest poured the steeped tea, using two other cups pressed tightly together as a strainer. No milk, no sugar is ever used. In the Mandarin Tea House with its famous dragon wall winding about and ending with two fierce dragon heads, large saucers of peanuts were served, *an unusual combination, but not*

half bad as our English cousins would say. Crowds gathered around two performing jugglers and mountebanks, who were doing clever balancing, at which they were very clever. But their legerdemain was commonplace.

Sheltered under a little piece of bamboo matting was that strange institution of both China and Persia, the professional story-teller. The business is followed by old men, who by long practice have acquired wonderful mobility of feature and intonation, and really seem to so perfectly identify themselves with the characters in the story as quite to lose their own personal identity, for the time being.

If anyone believes the oft repeated tale that the Chinese are stolid and unemotional, he has but to watch the group gathered around a story-teller! As the story progresses, from sad to gay each change registers itself in the faces of the little audience, who laugh heartily at all humorous parts, though I must confess I have never seen them weep at recitals that were sad. The Chinaman can laugh but he cannot cry, at least I have never seen a native crying anywhere within the thousand miles of China I have seen. Perhaps they feel like the little girl in Brooklyn when she saw her mother weeping, and said, "Mama, please do your sorrow in your own room."

Although we had been told that a visit to the native city would expose us to many indignities and rough treatment, our experience was quite the contrary, and though no friendliness was manifested we were allowed to go about unmolested. The large force of foreign troops now quartered in the European portion of Shanghai very effectively serves to overawe and control the native population. The Chinese are great cowards and quickly submit to a show of force. It is the opinion of all who have had long experience with the Chinese that they are amenable to no other argument, and that it would be a serious and perhaps fatal mistake to introduce any other element into the settlement of the Chinese Question. It is very difficult for those who are many thousand miles away from the sphere of action to rightly judge the needs of the situation in China, especially when those who have long been resident here are themselves in profound perplexity and doubt as to the true solution of the problem.

"The Allied Forces in China" was the headline for the next report to the **Portland Oregonian.**

The presence of large bodies of armed foreign troops, upon the soil of China and in possession of some of her most important cities and fortifications affords a striking commentary on the frequently repeated statement that 'we are not at war with China.' During the writer's visit to North China points — Port Arthur, Newchwang, Taku, and Tien-sin — transports were constantly arriving, troops disembarking, marching and countermarching and all the panoply of war was very much in evidence.

He then quoted from an article by a correspondent of the **Times of India** which he considered in the main so truthful and well-expressed that he believed it would be of interest to the readers of his articles.

Speaking of the memorable march of the Allies to Peking and their capture of the Imperial City, the correspondent says, in part: As far as generalship was concerned the Allies were so uniformly successful that there is no opportunity for criticism. Courage is a quality so universally prevalent that its absence could only cause surprise. In fact the only people that showed themselves wanting in courage were the Chinese, and even among them, there were many who would rather die than run away. Under fire, the British were steady, the Americans cool and courageous, the Russians stolid and the Japanese daring and self-possessed. Some folks spoke vaguely against the French, but I think such remarks were ill-natured and unfounded, as I saw French marines under fire and nothing could exceed their composure and sang froid.

With general regard to the discipline of the troops, by which I mean strict obedience to orders, self-respect and regard for the traditions of humanity, the general conduct of the troops was excellent. No prisoners were tortured, no defenseless people shot down in cold blood, and few women shamed.

The correspondents used to speak with amazement, admiration and disapproval at the same time. On occasion we felt inclined to take off our hats to every American soldier we saw, and at other times the army seemed almost a mob. An American officer told us that Americans believe the "fighting unit" is the man, not the company nor the regiment, and that therefore they encourage self-reliance and individualism.

Of the Russians this correspondent of India says, "If the American army was a source of wonder and admiration to Europeans, the Muscovites were something more, a profound mystery. The Russians were always polite and obliging and yet in some way seemed to be always holding aloof. We saw them in camp at Tiensin, we saw them on the march to Peking, we saw them in battle, and yet notwithstanding this very few would venture an opinion of their real fighting efficiency. There was always an air of alertness and expectancy about the Russian camp. It was guarded with a double line of sentries. The Russian soldier never unfoxes his bayonet and the Russian officer never unbuckles his sword."

He continued to describe the Russians and remarked that whenever they entered a Russian camp, they felt as if a thousand eyes were furtively watching. The soldiers paid as little attention to "Smartness" in dress and equipment as the Americans, but they had all learned one cardinal principle — they had to obey and obey at once, which makes them a formidable instrument. What they would do deprived of such officers is another matter. Behind the Russian wall of reserve and suspicion, they may be holding a mighty engine of warfare.

The Japanese soldiers, the correspondent found, excited almost universal admiration and friendliness, and were in turn very friendly to the British and Americans. Even the little Japanese soldiers, with their quaint white and red uniforms, would grin with pleasure when they passed or met soldiers of these nationalities and would show dazzling white teeth as they saluted. They were trained in European fashion, but until one saw them in actual fighting (when they showed up splendidly) it was difficult to get over the feeling that the men, horses and guns were toy things and not real. They were all so little.

It is said the Japanese warships are built so low between decks, that if captured by another power they could never be used. But these little Japs in battle arouse only respect and admiration. They never turn back, and they fight like the famous hill Gourkas of India.

Frank goes on to describe the Indian soldier, probably the most picturesque of all foreign troops in China.

These strange swarthy soldiers which England has formed from the races of India, and is now employing against China (never against Europeans) were not sent against the Boers in South Africa. They probably number fifteen thousand here now. They have English officers, and follow modern tactics.

So far as I have seen them at Tientsin and Shanghai, these Indian troops consist chiefly of Rajputs, Gourkas, and Sikhs. The Gourkas are short, thick-set, stocky little fellows somewhat like the Japanese. They are said to be splendid fighters. Being a hill tribe they march to the music of highland bagpipes of Scotland and seem to like the peculiar music.

The Sikhs and Rajputs are much larger built men — many of them exceeding six feet in stature — handsome, soldierly statues in bronze, fine broad shoulders and curiously spindle shanks. It is a question how these troops from the hot Indian climate, will stand the sharp biting cold of the Chinese winter, especially as many of them seem to have no other shelter prepared than the little bamboo sheds, covered with straw matting.

The Gourkas wear little brimless caps similar to the English soldiers, the Rajputs have dark blue turbans made of voluminous folds. (We saw the material of one such turban unrolled and stretched out on the ground. It is no exaggeration to say that it was at least thirty feet long.) The Sikhs wear similar turbans but of the most vivid scarlet. In summer Kaki is worn for uniforms, but the winter coat is of the usual brilliant English scarlet, making these troops a brilliant spot of color in any background where they are grouped.

Little has been said of the German troops, who however deserve mention. About 10,000 arrived in Tientsin while I was there, and probably many more since. A rumor is in circulation that still further troops are to be sent, but we do not know if this is reliable.

One thing is certain, the Germans are out here for business and whatever indifferent or shilly-shally policy may control other cabinets, the Kaiser proposes to teach the Chinese a lesson that they will not be likely to soon forget. They are sturdy looking . . . and with their Minerva helmets and dark blue uniforms, look very martial. Their order and discipline seem perfect. I have never seen a more remarkable operation of military machinery than the disembarkation of 10,000 German troops at Taku. It seemed like a piece of well lubricated clockwork.

It was estimated that there were fully one hundred thousand foreign troops in China at that time, with full supplies for a winter's stay and also not less than a hundred and fifty naval vessels of difference classes, at various Chinese ports.

If thought can penetrate the dense ignorance of the Chinese Court mind and the reactionary officials connected with that antedeluvian institution, it might just begin to dawn upon their medieval understandings that China against the world is a difficult contract to carry to a successful consumation. Paper lanterns, tom-toms, and old moth-eaten superstitions are slightly inadequate for the task.

He closes:

It may astonish Oregonian readers to learn that at this very moment, with Peking, the Taku and Pei Tang forts, and almost every important city and fortification along the China coast under the absolute control of the Allied Foreign Powers, the great masses of the Chinese still blindly believe that their government is still in supreme control and that foreigners are in China only on sufferance. My tableboy came to me yesterday to tell me the important news that the Emperor and Empress Dowager had decided to remove from Peking for a short time "in order to get better air in the mountains!"

One hundred thousand foreign troops in China is really the only argument that counts for any thing in the settlement of this question. No consideration but force, and no motive but fear, will ever

have weight with the ruling class in China.

The dramatic flight of the Empress Dowager from Peking ("that old vixen," Aunt Isabel called her with good reason) is an intriguing story and incredible Uncle Frank tried to visit Peking right after its capture but there were too many bands of Boxers still around. They did not reach it until March, 1901. On November 3, 1900, they were still in Shanghai; and Frank wrote of his preoccupation with *establishing a Branch House and all the responsibility rests on me for the work. I have also just closed successfully a fifty thousand dollar sale of lumber that has claimed much time and attention.*

They were living in two comfortable rooms at No 5 Nanking Road in the house of an English family, *who charge us very high prices and serve us very poor "chow" which means feed. The good old days when everything was cheap in China have passed and living is now horribly dear and bad. We have a little China boy named Chu Yu Dong to bring our meals and wait on us, for which we pay him five dollars a month and he furnishes his own chow and sleeps at home somewhere over in the Chinese quarter. This is the way he talks: "Misse you wanche me catchee one pieces rickshaw makee walkee bottomside?" or "Me belong ploper No. 1 boy, me makee work ploper fashion, etc." He has a long black pigtail of which he is very proud and finger nails as long as cat's claws, and wears a long blue nightgown about the house. Altogether he is a very good specimen of a nice young Chinese and perhaps if we can get him in we may bring him with us to America, where he is very anxious to come, says it is "more better."*

Life, they found, was dull and uncomfortable; but with many gunboats anchored in the river opposite the city, they felt safe. Even going through the native city of over a million inhabitants, accompanied by a friend and Chinese guide they experienced no rudeness. The people seemed quite indifferent to their presence.

Anyone seeing the average Chinese here at home finds them very amenable to control and on the whole quiet, industrious and excellent people in many ways, but they have been wretchedly misgoverned, squeezed and misled by an utterly corrupt and fanatical lot of officials. Give China good honest and enlightened government, and all who know her powers say she would become a great and prosperous and happy nation. With all their ignorance, superstition and strange reactionary ways, everyone living in China comes inevitably to feel a sort of respect and sympathy for the masses of the people. Don't think this is a pro-Chinese argument, but there are two sides.

Having said this, you will realize there is no harshness when I say, with those who know far better than I, that China must be dealt with firmly and securely now, or foreigners will never live here in peace and safety. That is, the Official class, who have caused all these troubles, must be sternly punished and taught a lesson not soon to be forgotten. But the great hard-working masses are not the ones to make suffer. The Mandarins, Viceroys, Taetais, and the Court officials are the ones to be punished.

The winter in Shanghai was as raw and cold as in New York; and overcoats sealskins, and heavy wraps were in use. The natives wore funny wadded clothing that made some of them look like beer barrels or inflated balloons. *The little children are especially comical looking, about as broad as they are tall.* He closed with the good news that

Isabel is in better health than in many years past and free from pain. She joins me in love and best wishes. So chin-chin me too muchee talkee so fashion suppose I no belong ploper bedtime. Chin-Chin. Yours from the bottom side of the world.

"Some Chinese Peculiarities" is the title of the next article published by the **Portland Oregonian.** It states that the longer one lives in China, old residents say, the less one knows about the Chinese, *an apparent paradox that involves a truth.* Chinese servants, for instance, who had been employed for eighteen years with uniform kindness, living in Tien Tsin, utterly failed to give warning of the impending danger of the Boxers or in any way show interest in their employer's family, although they were informed of the danger.

It is frequently said, the Chinese have no such sense as gratitude. On the contrary, others have found them occasionally most devoted to their interests and ready almost to lay down their lives for those they served. These strangely contradictory testimonies by experienced residents, gives one clue to a most remarkable Chinese peculiarity — they are a people of contradictions. With them it is the unexpected that happens.

From an occidental point of view they live on the bottomside of the world. So their mental and ethical standards often seem inverted also. For instance, I have yet to see the first Chinaman who is embarrassed or ashamed if caught in a lie. A lie seems to him to be a perfectly natural and proper kind of "Diplomacy" and if the other party is shrewd enough to discover and unmask it, the perpetrator simply grins goodnaturedly, but without a blush (no Chinaman is ever known to blush) and simply gives increased respect to the superior acumen of the other.

In bargaining, no one ever takes a Chinaman's first named price as final or as bearing any relation to what he is willing to take. Ladies shopping make it a rule never to pay more than one third to one half the price demanded by the dealer.

Obliquity of both moral and physical vision seem associated with these almond-eyed people. If, as the Good Book says that heaven contains no one who loveth or maketh a lie, there will be very few Celestials up there.

Another peculiarity that attracts foreign attention is a certain lack of sensibility or "nerves," and consequent indifference to physical suffering either in themselves or in the people and dumb animals around them. I have seen a Chinese coolie carrying a lot of fowls to the market, tied by their up-beat wings to his bamboo pole. It never seemed to occur to his mind or to the bystanders that such a method was cruel and barbarous, and the strangest part of it is that the fowls themselves made no audible protest. All through the Far East, animals of all kinds — cats, dogs, horses, the water buffalo, fowls, etc. — all seem to grow stolid and indifferent to physical pain. Possibly Darwin's theory of long inherited instincts, developed by special requirements, would account for it. Certain it is that a Society for the Prevention of Cruelty to Animals would have its hands full in China.

The strange contradiction of the Chinese indifference to pain is the remarkable responsiveness of his body to the influence of European medicines and stimulants. One half or even one fourth the dose required with us, will produce an equal effect on the Chinese. I have seen a Chinese merchant, after sipping less than half a glass of port wine, complain of tingling and burning sensation running even to his fingertips. Drugs have an immediate and marked effect, and a native, changing from his usual diet of rice and vegetables to the stronger food and meats of Europeans, is made acutely and often dangerously ill . . . thus illustrating that "what is one man's food is another man's poison."

The most marked peculiarity noticed is Chinese conservatism, or slowness to adapt to new and unfamiliar ways and ideas. In this he is the *byword of the civilized world and the epitome of non-progressivism. His 'No savy so fashion' seems to him a perfectly adequate and reasonable excuse for rejecting anything new and strange.*

Custom, handed down unchanged and unchanging from time immemorial, binds his mind, as the wonderful little shoes bind the feet of the Chinese women, and speaking of these, we have a number of pairs purchased at random from ordinary Chinese stores that measure four inches long and are worn by adult women. Probably nowhere in the wide round globe can there be found a land where Custom (spelled with capital C) stands so rigidly fixed and unalterable through the long centuries as in China. Australia is sometimes called the land of "never-never" but China is the land of "ever-

ever." If Napoleon, standing beneath the Pyramids exclaimed "Forty centuries look down on us," what would he have said and felt in China!

They took tea in a teahouse that had only been serving successive companies of patrons with the beverage that cheers but does not inebriate, for the comparatively short space of five hundred brief summers, and apologies were offered by the comparative youthfulness of the teahouse. *Such is China* wrote Uncle Frank, *which the Powers expect to reconstruct in a twelvemonth.*

Reverence for the aged and for the dead was ever present. The young wife is a servant but the old mother is a queen, and the dead are more highly esteemed than the living, chiefly, Uncle Frank thought, because of a fear that neglect to propitiate the dead might lead to being *Ha'nted.*

When our friend, Dr. Lincoln of St. John's College, first showed his Chinese students an articulated skeleton, used for purposes of demonstration in anatomy classes, they exclaimed, 'How dare you treat him so irreverently? Are you not afraid of his coming to haunt you?'

Graves all over China are most carefully and reverently preserved and at stated periods offerings are taken to them. Steaming foods are left upon the graves for an hour, while all withdraw, so the Spirits can feast upon the immaterial portion of the food. This attention is rendered the dead only on the first anniversary. After that, there is held each year in the Chinese home, what is called "The Spirits Festival" (Chung-Yuan-Chish) on the fifteenth day of the seventh moon. A table is spread with many delicacies and all the seats about it are left empty, for spirits to occupy, while they feed on the sublimated essence of material food spread out. The paper copies of the silver shee sycee (money) are burned, so that the spirits may have ready money to pay their way in the spirit world for the coming year. After all this the practical Chinaman says, *As the spirits of our revered ancestors have taken their fill and are appeased for another year, we may as well utilize the remaining material portion of this devout offering* and so they gather around the festive funeral board and apparently discover no dimunition of the original supply

and both dead and living are satisfied and fed. Until one has personally seen the reverence with which the resting place of dead ancestors is regarded, it is impossible to realize clearly one of the most powerful causes of hatred of foreigners and especially the march of western progress in railroads, parks, drives, villa sites, etc. All outside any city in China, the environs are thickly dotted with thousands and thousands of burial mounds. Now whenever the Foreign Devils start to lay out a town, build a railroad, etc., they run their abominable foreign pathways straight ahead by compass, regardless of these ancestor graves,

and forthwith there is a pretty how-de-do, and the deepest traditions and feelings of the Chinese are ruthlessly overridden, graves desecrated, bodies disinterred, etc. Of course proper arrangements are made for reinterment elsewhere, but this really constitutes one of the chief objections on the part of the Chinese to the march of modern improvements. In riding over the railroad from Taku to Tientsin, it seemed to me that we travelled through one great, continuous graveyard for many miles. It is a very strange feature of the landscape, this stretching vista of high burial mounds. Dead China seems more potent than the living portions of the nation.

The funeral procession of the late Taetai Shan Pte-jen, third uncle of His Excellency Sheng, Director General of the Imperial Telegraphs, of the Chinese Merchants Steam Navigation Co., and of the Imperial Railways south of the Yellow River afforded a very striking illustration of this profound Chinese reverence for the dead.

Sheng Pte-jen died suddenly of apoplexy, October 10, 1900, at the house of his nephew Shenh Taetai. The body was kept in state until November 8, when the gorgeous funeral occurred. First came a large retinue of probably a hundred servitors carrying gaily colored banners and some beating gongs and tom toms. Then there were twenty carriages (four wheelers) filled with factory girls from the cotton mill at Yangtzepee, of which the deceased was a large shareholder. These girls had each been presented with a new dress of Prussian Blue colored cloth and wore long strips of white cotton over their head dresses. They looked quite neat and picturesque. Then, we are told, there came 120 sedan chairs, each carried by a uniformed coolie, each chair containing a single clansman or female relative of the deceased, the women holding white handkerchiefs rather demonstratively to (supposedly) dry eyes.

Following these came a large number of open stands or platforms bearing floral designs and many large funeral wreaths, the gifts of the foreign friends of the deceased and of his nephew, His Excellency Sheng. Under a panoply of pure white cloth marched the six chief mourners (sons and grandsons of the deceased) following immediately behind the richly embroidered pall of purple velvet which covered the immense and very costly coffin. In China, coffins are made of six-inch thick teak lumber and are about as large as a wagon and as heavy as a ton of coal. Behind the chief mourners walked His Excellency Cheng and the members of his branch of the family, while bringing up the rear of the procession rode His Excellency Sheng-Haie-jen, the eldest brother of the deceased (over 80 years of age) and for many years the acting Provincial Treasurer of Hupeh. In all there were over a thousand people in the procession which passed through many of the leading streets of the foreign set tlement of Shanghai, and finally came to the "Ping-chiang Kungse" or mortuary temple of the Cheng family in the Ch'angchou prefecture. Here the coffin was placed for at least a year, until a new tomb was built, when it would be sent thither with pomp similar to this just completed display.

One peculiar detail of a small family funeral procession witnessed on the first day of arrival in Shanghai was concerned with a small merchant Chinaman being borne to his last resting place and immediately behind his coffin followed his four wives in four rickshaws, each following in the order of her relative position and importance in the family and most exactly modulating her grief to exactly correspond to her position and relation to the dear departed. The No. 1 wife was sobbing most demonstratively and floods of tears were pouring into the large white handkerchief she displayed. Wife No. 2 was similarly overcome with grief, but to a mathematically proportioned lesser degree as befitted a No. 2. The No. 3 wife was not crying at all but like an automaton placed her handkerchief to her quiet eyes at regular and proper intervals, while poor No. 4 bringing up the tail end of the procession, simply looked subdued and slightly pensive, like the ever-clouding of a pleasant April day, when the thin mists and shadows are liable to sweep away at any moment and leave the sun brightly shining.

Human nature seems about the same in China as in other parts of the world of the post-mortem grief to be strictly regulated by social convention. But in China, widows have reason to cry, as their condition is most unhappy and undesirable in many instances.

The duplicity of the Chinese was discussed further in the testimony of Bishop Meule whose experience showed how even breaking ground and building in a new neighborhood, in renting or purchasing land, the seller will pretend to hand over good title deeds, but all the time the vital fact is concealed that one or more of the part owners (whose consent is indispensable) is absent or non-participating. Sometimes a reprobate Buddist monk, in temporary charge of a convent, will profess to sell it for a song, but as soon as he has the dollars will promptly decamp and leave the buyer to the exasperation of the returning brother monks and possibly the whole neighborhood besides, who have no wish to see even a dilapidated convent given over for foreign occupation. This is a sample of the Chinese intermediaries through which foreigners are forced to operate.

Of course we do our best by cross questioning, by using the advice of those whom we have learned to trust and by submitting the various matters to the yamen for investigation and registration, to mitigate the effects of such assistants, but too often they leave their trail in every transaction.

Almost every old resident in China has had similar experiences, and has learned by bitter teaching to distrust the Chinese except in the case of some few of the most reputable merchants whose long dealings with the Europeans has taught them the necessity for commercial honor as the only basis for continued business. As before remarked, the Chinaman is a bundle of contradictions, and it becomes impossible to make any general rule apply.

Shanghai, November 10, 1900

Uncle Frank wrote about Chinese peculiarities and attributes in an article titled "The Real Chinaman. *The Chinaman at home is an enigma and a puzzle even to those Europeans that have lived half a century and studied him closely,* says Uncle Frank. This article may not have been published as the others were because a note says, *Needs careful revision.* He tried always, it seems, to confirm his own impressions and did considerable research. His conclusion, *Any old merchant, missionary or official whose arrival dates back a quarter of a century will say, 'The more we see of them, the less we feel certain that we know them in any true and final sense.'* Reading more recent books, and noting they are after the Revolution and currently after Mao Tse Tung, it may not be that Westerners understand the "real Chinaman" any better, but he himself certainly to a large degree has broken through old customs and many want Western ways. Frank says,

All that can be attempted therefore is to give with all possible fidelity, a series of mental photographs of the real Chinaman as he appears to the observant foreigner under the various changing conditions of his common everyday life following that excellent rule laid down in Shakespeare for all chroniclers, "nothing extentuate, nor set down aught in malice."

Then he enlarges on what he has said before under the heading, "Deceitfulness, Ignorance and Dirtiness." A few nuggets:

The trait of deceitfulness is shown not only to the foreigner but equally toward their own people and is manifest in their "Joss Pigeon" or religious rites, intricate and complicated series of shams to deceive the gods or spirits. For instance everywhere are countless strings of silvered or gilt paper money, copies of shee sycee — which is burned before the joss as a supposed means of concerting "the mammon of unrighteousness" into celestial currency. So also various paper effigies of horses, houses, servants, etc., are similarly burned before the joss and thereby sent on into the spirit world to serve their masters there.

Confronting them with wrongdoing elicits only blank stares and a response "me no savy." You can't penetrate that stone wall of China. Servants screen and protect each other. For a force of fifteen house servants, a quite usual number in an ordinary household, the servants' food is given to the No. 1 boy or to the cook; and as he passes it on, he takes out a portion as his *squeeze* and then *these many littles make a muckle,* he either smuggles it out to relatives or to a buyer.

Passing upward in the social scale — the shraffs and compradores in the business offices carry on with the same industry and duplicity the universal "squeeze pigeon" and levy a tax on everything passing in and out. The compradores as a class are generally well-to-do and are past grand masters in the gentle arts of lying and squeeze. The only thing to be said in their favor is that while they cheat you themselves, they rarely allow others to do so. Newcomers to China at first struggle against these delightful little Chinese peculiarities, but in course of time learn to submit to the inevitable and take it philosophically. . . . There is one fine word in universal use throughout China, it is "maskee" never mind or it does not matter. In that one word has crystalized the accumulated experience and wisdom of all the foreigners in China since the country was first opened to them, maskee.

Many here strongly believe that the ultimate outcome of the present peace negotiations at Peking will afford a fresh and astounding evidence of the duplicity of the Chinese and the credulity of the Foreign Powers. It is astonishing to people here that Minister Wu in Washington has succeeded so completely hypnotizing the Administration into childlike faith in his protestations of Chinese good faith and sincere desire for peace, while all the time it is well known here that the Empress Dowager is simply prolonging peace negotiations until the coming of Spring weather permits her to complete the gathering of her forces and that then she will cast off all the shallow disguises and once more resume her true attitude of fierce hatred and resistance to foreigners.

The essential ignorance of the Chinese gradually impresses the foreigner. They have a certain type of knowledge and cleverness that gets them by but

when it comes to the exercise of the intellectual faculty in original analytical and synthetical processes and the mastery of new and unfamiliar things — then the Chinaman is at a very great disadvantage. . . . They are great imitators and have remarkable powers of close observance and memorizing and often the results are mistaken for evidence of higher intellectual qualities. . . . As long as their learned men can quote passages from their books they show surprising ability, but the moment you take them off the beaten path and ask them to give reasons or explain the meaning of certain passages they show how largely all their facility and supposed learning is mere parrot

talk and how little real intelligence there is beneath this veneer. One justly said, "The student wanders through dreary miles of superficial generalities only to arrive at last in a desert of formal platitudes and moral precepts unrelieved by originality or imagination." . . . So it is with the Chinese literati, but this letter deals with the common people. . . . If I were to summarize in three words the chief characteristics of the great mass I would say, deceitfulness, ignorance and dirtiness.

Take as a single illustration in the household servants, and here I speak with confidence born of personal observation, confirmed by householders twenty years resident here. . . . The various classes of household coolies are necessarily more intelligent and better trained than the great mass of laboring coolies employed in the outside world. . . . I have seen a force of fifteen coolies connected with the house in which I live for a period of several months.

Surely fifteen house servants for a family of four (not counting the dog) is an adequate force and no one is overworked. Well, to begin the dawning of day, the No. 2 upstairs coolie comes slamming and banging through the dressing room at seven o'clock and though instructed to be quiet, opens Venetian blinds on the veranda and performs his other chores with that peculiarly Chinese disregard of mere niceties that effectually ends our last sweet little after nap before rising. A bull in a China shop would be quite as gentle and quiet. Portieres closed against a severe cold spell are forever after kept closed by No. 2 coolie.

Though the household had two cooks, No. 1 coolie does not come to cook the breakfast and so No. 2 cook taxes his knowledge to the utmost to prepare the simple dejeuner of coffee, toast and oatmeal. Recently we added eggs and struggled with the No. 2 for a week before he could learn to cook them properly. Later a non-egg-eating member of the family circle thought he would also eat an egg for breakfast, but this required changing the number cooked and threw the cook into profound perplexity and confusion. "Why so fashion?" he indignantly exclaimed, "my catchee four pieces of egg, all lite, what for you now change six pieces?" The No. 1 table boy, a tender youth of only sixty summers is equally a slave of old custom, and anything unfamiliar throws him all to pieces and he loses his head. Equally true of all the servants — the mafoe in the stables, the gardeners are all good monkey imitators, but poor initiators or original thinkers.

The superstitions that dominate the Chinese mind thrive in the atmosphere of ignorance. They live in continual dread of the vengeful spite of the gods, spirits, and various occult influences. They have crude and barbarous notions regarding western inventions.

The house boy tried to explain the telephone installed in the house.

Quoth the boy, "This ting belong ale samee lectic lites. S'pose dogs eyes no hab got, how fashion? No get lectic lites. Plenty Chinaman talkee dogs eyes no got, no lectic lites." This strange belief grew from the fact that the dog pound happened to be near the electric light works and the natives concluded the dogs' eyes were used to make electric light. All Chinese junks have two great eyes painted on each side of their bows. The Chinaman reasons thusly, *"No hab get eye how can see? No can see how can makee walkee over water?"*. . . . The Chinese are yet in their childhood, notwithstanding their six thousand years of peculiar and one sided development and history.

Everywhere dirt reigned supreme in that strange land. Uncle Frank said in nearly half a year in China he never saw a lower class person clean or washed until their great annual festival of Chinese New Year when most of them seemed to take their annual bath, or at least washed their faces. This was in regard to the laboring classes. The poorer classes wear ancient wadded cotton garments that have been handed down year after year and perhaps from generation to generation without washing. They put them on early in the fall and wear them night and day without ever removing them, Uncle Frank reports. When the warm summer returns, they throw them into some garret in a foul sweltering mass and leave them until fall. (One wonders what the situation would have been like if all the hot springs and water available to the Japanese had been equally available to Chinese natives.)

Happy Christmas and New Year to you, dear sister, Frank writes from Shanghai, November 23, 1900.

As this will find you no doubt at Charlie's you can see also my fuller notes. I am having a race with the clock before the steamer sails. We have sent you as a Christmas remembrance some of the celebrated Chefoo Silk Lace — hand made — which I bought when I was at that point last summer. It is made by Chinese women and is an exact copy of the well known Malta Lace, except that its material is silk.

This is especially interesting as I was given this lace after Auntie Floy died and used it on my wedding dress which I made.

Isabel also sends you a piece of Chinese embroidery, worked in silk and gold thread on a black ground. This is what certain high officials wear on the front and back of their outside robes when in public to show their high estate and make all common people bow down to them.

You can make it into a sofa pillow or a chair back or for your own back, or use it any ornamental way. There is also a "Fukusa" or small cover used when sending a ceremonial present (which in Chi-

na and Japan must always be returned), but not so in your case as we are only "foreign devils." This will make a little stand cover.

Among the other gifts sent and which I also remember and own, Uncle Frank listed *one of the regular Chinese shoes ordinarily worn by all high class Chinese women.* Another must have been sent to Charles' family as I have two besides a smaller one bought from a returned Chinese missionary. He explains:

The true foot is not really as small as this but in childhood is bent and distorted by foot-binding, whereby toes are all bent in to a point and doubled under the ball of the foot; the heel, while bones are soft, is crowded back into the instep, and the whole foot twisted from a permanently horizontal angle. If you, as I, many times had ever seen a ballet dancer in Paris or elsewhere, you would at once recognize the thing I mean. She learns to walk on her toes. And just so the poor Chinese woman waddles and stumps along in these little shoes.

Isabel and I enjoyed reading Mrs. Skidmore's "Jimrikshaw Days" that we sent you a copy of by last mail. It will give you a very accurate idea of the Japs who are a much more likable people than John Chinaman. Ask Charlie and Lizzie to exchange with you the various notes and letters I send from time to time. With all my pressing business affairs, it is impossible for me to go on duplicating these things. My business mail with North China and Portland is large and exacting. *Next Sunday I am to deliver an address to a large group of partially Europeanized Chinese — some graduates of English and American Colleges, others heads of large affairs here etc.,-topic* **THE LARGER FREER LIFE AND GROWTH POSSIBLE UNDER WESTERN THAN UNDER ORIENTAL STANDARDS AND TRADITIONS** — and I am going to give it to them **"hot."**

Their minds are as cruelly bound as their women's stumpy feet, but it won't do any good. You can as well expect to move the Catskills as these stolid Chinese, bound by 4000 years of custom and tradition. They amuse and irritate every moment of my life.

The same day he wrote to Charlie, Carrie, and the little Wardles *From ten thousand miles directly under your feet,* with more Christmas greetings, and word of a little package sent per S.S. Empress of India due Vancouver, B.C., December 12. *As it goes first to Portland it will reach you about Christmas.* He told of a *true Chinese pipe for Charlie* that they could not get into the box and would bring back with them. *That's rather Irish, but then we are bottomside down here under your feet.* I have the opium pipe; one part has been broken. Dad used to put a cigar in it and try to draw smoke. There was a place to put some water, and I don't know the opium was used in it. The description of other gifts has meaning since I still have some of them, and it was quite a thrill to find them mentioned and described in these letters, even though I did remember them.

There is a piece of very old and fine Chinese embroidery for Carrie that she can hang on the wall, [I do not remember that Mother did so but later, I did], as many do here, or make into a mat or a cushion. Its original use among the Chinese Mandarins is as a badge of his high rank — fashioned on the back of his robe — and as he passes along every ordinary Chinaman "kowtows" or knocks his head on the ground three times in token of respect. Perhaps it may have the same effect on Catskill people if you wear it outside in the town. Try it. If the police arrest you, I'll pay the fine.

For Carrie there is a belt buckle of Chinese workmanship representing the two characters — Good fortune and Long-life — and as long as she wears it she will always have silver on hand and be alive. These belt buckles are quite the rage here — every woman has one, but possibly not so much so in Catskill. [This too I remember and wore on a belt I owned. It disappeared.]

"Sleeve buttons" made of the same Chinese characters were sent to Charles.

The dealer guarantees that every time he wears them, a customer will at once take out a large policy of insurance at a high premium. [Charles was an insurance agent at that time.] This without any necessity for talking, and will pay the first five years premium down spot cash in advance —so it will pay to wear them. I don't quite know how you will collect the guarantee if case results should not fulfill promises, but as Kipling says, "that's another story."

Thinking there cannot be too much good luck and

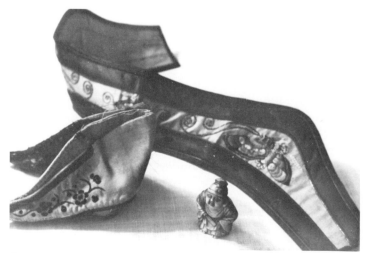

Chinese winter hat, Chinese shoes for bound feet, and children's Buddha. *Photograph by Winifred J. Clark.*

long life in the Wardle family, Isabel has bought the same kind of sleeve buttons for both Gerald and Francis — being at her wits end what to get for 35 nephews and nieces on her list —and I am no good and absorbed in selling lumber (sold 2,000,000 ft. last week) so please excuse.

There is a winter cap or bonnet such as young Chinese girls wear here, embroidered. It's really not bad looking in actual use — much less ridiculous than our spreading hat creations, decorated with the tail feathers of a Lulu bird. [This was given me and I have it. I never knew if one wore it like a crown or more probably down over ears for warmth.] Among the little toys or wooden models, there are a Japanese kitchen — a perfect facsimile of the real thing, even down to a shrine. [This belonged to my sister Constance, and I don't know what became of it. It was so tiny and such fine workmanship. We always laughed because a little dustpan hung right over the kitchen table.] A Chinese wheelbarrow [no recollection of this] on which everything is moved, people and things. One day we saw two Chinese girls loaded up on one side of one of these wheelbarrows and a fat black pig on the other side — all parties apparently perfectly satisfied. I have seen as many as six Chinese women riding in one wheelbarrow and propelled by one staggering coolie. That and the jinrikisha are the two universal means of plebean conveyance. The rich, they ride in chaises and the poor, they walk.

Three little Jap costume dolls were sent and also a string of Buddhist beads by which prayers were counted, *much like our Catholic way. The views of Shanghai which he included however*

give a very wrong impression, as amid all the fine buildings there is a strange Chinese element and beyond in a city of half a million Chinese quite un-Europeanized and in all their native qualities, dirt predominating.

It was noteworthy to me on my visit in the Far East that there were not slum sections separate from handsome homes but always here and there and often right next door.

One pleasant piece of good fortune has just befallen us. Mrs. and Mr. Hunter — two of the nicest people in Shanghai and with a large, fine house — are going to take us in with them, December 1st, giving us two fine large rooms to ourselves and all the run of their delightful home. So if I have to go to Manilla, Borneo, Corea and back up to North China on another trip, as is possible, Isabel will be well taken care of and have a nice home.

A great gap now appears. Perhaps letters were sent on to other members of the family and not returned. But May 14, 1901, Frank wrote in longhand a short note saying he was

in the midst of a long and difficult lawsuit, $6,500,

about demurrage or overtime rent of one of our ships and it is taking all my time. Then to cap the climax I have just received a cablegram from Portland saying, "be ready to go to Manilla and the Philipines, May 27th, probably a month trip as the sea voyage alone is 14 days. So all I can say is I hope to write you all at length bye and bye.

A week later he wrote to sister Florence that he would be leaving in two days for

another of those five thousand mile flying trips this time about a big government contract to Manila and the Philippines and will be back in Shanghai about June 23rd, my birthday.

En route he would visit Hong Kong, Canton, and other places in the south.

When I return to Shanghai, I expect to take another long trip north, going first to the mouth of the Amoor River above Vladiwostock, [Russian spelling] in Siberia and thence to inspect timber lands in Northerj Siberia with view to see if we can use the timber.

So you see in two months I will travel from the equator to the pole due north and south. I could not make these trips in any comfort of mind if Isabel were not so perfectly comfortable in a beautiful private home. It is one of the loveliest country seats in China — about six acres of beautifully kept grounds — full of trees and flowers — and the house an ideal one. We have half the house — three big rooms — two baths and every comfort and the two people, Mr. and Mrs. Hunter are most kind and agreeable. I took Isabel on my last trip to Peking and it almost killed her — much dirt and discomfort and now she is content at home. I must stay in China another year, until April, 1902. I have renewed my contract to that effect until June, 1902.

A Hong Kong Club Letterhead dated June 6, 1901, tells of being 1000 miles on his way to the Phillipines. The stop-over was for a week *with many friends and customers.* It was one of the *most beautiful and romantic islands* he had ever seen, with high mountains coming right down to the sea. (He would hardly recognize it today built up with hundreds of skyscrapers.) The Plague was ravaging the place and spreading terror among the inhabitants.

Every morning when I go out I find the streets and doorways sprinkled with carbolic acid and chloride of lime and the air so heavily charged with disinfectants that one can hardly breathe. Over a thousand people in Hong Kong have died of the Plague recently and fresh cases to the number of thirty or forty occur every day. The Bubonic Plague is a strange thing — attacking Europeans and Asiatics alike and a man may be well at noon and buried before sundown. Its action is almost as rapid as lightning. I have seen many strange sights since I came here. Yesterday morning there were twenty dead bodies found lying in the streets at daybreak.

It seems the authorities have a rule that every house in which a death from the Plague occurred must be thoroughly fumigated — a thing which the ignorant and stupid Chinese don't understand or see any reason for, so when one dies from Plague in a Chinese home, the family watch their chance and take the body out and dump it somewhere in the public streets far away from the house.

To combat this, the Municipal Council made a law that four houses immediately nearest where a body was found should be fumigated. So *these wily Chinese* watch their chance and dump the plague stricken before various public municipal buildings and vacant lots. *There is no such thing as getting ahead of the Chinese,* says Uncle Frank, quoting Bret Harte's "For ways are dark and tricks that are vain, the heathen Chinese is peculiar."

He sailed for two days and three nights to arrive in Manila on June 10. He found the climate in June throughout the whole of South China and the Philippines *horrible. One is always gasping for a breath of air and feels as if strangling. There has not been an hour day or night that I was not dripping with perspiration as if in a hot Turkish bath!*

This second summer in the Orient, he learned how to dress, though it did little to lighten the discomfort. *Don't be astonished when I tell you I buy my white linen suits by the* **DOZEN** *and wear from one to two suits every day.* A suit was only two garments, trousers and military jacket buttoned up to the throat and *cost complete only $3.50 gold and 1½ cents to launder.* The only underneath garment was a *singlet* or undershirt and open mesh stockings — no collars, cuffs, shirt, drawers or any other

superfluous frills. I very much doubt if Haedes is much more uncomfortable to live in. You can't imagine it unless you try it yourself — a thing not very probable since I seem destined to do all the Globe Trotting for the Wardle family.

Sometimes when I sit down in quiet and think of all the thousands of miles I have travelled over this world — and the thousands of places I have seen — I wonder at myself — a poor beggar who can not yet pay off all his debts, though that is coming along better now and will be accomplished by two more years of hard work. I only owe about three thousand dollars now — mostly repayments to friends of their losing investments — every penny of which I assume and will discharge . . .[This refers no doubt to shares friends bought in the Jupiter Gold Mine.]

In these later years I have got to the point where I can pull steadily under the yoke of other people's burdens and without fretting. I have ceased to expect anything much for myself in life, and am content to do the day's work as well as I can and having food and raiment therewith to be content. Belle has already given me one of her two lots in Greenwood — so that living or dying I am provided for and why should I complain. [Greenwood Cemetery in New York. There is a map among the papers.]

He was hoping for extra profits from the lumber business, but they lost so much on some of the big steamer charters that there was little chance of that.

I have sold **HALF A MILLION DOLLARS GOLD OF LUMBER.** *Not a bad year's work — so everyone says — and it ought to have netted me at least Ten Thousand Dollars, instead of which I have had out of it a bare living and expenses. However,* **MASKEE** *(that is a word embodying the highest philosophy of the East meaning Never Mind).*

Well, good bye, old man and God bless you. My love to all.

> *Affectionately your Venerable Elder Brother.*

> *(My Chinese title)*

Back in Shanghai by August 6 at 165 Bubbling Well Road, a long letter describes the recent places visited including Peking. The former Manager of the Shanghai office had gone home to the United States *sick of China and the Chinese,* and his work has been added to my already heavy load.

KIAUTSCHOU

We first visited this interesting new experiment in colonization by the Germans. The port is about 500 miles north of Shanghai on the Shangtung promontory. I will not attempt to give you any description of Kiautschou, as I have sent an illustrated article on it to Scribner's Magazine, which will shortly be published, I suppose.

CHEEFOO

Next we visited this port — the headquarters for missionaries and education. Foreigners from all over China send their children here for their school training which is excellent. My article on "A Winter Morning" describes Cheefoo somewhat and was written at that place. We stopped only a short time on this trip.

A VISIT TO PEKING

As the Forbidden City, the Temples of Heaven and of Agriculture, the Summer Palace and many other places of great interest will shortly be closed, upon the return of the Court, we felt our chance was now or never and so went to peek in at Peking, notwithstanding all the hardships and discomforts of the trip.

A year ago when at Tientsin I tried to reach Peking but failed and was turned back. This was immediately after its capture, by the Allies and roving bands of Boxers made it very difficult to get through. The country from the seaport of Taku to Peking, 80 miles, is as level and monotonous as our western prairies, though in ordinary times every inch of ground is carefully cultivated with three crops of millet or other grain. When we went through on the train (five hours) the country was under partial cultivation only — many wide stretches being deserted and hundreds of villages burned and desolate.

The greatest cruelty and wrong of war, he continues, is that its blight fall heaviest on the unoffending peasantry and poor who cannot flee. In North China, over three million peasants perished from famine and exposure during the preceding winter, from the ravages of war.

> *Meanwhile the chief instigators of the whole trouble live in peace and plenty, far off in the mountains of Shansi, at Sian-fu and from there listen to the beseeching of the Powers that they will condescend to return to Peking. Oh, it is the greatest Comedy of Errors ever played on any stage.*

The Empress Dowager, Tzu-Hsi, and her Court fled Peking in the early hours of August 15, 1900. Manchus had been fleeing for several days as the Allies' Relief Force for the Legations drew near. They arrived between 2 and 3 in the morning of the 14th. More trickled in, hot and exhausted, the rest of the day. Chinese soldiers quietly evaporated.

The Empress could scarcely believe this was happening to her, but she finally gave the order and changed clothes and hair to look like an ordinary peasant. The Pearl Concubine, favorite of the young Emperor who had been taken from him, had been weeping and falling on her knees. The Empress was so annoyed with her she commanded her eunuchs to throw her down a well.

The Imperial procession started in Peking on a lengthy, roundabout route to Sian, 700 miles away. And escaped just in time. She was in Sian for one year in splendid exile. Only the British Legation in Peking crowded with 3,000 refugees had not been destroyed and continued to resist with great bravery. Thick walls had to be blasted in order to enable the relief troops to enter Peking. They were about to do the same to the walls of the Forbidden City within but a Russian Commander-in-chief insisted that the rape of the holy of holies would sew seeds of resentment and trouble far into the future. At first, Emily Hahn says in **China Only Yesterday,** "the men were angry in their disappointment, but they forgot it in the rapture of sacking the rest of Peking. Soon they were out of hand, and looting and raping and bestialty followed for weeks. The Forbidden City did not remain inviolate."

This Yehonola, Tzu-hsi, the concubine, the Empress, the Dowager Empress, was the last Empress of the C'hing Dynasty, 1048-1912, which followed the Ming Dynasty, 1308-1044. She held the fate of China in her hands for more than half a century. Her first big achievement was to give the weak, dissolute old emperor a male descendant and maneuver to have him chosen for the succession. She gave old China its last blaze of glory. Though her son died of smallpox early, she managed always, with machinations and deeds that put Lucretia Borgia to shame, to have a minor declared Emperor; and she retained the power as Regent with the help, of course, of the powerful palace eunuchs! So it was that the pregnant Aluteh, who might bear the departed Emperor a son, died mysteriously. Again, Tzu-hsi maneuvered to have a little boy, Kuang-hsu, become Emperor. Tzu-hsi's co-regent died suddenly, and the rumor quickly spread that she had been poisoned.

Tzu-hsi learned a lot about foreign affairs as her husband let her classify his memorials. As little Chao, from Pewter Lane, she early learned the realities of the life of the people as none raised in the palace ever could. She was unusually intelligent, amusing, a small woman of iron, extravagant, strong-willed, stony-hearted, with an equally good eye for fine embroidery or a rival to be chopped down. She could be most charming even when she was old. Money ear-marked to rebuild the Chinese navy was spent to enhance the beauty of the Summer Palace which was destroyed in 1860. She loved theatricals, and many performances were held for the Court's private delectation.

The Empress' love of nature found its outlet in landscape gardening, among surroundings that were peaceful and pastoral. Marble terraces and beautiful flowers were mirrored in the lake. The Imperial Barge was attached by silken ropes to boats that towed them so they glided as gracefully as a swan. When the Forbidden City was finally entered and the Summer Palace visited, the disarray and tawdriness amongst the myriad bejewelled and embroidered gowns was almost unbelievable. The return to Peking started in September, 1901. The empress and her entourage travelled 25 miles a day for over 700 miles. The trip was made in almost triumphal magnificence. The last part was by railroad, and a new station was built for the occasion.

Letters from Uncle Frank and Aunt Isabel describe their difficult trip to visit Peking before the Court returned. One letter of March, 1901, states:

Peking is strange and barbaric — with immense walls and towers. Its City Gates are defended. The Temples of Heaven and of Agriculture in the environs of the railway station and within its walled cities — three of them — lies the Imperial Forbidden City, surrounded by its own walls and in ordinary times entered by none but persons attached to the Court. When Peking was stormed, the American troops carried the first and second gates of the Forbidden City and could easily have rushed the third and last and have captured the Empress Dowager, the Emperor and all the Court, but through some freak of fate (represent-ed in this instance by General Chaffee's lack of grasp of the situation at a critical moment) all these Arch Rascals were allowed to slip away through a back gate and so escape. How different would have been the subsequent chapters of history had our boys gone a few steps further and grabbed the old woman, who is the cause of all the trouble.

The general impression one receives in visiting the various palaces of the Emperor and Empress Dowager and chief people of the Court is one of tawdry, cheap-looking splendor — grotesque and to a certain extent impressive, but rough and crude in its execution and details — nothing fine and artistic as in Japan. As Commissioner Rockhill said to me later in the U.S. Legation "China is a nation of Coolies — and the Coolies within the palace are much the same as the Coolies outside — ignorant, crude in tastes and habits, and without any true ideas of refinement or comfort. They are all barbarians."

Their chief interest was in the fact that they were walking in private palaces where Europeans had never entered before the capture. This fact was emphasized by

the hundreds of scowling eunuchs who stood around glaring at the intrusion of the hated foreigners — but controlled by fear and very quiet except for their covert expressions of dislike and ill-will. If they dared, there has not been a moment in the whole period of many months past, when the Chinese would not kill every European in Peking. That fact stands, a perpetual menace to all.

The Temple of Heaven he described as a blue dome of 300 feet in height; and to Uncle Frank, it was the most remarkable building seen in China. Next, he would place the Summer Palace — 14 miles outside of Peking. He found it a most interesting series of pavilions rising one above another up the steep side of a hill and crowned with a beautiful temple of Buddha — *the whole palace overlooking a charming lake.*

On May 3, 1901, from Bubbling Well Road where she had been staying, while Uncle Frank was traveling, Aunt Isabel wrote of the trip:

The trip to Peking was the hardest thing I ever did, the discomforts, the greatest, and the dirt and filth which we had to put up with in hotels and nasty Chinese boats, unspeakable. The hardiest traveller would flinch from much of it. And it really did not pay — it sounds well — but there is nothing worth seeing there, except perhaps that it is the dirtiest city in the world!!!

I am sending you a few faded flowers from the Temple of Heaven so sentimentalize over, and better still, a few morning glory seeds that I gathered at the Summer Palace. I think if you plant them you will certainly have something that no one else in Catskill has.

Something special was in the envelope I found among the attic letters. It was very fat. Inside was a carefully folded packet labelled, *Violets which I gathered at the Summer Palace of the Empress Dowager in Peking.* Another turned up marked, *I gathered these from the Temple of Heaven where the Emperor worships four times a year.* These I mounted and framed. The violets soon faded more than when first opened.

By comparison, Aunt Isabel's letter showed how much Shanghai had *improved* since they lived with the Hunters, and she compared it with Peking at this stage of its existence.

> *Shanghai is looking its best now. Bubbling Well Road is truly very pretty with its well kept places — fine trees on either side and Mrs. Hunter's place, the prettiest of them all. Winter hangings are now being taken out and cool mattings and summer curtains taking their place, waiting for the sultry days when "we must kick up our own breeze." For about a month the weather will be charming — and then we shall suffer. I hope we will stay here. Two bath tubs for our own use, with running water, ought to console one for much and the freedom from "dressing up" for dinner is great.*
>
> *The Company's agent went back to America last week. He begged to go and nkt being very useful, Dearest did not find it hard to say yes, but it made me feel very homesick to think we must remain here till next Spring. Ten thousand miles is a long distance to be away from our friends.*

By this time they were getting used to the Pidgin-English and sometimes quoted it in their letters. An old book titled **Fan Kwae** meaning "Foreign Devil" was written by William C. Hunter, Esq., resident in China from 1829 until 1842. One of the more fascinating parts which Uncle Frank quoted is on the quaint jargon called Pidgin English which is used throughout China. It is also called a murderous mixture of English-Portuguese and bastard Cantonese. It is strung together with Chinese idiom and

> *is a corruption of the word business and simply an attempt, chiefly on the part of the Chinese, to copy **SOUNDS** of foreign words and conform them to their own monosylabis mode of expression. There has thus been created a peculiar language, without syntax or logic and reduced to the simplest possible elements, but it has taken firm root and has beome the medium of communication, upon which have been based enormous transactions.*
>
> *Many of the words are of Portugese and Indian origin, such as Mandarin, from Mandar, to order, compradore from compra to buy, Joss from Deos, Maskei from Masque to never mind, or it doesn't matter, Scroff, a money dealer, Tiffin meaning luncheon, go-down from Ka-dang, a storehouse, Coolie, a laborer, Chit, a letter, etc.*

> *The Chinese word "chop" constantly recurs. It is from Cho, a document. Thus the Grand Chop is the tonnage certificate of a ship, a shopkeeper's bill is a "Chop." No. 1 chop means first quality. When a coolie is required to make haste, he is told, "Makee walkee chop chop." In ordering a meal to be served quickly, one says, "Chatchee chow-chow chop chop."*

Even more fun are the ones they quoted from their own experiences. *Your Great head top side — he savy my talkee true,* a curious recognition of our God. Regarding the piano one boy said *"one fine piece box my fightee-he (striking the table) be makee cry."* On one occasion the Chinese estimate of foreign music was expressed in the following manner, *"What for band makee so muchee noisee?"* to which the answer was given, *"That no belong noisee, belong music. You no likee?" My how can likee, all makee mixee. He too muchee foole."*

An amusing attempt at mutual understanding was in connection with a Chinese dinner, where the foreign guest fought rather shy of the slippery, unknown dishes, until what he supposed was roast duck was brought on. As the rhymster of the occasion expressed it:

> *Still cautious grown, and to be sure,*
> *His brain he set to rack,*
> *At length he turned him to his host,*
> *And pointing, cried, Quack, Quack?*

> *The Chinese gravely shook his head,*
> *Next made a reverent bow,*
> *And then expressed what dish it was*
> *By uttering, Bow-wow-wow.*

Cantonese Boat Life was also described in the book, ***Fan Kwae.*** It was not until 1745 that Canton was opened to foreign trade and for a hundred years thereafter foreigners were not permitted to land or trade at any other port. The Choo or Pearl River at Canton presented a most strange and animated appearance, as described by Mr. Hunter. It was crowded with all descriptions of boats including the immense, high-pooped junks that were engaged in the coasting trade with the Celebes, Borneo, Java, Singapore, and Manilla.

Long tiers of salt junks lined the Honan shore, bringing cargos of salt from Teenpak and the south and owned by an immensely rich and powerful Salt Merchants Guild, rivaling Co-hong merchants. The number of boats upon the river was prodigious (probably exceeding 20,000), cargo boats from far up the interior, Government cruisers, passengers and houseboats, queer up-country craft, flower boats, barner boats, sampans, and ferry boats plying to Honan, thousands of boats of vendors of every description of food, clothes, toys, household utensils, besides the many boats of fortune tellers, theatrical performers, musicians, restauranteurs, sing-song girls, and many others.

In fact, imagine a vast city of a quarter million population afloat, and you will get some idea of the incessant movement, the babel of noise, and the life, gaiety and tragedy of the river.

At the time of the Chinese New Year (February) all this was accentuated by the incessant beating of many thousands of gongs, the waving and fluttering of countless red and gilt banners and lanterns, and the universal visiting and merry-making of this vast floating population.

The Boat people remain in swarms in the harbors of Hong Kong, Manilla, Singapore, and the canals and river in Bangkok right up to the present. I presume they are not as numerous as they were in Canton, but I found them in 1967 an amazing mass choking the waterways.

"Regulation for the Foreigners" is another part of this book written about sixty years before Uncle Frank visited that area, and it bears out his contention that some of the merchants who had regular dealings with foreigners could be honest and reliable. Soldiers were considered the lowest stratum with merchants just above them. Farmers rated higher than either. Scholars were highly respected, but education and cultural opportunities were not within reach of the great masses of Chinese, so that the everyday contacts of the marketplace are not the whole story of this complex nation of millions of people through thousands of years.

In no part of the world was more vigilant care exercised by the authorities for the personal safety of the "strangers within the gate" who of their own free will had come to live amid a population whose customs and prejudices were so opposed to everything foreign. Although in those early days the Chinese government was bound by no treaty obligations, yet the care and solicitation of the local government never flagged, and foreigners, though admitted only on sufferance, dwelt in peace and safety and during that hundred years, transacted an incalculable amount of business, always with mutual good feeling and with a profound respect for the wonderful honesty of the Chinese merchants.

*Among the curious regulations made for the government of the foreign community in Canton, were the following patriarchal rules, "Neither woman nor fire arms shall ever be brought into China by foreigners. It is not permitted to foreigners to row on the river for pleasure, but on the 8th, 18th, and 28th of each moon, these foreign barbarians may take the air and visit Flower Gardens and the Honan Joss-house, but not **IN DROVES** of over ten at a time. When they have 'refreshed' they must return and will not be allowed to pass* the night out nor collect to carouse. They must always be accompanied by a Linguist (Chinese Interpreter) and should they disobey these rules, the Linguist shall be punished and the foreigners shall not be allowed to go out on the next holliday." These rules, Mr. Hunter concludes, read more like the regulations of a boys school, than the laws of a community of experienced men of affairs.*

Review of the book written for the **Port-land Oregonian** by Francis R. Wardle

On the return to Shanghai from Peking, cablegrams necessitated his going to Hongkong and Manila, June 1. It was a three-day sail to the *beautiful and romantic looking Hong Kong built on the steep sides of the Peak with terraced roads winding up the mountainside like the threads of a screw. I found the plague raging there and the streets and buildings drenched with carbolic acid and disinfectants — notwithstanding which, some thirty deaths occurred everyday — a few of them Europeans.*

Hong Kong is a solidly built English colony. It has a beautiful botanical garden — one of the finest in the world — a good hotel — and still better Club — and the Peak, reached by a steep cable tramway — a lovely mountaintop above the clouds and overlooking one of the most charming prospects I have ever looked upon.

Hong Kong at present affords a very good object lesson of what results can be looked for from a Sentimental Policy in dealing with the Chinese — to those held by the American Government. As an inevitable result, the native population of Hong Kong and environs have become cheeky, impertinent and almost impossible to live among. I have been hustled off the sidewalk into the gutter by a miserable coolie carrying a bundle of dirty linen, and if I had ventured to strike him for his impertinence, as I would do elsewhere, I would have been hauled up before the magistrate and fined or imprisoned. Sometime ago Gov. Blake went over to Canton and besought the Viceroy to send Chinese troops to prevent trouble on the mainland near by, when had he possessed an ounce of force he could have quelled the whole trouble in half an hour with the English troops and guns at his disposal. The English generally feel ashamed of their milk and water governer and his mistaken policy of treating natives.

After seeing the builders of the Naval Docks Extension and arranging to supply then with a cargo of our American lumber, I went over to

MANILA

a three days voyage and rendered most disagreeable by poor accommodations and hard downpour of rain all the time. One knows nothing of rain until experiencing a tropical rainstorm. It liter-

ally comes down in solid sheets and with a noise like a railroad train.

They sailed past Corregidor Island and Manila Bay opened up before them. An officer on board who had been with Dewey told them the vivid story of the attack on and destruction of the Spanish fleet at Cavite. *It does not matter how many times one has read of these things, the first fresh sight of the places and the hearing of the story by an eyewitness makes it all seem ten-fold more real and interesting. But it was a bad day for us when Dewey entered Manila Bay.*

The city of Manila is on low ground and at that time did not make much of a display from the sea — only two or three buildings standing out conspicuously, i.e. the Cathedral, the Palace, and the new Ice Plant. Twenty miles behind the town is a high range of mountains in which at that time many thousands of insurrectionists were still hiding.

We landed at the Custom House over which the stars and stripes were floating and at once began to realize that once more we were enjoying the glorious freedom of an American Citizen, by suddenly experiencing a more complete lack of freedom than at any time since coming to the Orient! Fifthrate pimply-faced boys and toughs swaggered about us puffing tobacco smoke into our faces and cavalierly ordering us to open our bags through which they thrust their dirty hands and rumaged throughout the contents and then after disordering everything, and not taking the trouble to replace them but walking off. Oh it was glorious to thus find ourselves once more under the highly civilized methods of real freedom, and away from the more courtesy and non-interference of less advanced nations than ourselves.

I waited in line an hour before a little window until a lazy little clerk condescended to issue me a permit to land and go to the hotel. Merchants all over Manila told me that even in the worst days of Spanish rule they were better treated, better served and less taxed and walked upon than under the carpetbaggers rule.

My ten days stay in Manila led me to be ashamed and sorry for the spectacle of mismanagement and constant interference with private rights, and the petty exactions and petty redtape that make one feel how great a blessing genuine freedom is. I have quite a number of testimonies from old residents — prominent merchants and others — all to the same effect — that the United States has brought in more mismanagement, more petty restrictions to trade and personal liberty than the people ever suffered under the Spaniards.

Had he not seen for himself the utterly unreasonable exactions and interferences with individual and personal affairs, Uncle Frank felt he would have discounted such a view of things. But he was forced to admit the American administration of civil affairs was not in any way creditable or ideal.

We have made a botch of it so far. When I hear of the condition of things in Porto Rico, and then see what is going on in Manila, I feel more strongly than ever that we ought to have staid at home and minded our own business. I very much doubt if the American political system with 'pulls and spoils' is at all adapted to good and effective administration of colonies.

He was further astonished to see in Manila how many old political hacks and hangers-on were given snug berths, and how poorly they served the interests of the people. His Captain told him that when he first entered Manila harbor a young inexperienced western farmerlike man came to his ship and demanded that he surrender into official hands his port clearance papers. The captain refused saying that all over the civilized world a ship's master was allowed to keep these papers as proof that he had properly cleared his ports. The answer he got was "Never mind what other nations do. This Great Yankee Nation does what it d--- likes." Such tales went on ad infinitum and ad nauseum.

Manila is full of men that I would not hire as fifth rate clerks at five dollars a week — all feeding from the government trough. This seems to be the trouble. Too few A1 men and the others "working the Philippines for what can be got out of them, quite a la Spaniard." It is all nicely covered up and nothing is said about it and the good folks at home think everything is lovely and "How Great and Good We Are" and why don't the Philippines appreciate us more? And why are they so blind and ungrateful? It is strange. **Very.**

He goes on to say that

Judge Taft is a fine man, and the other members of the Commission are mostly good men, and many of the army officers now engaged in Civil Administration are excellent men, but these don't know a fraction of what is going on undernaath the surface among the fellows who are working the country for their own advantage.

The largest merchants told him many things that would have shaken things up rather lively if they had been known at home. He believed they dared not speak lest they found themselves personae non gratae to the people in power.

Turning from our miserable bungling to other matters less mortifying and disagreeable, he did not find the Philippines themselves inspired him with much respect or sympathy. They seemed to him mostly idle, treacherous, immoral and unworthy. Most of the Philippines are now of mixed blood. They hate us and will continue to do so. They don't want what we are forcing on them. It will be many moons before there is any real sympathy or understanding between such alien races.

He did not find Manila an interesting place, even the Cathedral being without beauty. He got up to attend five o'clock Mass and found a thousand women kneeling on the bare stone floor and gazing adoringly at the great altar alight with hundreds of candles and with two score priests ministering there. *The Philippine men rabidly hate the Friars who have robbed them right and left of money, property, wives, and everything else. The women he found were superstitious and devout in a Spanish-Catholic sort of way — entirely disassociated from morals. The Lunetta was the only drive along the sea wall for about three miles and at sundown hundreds of carriages gathered there and drove slowly up and down while the military band played. It rained all the ten days and nights he was in Manila and it was hot! Hot! HOT!*

The back country is not yet "pacified" that fine ironical euphenism, and officers say there is ten years police duty and skirmishing and bush-fighting before we fully persuade them to quietly accept the blessings of the glorious civilization we offer them at the point of the bayonet.

When once we get the islands conquered, if carpet bag rule spreads as it did in the South, there will always be a sore spot in the Philippines, that honest Americans some day will blush over. Of course, it might be different if a sound civil service and merit system controlled the appointments.

A six days voyage to Hong Kong and Shanghai was full of *rest and comfort.* Isabel and he then started North for a short week's trip by steamer to the New German Colony of Kiauyschou (Tsingtau) where he closed a large contract for piling for the Government harbor works.

The next month, September, he planned a trip alone on a general comprehensive tour of the whole coast line of North China, Manchuria, and up to Port Arthur, with a possible trip from Chefoo to Korea. Then they arranged to go together on a business trip to India in November. It would take two months to visit Hong Kong, Manila, Singapore, Penang, Calcutta, Benares, Lucknow, Cawnpore, Agra (the Taj Mahal), Delhi, Lahore, Bombay, Hyderabadmadras, Madure (the oldest temples in India), Columbo, Ceylon, and back to Shanghai.

The trip to India is not positively settled yet, though it is more than probable, as we are arranging to send our steamers there with lumber and I hope to oversee the opening up of business relations. Still, nothing is absolutely certain in this world. Then I will make a farewell trip over North China ports again and about March 1st, 1902, we will start for home. Write often to the Shanghai address as we need to hear from you more fully to tide us over these last months of exile.

These past two years have given us much to remember with interest in years to come and notwithstanding the discomforts have paid us for all that has been suffered and endured.

One thing they will want to recall often is described in an article for **The Oregonian** titled "A Winter Morning in China." It was written from Chefoo where so many children of foreigners were going to school. For three days it had been blowing great guns. The harbor at Chefoo was crowded with belated shipping. The sea was whipped by the lash of the wind into a seething, tossing mass of white foam. Landward the prospect was even more desolate and drear. An endless succession of rolling, barren hills, without a tree or a bush to relieve their wearisome monotony. The night settled down upon the deserted streets, and the storm reigned supreme.

Rousing at intervals I heard the fierce rush of the wind and the pounding of the surf. Burying myself more deeply in the warm blankets I thanked God for shelter, and softly drifted off again into the pleasant land of dreams.

When I awoke in the morning what a wonderful and beautiful transformation had come to the dreary little port of Chefoo! Had I been transported like Aladdin into some wonderful palace of beauty built by the Genii who were always slaves of the lamp.

As far as eye could see there flashed and glistened a dazzling white carpet of virgin snow, while from every tree and branch hung myriads of shining crystals,

and such was the magic of the ice kings wand that even the ugly walls of the compound opposite my window seemed changed into fantastic battlements of some old castle pierced here and there for the culverins, while the rough black tiles of the French convent below became a miniature copy of the seven thousand carvings of the Milan cathedral.

All about me was a fairy land, brilliant, spotless and exquisitely dainty in form and coloring, fresh from the hand of God. The leaden sky of the past week was exchanged for one of softest and deepest Italian blue, without even a trace of feathery floating cloud. Nowhere have I seen the peculiar and delicious blending of brilliancy and exquisite softness that one finds streaming down from the blue vault that spans this far off China, a mingling of the skies of Lombardy and the Alps.

As I looked forth from my window entranced and a suspicious lump rising in my throat as the loveliness and strangeness of it all came over me, the sweet toned convent bells rang out for matins and a procession of white robed Sisters of the order crossed the cloister to the chapel. Prayer must have been easy for the good Sisters that morning.

Almost at the same moment, Uncle Frank became conscious of a great contrast as a hundred coolies came swinging around into his quiet street, bringing great baskets of coal from the harbor to the storeyard. As they filed along under their heavy burden they chorused the porters' cry, without which no coolie in China seems able to accomplish his daily task — "eeh yhe hahn yeh."

Here he felt the first discord intruding itself into the harmony of the lovely morning. He noted the strong contrast of the great baskets of coal against the background of pure snow, not more pronounced than the squalor and misery of the toiling coolies amid the bright joyousness of the morning.

In China one must always be more or less conscious of this undertone of stress and pinching want in the lives of the great multitudes whose constant and heavy toil barely keeps them one day off from hunger and the poorhouse. It is pitiful to see the hard pressure of the struggle for existence that bends all shoulders to burden-bearing, even the feeble bodies of old men and children. Life is hard in China.

He sallied forth into the crispy, tonic morning air. Friends looked smiling and happy and shouted joyous greetings, followed perchance by a snowball. Even the sober-minded merchants seemed to him infected with the high spirits of youngsters and cast off the dullness of the office to enter into that pure joy of being alive on such a day. The fresh snow crackled under his feet. His eyes were dazzled by *a million flashing mirrors above, below and all about.* His cheeks tingled and glowed from the fine sharp touch of frost. The air was vibrant with sounds of life and joy.

It is astonishing on such a morning how far sounds carry with wonderful distinctness. Far out across the bay the U.S. Cruiser New Orleans is sounding eight bells and the boatswain is piping orders to the watch. The sounds come over the miles of water and echo faintly but clearly in the town.

Oh it is good to be alive, this day of days, but even as the thought rises in the mind, the ear catches the deep boom, boom of a Chinese funeral gong and a moment later a most strange and fantastic procession turns into the main street, such a spectacle as one can see nowhere save in China.

A motley group of ragged beggars came first, carrying large paper figures of horses, servants, houses, and various symbols of comfort and pleasure that surrounded this rich man during his life. These gigantic figures are burned at the grave or the temple so that the spirit of the dead man may have the spirits of these things with him in the spirit world. Two city blocks long, this part of the procession is followed by two hundred or more members of the Beggars Guild.

Until this winter morning in China, I had cherished the opinion that in Italy I had seen the very climax of beggarly misery or miserable beggary in the tattered and loathsome vermin that swarmed my steps at Fiesole, but after seeing the tattermalions of Chefoo I changed my opinion. It said that the deceased gave frequent largess to this beggars

guild and they had most cogent reasons to mourn his loss.

The third section of the great procession, Uncle Frank called the *gastronomic department,* because it consisted of large gaily decorated ceremonial tables turned upside down and filled with a great variety of foods to nourish the departed spirit. Upon one was a whole pig weighing several hundredweight, roasted to a glistening brown in sugar. Then a pitiful little deer or antelope *postured as if in the very act of springing and with a bloody knife sticking in its throat, a horrid sight to make one shudder.* Next came roast ducks, bowls of rice, bottles of samshu or rich brandy, and all the other delicacies of a rich Chinaman's table.

A strong bodyguard of Chinese soldiery — maybe even some original Boxers — followed with men blowing horns at least ten feet in length to frighten away the evil spirits. Last came the only son of the deceased following beside the gorgeously bedecked bier, and surrounded with sympathizing friends and relatives, all dressed in white which is full mourning among the Chinese. (Blue is half mourning.) The son had a piece of rough gunny sack or sackcloth tied about his shoulders with heavy rope.

With true Chinese etiquette this young man pretended to be utterly bowed down with grief so that he could not walk without being supported on either side by two friends that poured consoling words into his heavy heart. As the actual death of his father had occurred several months previously and the body had been kept until the priest could find a lucky day for its burial, it is not unreasonable to suppose that the faithful son's grief had during the interval had ample time to exhaust its first uncontrolled poignancy. But the Chinese are great actors and all this was the proper stage pigeon (business) and so had to be followed.

The body would lie in state at the temple several days. With the disappearance of the motley crowd it seemed that all the beauty of the day had vanished — spoiled by this barbarous and fantastic spectacle of Chinese superstition and materialism.

The rest of the day was spoiled even when Uncle Frank was far out on the broad white fields beyond the town, in friendly silence. He still heard the booming tomtoms and before his mind floated the flaring banners. The charm of the day was gone. It was a *Winter's day in China, and not beneath the old flag at home.*

Dates of letters do not coincide with the itineraries described in them. Articles for the **Oregonian** are written and printed when convenient. In a letter written around Easter, 1901, Aunt Isabel says,

Dearest has been gone ten days again to Tsingtan. He will use the opportunity to study the Henry George system of 'single tax' as instituted in that German settlement.

An article was written by him for **Scribner's Mag-**

azine entitled "Something New in Old China." (The land laws of the new German colony at Kiautschou were based on the theories of the late Henry George.)

At the International Geographic Congress in Berlin, October, 1899, Mr. Poultney Bigelow first called public attention to one of the most remarkable and interesting economic experiments now in process of practical evolution in any portion of the civilized world.

Bigelow lived in my time in Malden, New York, near Catskill, close to West Camp where the Palatines landed. Mr. Bigelow says:

The responsibility for and the success of the introduction of these advanced principles relating to the tenure and taxation of land in the new German colony of Kiautschou in Shantung, China, rest largely with a learned and progressive doctor of philosophy of the University of Leipsic, Dr. Schrameier, who holds the post of Colonial Secretary in that faraway colony. He is a hard student and a close and clear thinker on matters of economic and sociologic science and has long been an earnest believer in the theories of the late Henry George in regard to land tenure and taxation.

When this new colony was founded four years earlier, Dr. Schrameier finally succeeded against much opposition in getting permission to give the theories a fair trial. Even opponents never denied that if Henry George's theories could be put into practice they would bring untold blessing to the human race. The contention was that they could not be successfully adapted to the practical conditions of life as they existed. Even though China was the oldest and most conservative nation on earth, conditions in the new German colony were favorable to the exciting experiment. The colony consisted of a few scattered villages of farmers and fishermen and no vested interests. A large portion of the ceded territory was unoccupied and of no value. All private title was extinguished and vested in the government — that is to say, the people — since it was a self-governing colony. The transfers seemed entirely fair to the natives who were pleased to have a few dollars for their miserable huts and holdings.

There are thirteen pages of explanation of the workings of the colony. In brief, the government auctioned off to the highest bidders among the European colonists the perpetual use of the land, but only in small parcels. There were stringent rules for immediate improvement. Landgrabbers and speculators were at a disadvantage and there was no chance for wealthy individuals or syndicates to move in as in the United States when a new town starts up. The best corners, rail and water frontage, etc., are acquired and the land is left idle until the absentee owners can cash in on the improvements made by the hard work of others. Improvements in the colony made at the owner's expense were never taxed. The original land

alone was taxed at six per cent of its actual value from year to year. The constant effort of the government was to keep down values and make land cheap and thus stimulate a natural healthy growth. There were some objections to the rule for resale of land every twenty-five years and one third the profits going to government. Theoretically, the land regulations seemed wise and just and beneficent. After four years the young colony, the port of Tsingtau, was rapidly becoming a very beautiful and attractive place.

There are some hundred or more substantial and handsome brick and stone structures, chiefly along the Bund or seawall and the main street parallel to it . . . . The foundations of a fine and modern city are being laid and well laid . . . . It is a moot point among Tsingtau's citizens what relation the land laws and single tax have had to this development. Some claim that early progress and prosperity have been repressed to the disadvantage of the place.

On the other hand supporters of the present system claim — not without reason and justice on their side — that all booms eventually boomerang and hurt rather than help a town. If the initial progress is slower the community expects benefit later on in the life of the community.

I can do no better than here quote the substance of a very interesting interview I had with Dr. Schrameier. "The intention of the German government is to create here a lasting and prosperous mercantile and industrial city, built and managed in European style, that in time will become the centre of the trade of Shangtung province and beyond, a hinterland of a hundred thousand miles of rich productive country and peopled by a frugal and hardworking population of probably forty million souls. We shall penetrate every part of this hinterland and with branches of our Shangtung railroad, and we shall connect its Tsingtau terminal with direct steamers to Europe . . . . To prevent private encroachment upon the profits . . . a duty is imposed upon the government to so administer this great trust, the land, so that all might equitably share in the profits accruing and so that the few might not get rich at the expense of the many . . . . also to guard against selfish speculators residing outside the community and indifferent to its immediate interests . . . we believe that huge and reckless speculation in land and absorption of the best locations has been effectively prevented and great prosperity and future good secured to this colony by the practical application of Henry George's theories."

The article closed with contrast of this *earnest and brainy man, thoroughly devoted to the interests of that community and Tammany's Chief in New York and municipal boodlers in general.* Uncle Frank also cited the problem of bad weather, exposed anchorage, and poor facilities for discharge. A new harbor was being built but slow, careless, costly, and inefficient handling of valuable merchandise was a serious disadvantage to Tsingtau as compared to its neighbors. Red tape was another drawback and had already cost the port a half million dollars loss. The practical men of affairs resident on the colony and familiar with its real need were not given sufficiently free hand, a generic fault of German administration.

The more influential Chinese merchants of the interior and the treaty ports are absolutely essential with their cooperation to secure large trade in the hinterland, but are not attracted. There seems to be a certain lack of mental adaptability about the Germans that may work against their success. In many ways they are splendid fellows, substantial, hardworking, thorough, and highly intelligent, but it remains to be demonstrated if they are adjustable and adaptable to the very peculiar conditions and people. I find myself hoping with all my heart, for it will be an immense gain to the Chinese of Shantung Province, to have a flourishing German colony at Kiautschou. It means the eventual emancipation of many millions of people in one of the most primitive and backward provinces of North China. And this is why I wish the Germans success and hope most sincerely they will attain it.

During this same period Isabel tried to carry on the personal correspondence for both of them. Uncle Frank, when not away on a trip, often brought home an old typewriter and hammered out interminable business cables and letters until ten o'clock. Isabel wrote to her sister-in-law, Florence Wardle, explaining the great postal difficulties in mailing packages.

It is not worth while as you can purchase at Vantines any of those silver things quite as cheaply as here. You surely do not imagine they cost but ten cents each and are even worn by the Chinese! They are made entirely for foreign trade .... Foreign goods are 1/3rd to 1/2 higher than in America.

She describes life there as very prosaic and had previously described about all that was not commonplace.

Society is so empty here. Mrs. Hunter and I are going today to return some calls. We will drink a poor cup of tea and talk about Mrs._____'s new jacket or Mrs._____'s pain in her side. Someone recently described Shanghai in the paper.

1. *Shanghai incomes are insufficient.*
2. *Shanghai displays money, nothing else.*
3. *Shanghai holds intellectual culture at a discount.*
4. *Shanghai professes little religion, practices none.*
5. *Shanghai expects no hereafter, deserves none.*

Add a dreadful amount of scandal and the picture is

complete. I think it is the wickedest place I was ever in. The weather holds very raw and cold so the trees and shrubs do not venture to bud yet, but we have had heliotrope and violets all winter from the little greenhouses. Just lately I have discovered the absurd little forts the people build on their roofs and mount empty wine bottles on the forts for guns to frighten away the evil spirits supposed to be always hovering about. Little crude shrines are very common on roofs. One day I saw a very poor funeral. Unable to pay for drums and tom toms, to scare the spirits away, a man riding on a wheelbarrow was preceding the coffin scattering the silver sycee, or money to buy off the spirits. I have seen this twice. If a Mafoo (coachman) wants good luck for his horse, he takes a tissue paper horse to the temple and burns it. Millions and billions of this paper money is used every year. For a few cash one may buy a dozen. They look like little boats or shoes — Chinese shoes.

Recently they saw the whole process of preparing the silk for weaving from the sorting of the pretty little cocoons to the packing of the glistening skeins in eight-pound packages for market. In the room where the cocoons were unwound there were about 400 girls and women from nine years upward. They sat there twelve hours daily in a steam laden atmosphere, their fingers whitened or parboiled by constant handling of the cocoons as they bobbed up and down in the hot water where they were being softened. Five or four cocoons made one thread and these were guided over little pulleys to the skein reels. Each cocoon furnished about 200 yards of filament. The temperature was about eighty degrees in the room they visited, and they could not imagine what it would be in the summer. The girls got paid two and one half cents gold a day an furnished their own food. Some of the women were married and had children.

The manager said to us that labor is getting so dear there is little profit in the business! Yet these girls do not look unhappy and seem contented. They are warm, about the most desirable condition a Chinese can imagine. Work they must and this is easy work though very confining. Labor of all kinds is very cheap. Women come here now to cut weeds out of the lawn. They get five cents a day. Common street coolies get 10 cents. They do almost all hauling in barrows, the wheel of which is in the center, thus bearing most of the weight. It is a common sight to see 8 women, four on each side of these barrows and only one coolie. All furniture is moved in this way, as well as all building materials. Horses are most rarely used. Coolies are cheaper. Lighter merchandise is carried in baskets suspended from the ends of a bamboo pole over the shoulders.

At the Chinese New Year, February 19, every coolie and servant wanted his wages advanced and for two to five days gave himself up to such luxury as his means allowed; regardless of the pinching that would inevitably follow. Every man, woman, and child procured some new garment at this time, thus deceiving one into thinking they might be a shade cleaner. But all the dirt was still there underneath. Everything that came home from the cleaners had to be hung out of doors for a week, before one could endure it in the house. They seemed to like themselves just as they were, unlike the Japs who were eager for change and foreign ways.

The Chinese will learn English because it enables them better to trade, and in this connection I believe from what I hear and observe that they dislike Americans less than any other nation because all we want is legitimate trade. We do not seize their lands and impose our ways upon them. I speak from a commercial viewpoint only. The missionary is another story which we will not discuss.

A summer unusually cool for July is compared in Isabel's next letter to the extreme heat New York was experiencing.

The hot weather was due a month ago. It has rained constantly for a fortnight. Today with the first sunshine, I have had everything out on the balconies. Even garments wrapped and put away are quite spotted. Our shoes look like potato patches. We shall be more glad than you can possibly be to get home again.

Siberia was next on the agenda for August. Isabel wanted to go with him as far as Vladivostok, but so dreaded the four-day trip on dirty Chinese boats to a place *with nothing interesting — only cooler weather.* He was to go into the forests of Siberia to see in they could use the lumber there.

In November, Mr. Wheelright wants Dearest to go to Calcutta. The weather will be tolerable then, **perhaps,** *only perhaps. If I can manage that trip I should delight in it for the Indians here are the most pleasing feature of all the strange sights.*
I enclose some samples of Japanese maples, the fine, lacy leaf is red always. The others turn in the Fall. I like the one with seed pods. The trees are small, not larger than a lilac bush of average size. Do write and share our letters with all who care to hear.

Four months later, there is a letter dated November 11 and written from Shanghai. Uncle Frank had been very ill; in fact he had not been well for several months, *much neuralgia from eye strain, causing headaches much of the time. Also the bowel conditions persisted all the time more or less.*

On October 16th he went to Hong Kong on his way to Manila. He was taken very ill there after a few days in the Hotel and could get no attention whatever from anyone — not even a doctor summoned, until finally by giving a big "cumsha," he got a cit or note sent to a friend, who came as soon

as possible. He had him moved at once to the Peak Hospital where he lay for a week before letting me know and sending for me. He had what the physicians called a severe case of influenza with complications which might develop into either Typhoid or Dysentery. He had high fever for three days, much abdominal pain and no appetite for poor hospital food. When I arrived after a trying four days sail, on the 29th I found him sufficiently better to be able to be taken to the steamer and brought home very weak. We reached here November 3rd and he has been in bed ever since — today walking to our dressing room for the first time to have his bedroom thoroughly aired and cleaned. He has been more or less flighty a great deal of the time and still has some pain in the lower bowel where some slight inflammation seems to persist resulting from his attack of dysentery in Chefoo a year ago last August.
We are feeding him now entirely on liquids — milk, broth, beef juice, etc. He is very weak and finds mental effort very trying and fatiguing and worries correspondingly as very important business is at hand. Telegrams come every day to which he cannot give proper attention. There is no one to help him. I write for him for an hour or less and then he is too tired to continue. I translate and make up code telegrams for him but I am such an ignoramus about business that I am little use that way.

The doctor did not think him in any condition of danger and since he was gaining slowly and Isabel was well, she was able to do everything for him. He had lost forty pounds. The servants were all willing and got big *cumshos* so they were entirely comfortable. Isabel saw Hong Kong only by moonlight the night she arrived and the night they left except for a chair ride *which Dearest was so set on my having that I found it made him worse to resist. She went for an hour's ride around the Peak and if my heart had been at rest I would have thought it one of the loveliest sights I have ever seen. The Catskill Clove, the Pali at Honolulu are enchanting.* She was glad to find some part of China that was truly beautiful. *If ever I do get back to God's country, I shall never ask to leave it again.* (however, after Uncle Frank's death she lived for several years in Florence, Italy. I have many postcards and a scrapbook Mother made for me of Florence. When I came home from Europe by way of Italy, the chief place I wanted to visit was the Ponte Vecchio in Florence.

I sent you Florence a blouse length of silk. [I was given some blue silk out of which I made a blouse for my trousseau. I believe it was the same.]
We came up on the steamer from Hong Kong with Prince Chin. I saw his Highness everyday — a very plain looking youth. But for his silk clothes

and fine pearl in his hat, he was quite like all the rest of this nation of coolies.

The family pack rats were slipping and not saving all letters, but by good fortune there was a fairly consecutive account of their Far East trip. It was soon to end. By good gortune, Aunt Isabel's last letter, dated Shanghai, March 10, 1902, fills in the final months.

Have I acknowledged **any** *of your welcome letters, all of which I found awaiting our return from India, the 22nd of February? I cannot be sure, but then I found 26 letters, lots of parcels and books and papers, so I am a bit puzzled. I only know all were very good to get, the children's and Floy's and yours, and your book (which we enjoyed hugely) and the pretty little bit of drawn work and all the good wishes.*

These last weeks are very busy. Friends are kind with their invitations. I got **no** *sewing done for Fall or Winter because of Dearest's illness and our two months absence. And now I am trying to put together, hastily, a few blouses. Skirts are beyond my present power — they must wait for home leisure. And Home begins to loom delightfully as we leave on the 28th of this month (16 days more!)*

They were to sail on the Doric which would be due in San Francisco on the 22nd of April, 1902. This was as close as they would get for awhile *to our heart's home. We will still have a continent between us, but a week is much nearer than a month away.* She also said she had written to Carrie from Calcutta and told them how they had given up all travel in India.

Dearest was too ill and I was so tired that I was most grateful not to have to make the hard trying journeys by wretched railroads. Now I am beginning to regret it.

They felt it was not to be. Frank improved rapidly after they left Calcutta, so they enjoyed stoppages at Pengar, Singapore, Hong Kong, and most of all two days at Canton. They had to wait for a steamer at Hong Kong so went up to Canton.

We had a good guide, went all over this most Chinese-y of cities. We ate our tiffin in a Pagoda 1200 years old, looking over this vast city which seems all one roof! so narrow are the streets.

One evening we took a sampan and visited the Flower Boats. They are places — sort of tea gardens on boats wherein greater or less magnificence, rich (or poorer) Chinamen go to smoke, gamble and be entertained by the Sing Song girls — The Flowers. All is perfectly decorous, some of the girls very pretty. Poor things. Their highest ambition is to have some rich man buy them for slaving. [Make your own interpretation. Perhaps the word should be bye, but that's not the way it is spelled in the letter. And there seems no doubt the word is "slaving." Sha? Moen? also hard to read, is called the foreigners portion "is the prettiest little spot in China," that is of the towns.]

We "tiffined" with some young bachelors in their "mess" over their "Hong" or business quarters. Then once more on a big steamer, (I wonder how many I have been on out here) headed for Shanghai and a warm welcome from our hosts whose picture at their doorway I enclose.

So ends the saga of the Far East. Instructions are to write from then on "Care of the Pacific Export Company in Portland, Oregon," though they planned to stay a few days in Frisco. Frank was desparately busy *finishing up.*

The adventurer of the Wardle Clan was back under the Stars and Stripes. He wrote his brother Charles (my father) from Portland, Oregon, on July 25, 1902:

We have just returned from a trip up into the Olympic Mountains of Northern Washington and have had a fine time. We stayed some time at a lovely lake called Lake Cushman in the midst of the great forests of fir that cover the country for a thousand miles. The fishing was good and so was the food and both Isabel and I have regained our health and feel once more the blessings of well bodies and buoyant minds.

After my two years of hard work in China and my long illness there and rundown condition on my return, I felt the first necessary thing to do was to get well and strong and then I could tackle anything on this earth and make it go.

His friends told him he looked brown as a berry and well and strong enough to lick his weight in wildcats. They planned to leave Portland, where they had made many pleasant friends, and take up permanent residence in San Francisco. He would rent a house after Isabel returned from her

proposed Fall visit to her brother Judge Church at Evanston, Illinois, and then on to New York. I shall be obliged to stay in San Francisco attending business while Isabel makes her Eastern trip, though I would greatly like to come with her.

His former company, the Pacific Export Lumber Company, offered him entire charge of its business in San Francisco, so he planned to continue to look after its interests as he had for the last two years. But he also planned to take on other interests on his own account, and he hoped to do fairly well. Mail was still to be sent to the P.E.L.Co. in Portland until he could open his office in San Francisco, and also find them a home in which to live.

As last June was my 50th birthday, I shall be starting anew in undertaking my San Francisco business — a man beginning all over again after he is fifty years of age. Still it does not turn a hair with me and I am strong and able to win my way as ever — that gives me not the slightest concern.

They both found they were growing to like *this lovely California climate and the many nice, quiet, refined people whom one can come to know. There is a fine element on this coast and the climate is perfect both winter and summer.*

A Wardle Genealogy was compiled by Francis Robert Wardle during the next few years. The latest date recorded in the genealogy is 1904. The date of his own death is not recorded there, but Frank died in 1904 before the San Francisco earthquake of 1906. I remember well hearing that Aunt Isabel, at the time of the earthquake, put into a small bag a change of underwear, her Bible, and a picture of her late husband. She crossed the bay and went to be with cousins who lived in Berkeley. The Genealogy (there is only one copy) must have been sent on to my father after Frank's death and so escaped the earthquake destruction. This copy is now in the Library of the Bronck Museum Library, Coxsackie, New York.

In a 1902 letter to Charles, Frank requested this group picture of the six Wardle children (taken in 1900) which he wanted to include in this genealogy. *L. to R.* Alma, 2; Philip, 3½, Constance, 5; Winifred, 7; Francis 9½; Gerald, 14½

This picture (taken around 1912) includes Charles Athow Wardle, Jr., who was born in 1904, the same year that Uncle Frank died. *L. to R. 1st row:* Constance, Charles, Francis; *2nd row:* Winifred, Philip, Gerald, Alma

Winifred Wardle, 2 years old in her red coat.

Winifred and Francis West Wardle (I have the sailor suit.)

Charles Athow Wardle, Sr.

PART VIII
HERITAGE

The quest for one's heritage and ancestry is epidemic. Few people want to be without roots. The amazing success of Alec Haley's book, **Roots,** which traces his ancestry back to the slave ship and his tribe in Africa, has sparked interest among all of us ethnics.

Running like a thread through the letters of 1854 to the 1900s is a strong sense of "Who am I?" Those readers without packrats for ancestors or whose relatives have slipped beyond the Question-Answer Stage gain some sense of their background from these and other letters of old before the often regretted, "Too late."

Our heritage in all the decades of living recorded shows how highly they prized education in a very realistic fashion in all the family lines including the many dirt farmers.

On the Dutch side, the Dutch Reformed Church from earliest days to the present insisted on an educated ministry. Its early church in Catskill paid for the theological education of one of its first ministers, Dominie Schuneman. He went back to Holland because there was no theological seminary in the New World until The Dutch Reformed Church founded New Brunswick Seminary in New Jersey.

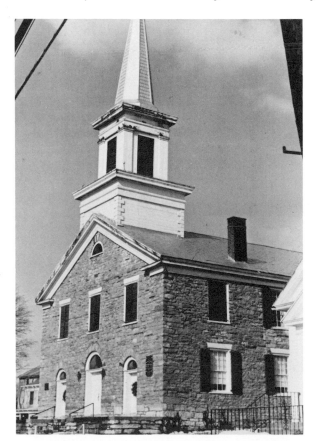

Leeds Reformed Church. Members of this church built a new church at Catskill Landing in 1832 — the First Dutch Reformed Church of Catskill.

A book, **Dutch Dominie of the Catskills,** was based on his life. His red brick home and gravestone are well preserved near Catskill's Jefferson Cemetery. Schuneman is a name found in the Van Gelder Genealogy — an example of how tied togeher are most of the older family lines in the Greene County area.

Born-againers of today find many of the letters of friends writing James Harvey Van Gelder have common feelings and express themselves with the same effusive manner.

Our own Methodist background, however, is tempered with restraint which shows up in the quotes from family publications, as well as their letters.

Evocative of the times, are quotes from **Bridal Greetings,** a book given by Methodist Ministers to their parishioners on their wedding days. My copy was handed down by my grandmother, Rebecca Pine. It has her wedding certificate in the front. An excerpt:

> If the reader expects to find highly wrought sentimentality or romantic fancies in the succeeding pages, he had better lay them down . . . But if a desire to learn somewhat of the stern realities of rugged life and profit by timely cautions, then the author can cordially invite his reader to a more intimate acquaintanceship.
>
> Deceive not yourselves by expecting happiness in the married state. Marriage is not like the hill Olympus, wholly clear without clouds. Remember the nightingales, which sing only some months in the spring, but commonly are silent when they have hatched their eggs, as if their mirth were turned into care for the young ones.
>
> The first quarrel between a man and his wife, like the first glass of wine, is the only dangerous one.
>
> Very few married couples understand each other's tastes and peculiarities. Most courtships afford anything but an opportunity for gaining this knowledge. In general, courtship consists in mutual, though undesigned deception. Both labor to conceal their unfavorable points of character, both aim to please, and are determined to please.
>
> Only let the young couple resolve to begin their married life in a strictly religious manner, and all will be well. Let the conversation be spiritual, let the bridal chamber witness their prayers and their covenants to serve Christ together; let the social altar be erected at once, and their hearts cheerfully laid upon it, and Jesus will pronounce a nuptial benediction, which will bring them happiness and prosperity through the years of after life.
>
> If possible attend [services] at least twice on

Sunday. Make such arrangements for eating on the Sabbath as will not trespass on your time or that of your domestics. Avoid the guilty practice of many fashionable professors of religion, who keep their domestics at home, in the morning, to cook a luxurious dinner, while they are at church.

The same liberal and Christian feeling must influence them when they become parents, in the education of their children, though in this matter the wife is bound to remember that the husband is divinely appointed **HEAD** of the family. The right and authority to decide in their case, are unquestionably in his hands, to be exercised however with all mildness and discretion in the fear of God.

You have not only changed your relation to each other but to your respective families . . . By proper caution on both sides an harmonious union will make sweet music, may be permanently established.

Should there be a stepmother or maiden sister who previously acted as housekeeper for the bridegroom, the young bride may have a task . . . demand all her energies. In such case it is the duty of the husband to transfer fully and formerly all domestic management from his mother or sister to his wife. There cannot be two mistresses.

Only let the young husband and wife refrain from all acts and expressions that imply contempt of each other's relations . . .

Old friends of the opposite sex for whom strong attachments have been formed are not now to be received as intimate friends.

Have friends, few, select, worthy, but have only one confidant — the partner of your bosom . . . Learn that even innocent familiarities are not to be allowed between you and members of the opposite sex.

You can create a domestic heaven in the lowliest cottage; you can suffer the torments of social hell in the most princely dwelling.

I advise the newly married to do without help if possible. A servant brings greatly increased expenses, new cares, new moral element, new responsibilities into a family . . .avoid except in extremity . . . If needed, . . .pious servants truly devoted to God are to be preferred . . . rare.

Hired help should always be treated kindly, even respectfully. Treat her so she shall not feel her servitude. To do this does not require excessive familiarity, but only a kind spirit and respectful language. It is not necessary to take a hired girl so closely into the bosom of the family as to give her a seat at your own table or your own fireside. This may be done when there is suitability of manners and character.

There is no letter telling of Rebecca's father's admonitions for his daughter. But there is a copy of a

Kiskatom Reformed Church — Rebuilt by Frederick C. Fiero.

debate he had with the Dutch dominie of Kiskatom. Walter Pine, Rebecca's father, had never debated and was busy with several farms.

The debate was sparked by a series of doctrinal sermons by Rev. H. Compton (whose arguments on Predestination outdid for dogmatism any I heard as a teenager in the Catskill Dutch Reformed Church). When the minister of the Methodist Church would not argue with his fellow minister, great grandpa did his best.

Quotes show him very knowledgeable, and he must have read a great deal to so ably counter the dogma with a man who didn't wish to debate with a farmer.

Calvinism declares that Christ has redeemed only a part of the human family — a few souls so predestined.

Arminianism declares Christ has redeemed the whole human family.

Pine's object was to give the reader evidence on both sides so they could better judge the correctness of the theory.

The sentiments and advice of our grandparents on the paternal side of my family are in a precious copy of a book given be by my father. The book, written by my great grandfather, Robert Athow West, A.M., is entitled, **A Father's Letters to His Daughter.** The ancestry of this great grandfather is illuminated for us in Uncle Frank's Wardle Geneology compiled in 1904.

A **Father's Letters to His Daughter** is a small book with a lot of large messages. The daughter was Ann Eliza West, my father's mother. She graduated from three years of seminary, a girls' school equivalent to high school. The letters were sent when she was at the seminary.

In writing these letters, the father expresses his pleasure at his daughter's willingness to exchange thoughts:

You will, I feel sure bear me witness that my ear and my heart have ever been open to the story of your joys and sorrows, my tongue ever ready to counsel and my hand to help.

You may have many acquaintances, but you need and should have few companions . . . especially avoid closer acquaintance than courtesy demands with those around you whose thoughts dwell mainly on vanities and frivolities . . .

Be just to others as well as yourself . . . to your equals be affable and courteous, to your inferiors be generously civil.

There is one counsel I must neither omit or postpone. My beloved daughter "fear God and walk in righteousness." Learning is good but godliness is better . . .

Though he urges her to attend all public means of grace he says,

I lay little stress upon those adventitious aids which have come into use, such as standing up in the congregation . . . or bowing around those who conduct public exercises. I do not, I dare not condemn such proceedings, but I cannot conceal a misgiving . . . I think it likely, my dear, that you will profitably hit upon God in the quiet and reserve of your own place . . .

When she is about to leave the institute he writes:

You have but a few weeks to remain at the institute . . . a change of circumstance awaits you. You will no longer be subject to masters . . . and the formalities . . . which the educational institution renders expedient . . . You will assume your position among peers, and mingling with society, will have to speak and act on your own responsibility . . . Lean not to thine own understajding but in all thy ways acknowledge Him. I Ie shall direct thy paths.

You know the theatre is no fitting place for a young person of your sex . . . twice or thrice, as you know, I have been the unwilling spectator of a theatrical representation. For myself, I marveled much that husbands could take their wives, fathers their daughters, and brothers their sisters.

I am inclined to place dancing in almost the same category [as theatre] even though it might be considered a healthful exercise.

I know that ladies sometimes complain that gentlemen rarely address them as intellectual beings, but seem to think them as incompetent to converse on grave and important topics. I cannot dispute the fact, but if light and frivolous conversation has become the rule with men conversing with women, I fear it is because it has been found the shortest and most direct route to your favor and companionship . . . But it is in your power to change this . . . Teach us that we can only be enshrined in your good graces when we pay homage to your intelligence, rather than your vanity, when we challenge you to earnest and improving conversation rather than when we seek to amuse you . . . and we shall be willing pupils . . . Do not make a display of your educational acquirements or mental power . . . God has made no individual or class independent of others . . . The recreation of pleasant converse in needful to soothe the infelicities of life . . . Youth is entitled to indulgence of its vivacities, and sympathies, so long as you keep the fear of the Lord before your eyes . . . modesty, discreet reserve like the distance kept by royal persons contributes to maintain proper deference. Women can make their society too cheap . . .Remember that to God you are responsible for that wonderful influence over our sex with which He has endowed you . . . Men acquire habits of urbanity, courtesy, etc . . . Keep alive your taste for domestic occupations. A practical knowledge of domestic affairs and their management is both honorable and profitable to any woman, regardless of her wealth or social position.

Robert Athow West, A.M., was editor of several influential New York and Washington daily newspapers. Years later his son, Henry Litchfield West, my grandmother's half brother, was one of the editors and managers of the **Washington Post** and in Teddy Roosevelt's time, became a commissioner of the District of Columbia.

Further back, 200 years ago, John and William West, were co-laborers with Rev. John Wesley in the great spiritual revival in England. Later, Rev. Francis

Robert West   Rev. Francis West

Athow West, D.D, became president of the Wesleyan British Conference and both he and his son-in-law were governors of the famous Kingswood School of Bath.

In 1848 this same great grandfather, Robert Athow West, A.M., published a book, **Sketches of Wesleyan Preachers.** Two of the pen sketches are ministers related to the author. West's purpose was to strengthen the bonds between the two great branches of Methodism and carry out the purpose of the founder.

Uncle Frank wrote in the Genealogy in 1904:

Thus it will be seen that for 200 years the whole force and energy of the family have been devoted to human betterment and progress, along religious, literary, and educational lines.

From the days of John Wesley to the recent present there has been an unbroken line of Methodist ministers in our family, starting with my great, great grandfather, Francis West, who was born December 16, 1765, in Lincolnshire, England. He married Mary Frances Athow of Bedham, Norfolk, England. The Athow coat of arms was granted in 1586.

Grandpa Van Gelder once warned his descendants not to brag too much about the Van Gelder coat-of-arms. "After all, a Duke of Gelderland killed his brother." I know of no skeleton in the closet with the Athow coat-of-arms. A Fiero coat-of-arms was presented at the Fiero Reunion with the explanation that not all coats-of-arms were awarded as an honor. They were insignia which identified friend or foe.

No letters were found in the Fiero attic. My son did not inherit his pack rat habits from that side of his family. But like the rest of the ancestors, the Fieros had a long record of dedication to their religious heritage. My husband served many years on the Consistory, and I served one term as Elder (when I was in my 80s) of the Dutch Reformed Church in Catskill.

My husband, Frederick, inherited the skills of the French Huguenot artisans. At fifteen years of age, he built a grandfather clock case and kitchen cabinet. He also built a beautiful corner cupboard of old pine and a Chippendale mirror of old walnut for me. His natural engineering skills were passed on to our son.

According to my mother, my grandfather, Rev. John Knight Wardle, M.D., always handed his congregation his sermon in a nutshell at its close. In a nutshell, the quality I value most from the common heritage of all the ancestors is their open-mindness. They seem to have believed in opening the windows of the mind and heart to the fresh breezes of knowledge and revelations of the Truth. Do we need to be so afraid to venture, to take the risks of searching for Truth in unknown territory? We can still keep our feet on the solid ground which ancestors treasured.

First Reformed Church, Catskill, New York. Some member of the Fiero family served on the Consistory from the beginning until a rotation of officers policy was adopted.

First Reformed Church (Catskill), formerly First Dutch Reformed, ca 1910, when I became the church organist.

Frederick Clow Fiero

John Fiero, direct descendant of Valentine Fiero, father of Frederick C. Fiero.

Rachel Clow Fiero, mother of Frederick Clow and Florence Fiero

Golden Wedding Anniversary of James Harvey and Rebecca Pine Van Gelder, at Cherry Hill House, August 2, 1914.
L. to R.: Arthur Pine Van Gelder, James Harvey Van Gelder, Rebecca Pine Van Gelder, Carrie Van Gelder Wardle.

Fiero Dutch cradle, given to Derek Van Gelder Fiero

Peter Van Gelder's house on Walnut Street, Catskill, New York, built 1859.

Katsbaan Church — stone marked "CM" stands for Christian Myer — erected 1732, rebuilt 1860.

SUMMER BOARDING HOUSE,

Early photograph of Cherry Hill House showing Octagon House in the background. Before landscaping and Norway Spruce trees were planted.

From the oldest to the youngest — Great-grandmother Winnie and Megan Fiero — 1981.

John Robert, Ruth Wright, Derek Van Gelder, Sarah Elizabeth Fiero, 1961. Octagon House in rear.

Derek Van Gelder Fiero, son of J. Robert Fiero, with his daughter, Megan Hope.

At the Fiero Reunion in Katsbaan, New York — **L. to R.:** J. Robert Fiero, Winifred Wardle Fiero, Robert Alan Fiero, Sarah Fiero Romo, Gilberto Romo.

Fred Herbert Wardle and his cousin "Bobby Jack" in the old Fiero Dutch cradle.

The Fiero Line

Valentine
Fiero
1690

Christina
Schram

Johannes
Fiero

Margaret
Elich

Johannes
Fiero

Lena
Schmid

John
Fiero, Jr.
1774

Mary Saxe
1774

Frederick J.
Fiero — 1801

Maria Saxe
1812

John R.
Clow

Maria Amelia
Wells

Rev. John Knight
Wardle, M.D.
1827

Ann Eliza West
1833

James Harvey
Van Gelder
1838

Rebecca Pine
1838

John Fiero
1846
Married
Second
Rachel Ann
Clow — 1856

Charles Athow
Wardle — 1865

Carrie Van
Gelder — 1865

Frederick Clow
Fiero — 1886

Winifred Wardle
1893

John Robert
Fiero — 1919

(Continued on other charts)

Arthur Pine Van Gelder
His Children

Arthur Pine Van Gelder
1873

Louisa Hunt Pool
1872

Elizabeth Pine Van Gelder
1903

Charles Pool Van Gelder
1907

Smith Pine — His Children

Smith Pine
1844

Married first
Luphema J.
Lawrence
18

Hattie Caroline Pine
1868

Walter Frederick Pine
1870

Sally Brunk Patterson Pine
18

Luella Amelia Pine
1874

Married
Second
Eva Shinn
18

William Lloyd Pine
1888

Elsie Howard
18

Laura Rebecca Pine
1889

Ralph Waldron Pine
1891

Lila Ruth Pine
1893

Eva Bell Pine
1900

Howard Smith Pine
1902

Carrie Van Gelder Wardle
Her Children

Carrie Van Gelder
Wardle — 1865

Charles Athow
Wardle
1865

Gerald Knight
Wardle — 1886

Ralph Harvey
Wardle — 1889

Francis West
Wardle — 1891

Winifred Wardle
1893

Constance Wardle
1895

Philip Van Gelder
Wardle — 1897

Alma Wardle
1898

Charles Athow
Wardle, Jr.
1904

To Whom Attic Odyssey is Dedicated

John Robert
Fiero — 1919

Married First
Ruth Wright
1918

Derek Van Gelder
Fiero — 1945

Married First
Janet Dreibelbis

Married Second
Tedi Lifton

Sarah Elizabeth
Fiero — 1949
Married to
Gilberto Romo

Aaron Fiero
Megan Hope Fiero

Married Second
Janet McGinnes

Robert Alan
Fiero — 1966

Janet had two children
Dawn McGinnes — 1953
David McGinnes — 1958

Ancestors and descendants of Rev. John Knight Wardle, M.D. and Anna Eliza West

Francis Robert
Wardle — 1852

John West
Wardle — 1855

Elizabeth Inchle
Wardle — 1857

Florence Turton
Wardle — 1860

Alfred Hill
Wardle — 1862

Charles Athow
Wardle — 1865

Rev. John Knight
Wardle — 1827

Hugh Wardle — 1802
Elizabeth Inchle (?)
1800

James Wardle, father
of Hugh
Dorothy

Ann Eliza
West — 1833

Rev. Robert Athow
West — 1809

Married first
Eliza Turton

Married second
Elizabeth Cook

Rev. Francis
West — 1765

Mary Francis
Athow — 1769

Rev. Isaac
Turton

Rev. William
West — 1710

Alice Rubins
1725

Son of
John West (?)

Ancestors of Carrie Van Gelder (Wardle), and Arthur Pine Van Gelder

Carrie Van Gelder (Wardle) 1865

James Harvey Van Gelder 1838

Peter Van Gelder 1800

Jacob Van Gelder 1771

Peter Van Gelder — 1737

Hendrik c1706

Annetje Vander Voort

Altie Hendrike or Hendrikese — 1729

Abraham Hendrick

Helleche Van Nostrand

Maria Mynderse or Maria Meinders 1762

Henry Mynderse of Meinders —

Treintje Van Wormer

Sarah Meyer 1800

William Meyer 1758

Johannes Meyer 1721

Christian Myer c1690

Ann Geertrug Theunyes (Gertrude Theunis) 1690

Maritje Osterhout 1734

Rachel Meyer 1764

Petrus Meyer 1732

Maritje Low 1736

Arthur Pine Van Gelder 1873

Rebecca Pine 1838

Walter Pine 1809

John Pine, Jr. 1773

John Pine, Sr. 1734

Catherine Chadeayne 1745

Ester Sutherland 1777

Levi Waldron 1879

Joseph Waldron 1765

Miriam Blaisdell 1759

Caroline Waldron 1812

Rebecca King 1793

Obidiah King 1764

Abigal Rundle 1764

Additional genealogical facts available.